MERLE HAGGARD
WAS A FRIEND OF MINE

a memoir

by Raymond H. McDonald

Ordering Information:
For details, info@raymondhmcdonald.com or
www.raymondhmcdonald.com

Merle Haggard Was a Friend of Mine
by Raymond H. McDonald

Print ISBN: 978-1-09835-307-0

eBook ISBN: 978-1-09835-308-7

Printed in the United States of America on SFI Certified paper.
First Edition

Book Cover:
Design by R.J. Shearin
Front photo of Merle and Raymond courtesy of Danny Joe McDonald;
background gentleman is guitarist Joe Manuel of the Strangers.
Back, top left photo courtesy of Brooks Liggat, and
bottom right photo courtesy of Chuck and Vicki Seaton

Photo courtesy of Dannie Ray Spiess

TO THE LEGACY AND MEMORY OF MERLE HAGGARD
with love

TABLE OF CONTENTS

TABLE OF CONTENTS *cont.*

INTRODUCTION

Bob Price, editor and brilliant writer for Bakersfield's only newspaper, *The Bakersfield Californian,* called me the afternoon of April 6, 2016, the day Merle Haggard passed away on his 79th birthday. He asked me to write a story about my life with Merle Haggard for an upcoming special edition on his life. The front-page story's header read:

MERLE HAGGARD, McDONALD REMEMBERS SINGER IN HIS OWN WORDS
Former Bus Driver Calls Country Artist His Idol and Father Figure

The excerpt below is from my story in which a subtitle described me as "the insider who regularly saw the size of Haggard's heart." The article appeared in the April 12, 2016 publication of *The Bakersfield Californian.*

I drove Merle's bus from 2009 to 2016, an experience that provided thousands of memories. The following is one of the most poignant.

While attending one of Merle's concerts at Bakersfield's Fox Theatre, I went to the lobby to visit with a group of friends during intermission. At one point, two dignified Black gentlemen walked up and we began chatting. When the older man learned of my connection with Merle, he launched into the story of how he and Merle had both been in the Kern County jail sixty years before. He hadn't seen Merle since then and said he would love to see him again.

I asked him his name. "Frisco," he said. I said, "That's your name?" He said "That's my nickname, and Merle will know it." I wrote down his number and we said our goodbyes.

The next day, as I was driving the bus down Highway 99 to L.A., I turned to Merle and mentioned this man Frisco. He nearly jumped out of his seat. He and Frisco had become immediate friends in jail, Merle told me. He said that Frisco was the self-appointed mayor of the jail cell, and he had decreed that Merle was the sheriff. He told all the other inmates that these were the facts and they had best not mess with his new friend Merle or they would get a thumping from Mayor Frisco. Merle laughed hard at the memory.

Merle called him soon, and they spoke for hours. Frisco turned his life around and had become a pastor for a church on Haley Street in Bakersfield. Merle was so proud.

Merle and Frisco (Lawrence Mackey Francisco) visiting on Merle's bus *Photo courtesy of Raymond McDonald*

Finally, at Cal State University in Bakersfield, Frisco and Merle met up the day Merle received his honorary doctorate. Merle's wife, Theresa, myself, and Frisco's family members visited together in the back of Merle's bus for a long time. We all went to Hodel's for lunch following the magical reunion. Frisco got up to speak and spoke eloquently about the Lord and, of course, his long-lost friend, Merle. We were family and friends, all united now.

Frisco called me about six months later. He had noticed that Merle was performing in Texas on Frisco's birthday. Could he invite some friends to celebrate his birthday with Merle at the concert? I said, "I'll ask. How many tickets do you need, man?" He said fifty! I was thinking four since that was the typical request. So I called Merle and told him. He said, "Give them fifty tickets and make sure they are in the first three rows."

That night Merle fed them and, oh yes, we had cake and ice cream, after which they enjoyed the wonderful concert. Merle sang Frisco "Happy Birthday" from the stage, with 4,000 fans joining in. I had seen hundreds of Merle Haggard shows but had never watched him sing "Happy Birthday" to anyone, ever. Frisco passed away about a month after that concert. Merle chipped in $5,000 to feed all the members of Frisco's church at his wake.

I drove Merle, his family, and his band for many years without so much as a scratch on any of them. I'm not saying I didn't scratch the bus! Merle Haggard was my idol, my father figure, my brother. I loved him very much.

Going to California

CHAPTER 1

Top steps: (LtoR) Raymond and Danny Joe
Bottom: (LtoR) Jolene, Mikey, Dad, Connie, and Mom
Photo courtesy of Raymond McDonald

BACK IN JULY 1950, I was born in the the Sunflower State, Kansas. My father, Joe McDonald, was a Native American Indian; his father, Henry McDonald, was three-fourths White Earth Chippewa from Minnesota. Joe's mother, Alice (Shipshee) McDonald, was seven-eighths Prairie Band Potawatomi; and my mother, Mary Sayler (her maiden name), was a descendent of English and German immigrants. My siblings and I became enrolled members of the great Prairie Band Potawatomi Nation of Mayetta, Kansas.

Halfway through the twentieth century, just about halfway through the year, I was born about halfway across the country. So I guess it makes some sense to say I'm about halfway 'nuts,' although seven decades later, it's still not clear which half. Maybe it's the half presuming interest in stories about my good friend, Merle Haggard, and my simple yet eventful life.

Posts about old folks shocked to find their life nearly over without much to show for it flood social media. This fear prompted me to put my brain and fingers to use, and get these stories down on paper (or onto the internet) where others can read and enjoy them. Fear of eventual death is a great motivator!

Now you might wonder how I came to live in California and how I ended up in the same town that would lead to my friendship with Merle Haggard. When I was about eight years old, our sweet mother told my three brothers, two sisters, and me we were moving to California. Our dad was a Linotype machine operator. His hands weren't as big as they were dense, from years of slamming the heavy metal keys used to create typesetting for the Topeka, Kansas newspaper. One day an opportunity arose that would soon lead our family to Hollywood! Even in Kansas, we knew about Hollywood. I was ready!

We rode a train for what seemed like forever, arriving in California on my ninth birthday in 1959. The day I saw palm trees for the first time was warm and sunny. There were movie stars, brand-new cars, and rock 'n' roll music piping from Hollywood windows into the streets. It felt like an entirely different world, and I fell in love with it right away.

We moved into a one-bedroom apartment above a drugstore near the intersection of Sunset and Vine. My two older sisters and one of my younger brothers shared a bed with me in the lone bedroom. My mom and dad slept on a foldout couch in the living room with my three-year-old brother, Mikey. Bob, my oldest brother, was a full-grown man in the Navy who lived with his wife nearby in San Diego, and I assumed one reason my mother wanted to live in Southern California.

My most vivid memory of that summer feels like a dream. It wasn't. Danny, my younger brother, was standing with me on the sidewalk just outside the drugstore, directly beneath our new home. A woman in a brand new Ford Thunderbird convertible pulled up to that famous corner of Sunset and Vine. She stopped right in front of us.

"You kids want to go for a ride?" she asked. It was the late fifties. She was blonde and beautiful, probably in her early thirties. We were two kids under ten years of age, with no adult supervision and without a care in the world. Hell yeah, we wanted to go for a ride around Hollywood with a pretty lady in a convertible! (But mainly because our family NEVER even owned a car.) With absolutely no hesitation, Danny hopped in back and I, as the older brother, took my rightful position in the front passenger seat.

Off we drove westbound on Sunset Boulevard. Our chauffeur had the appearance of a movie star: iconic sunglasses, perfect sundress, scarf blowing in the wind, and a magical smile. I peeked back to make sure Danny was in the moment - he was! I can't imagine the look of a more comfortable and smitten seven-year-old. In a stranger's car, he was sitting dead center on the bench seat with arms extended to either side atop the backrest, wearing a radiant smile with sunlight beaming off his glowing face.

Our impromptu guide readied us for our Beverly Hills mansion tour. I recalled someone in Kansas saying, "There ain't no mansions in Kansas; in Kansas, they call 'em farms." Well, I was quite sure there weren't any farms in Hollywood, and to my surprise and delight, we saw authentic mansions on every block.

Winding roads led us up to an overlook where we could view the entire city. It was surreal. Back in Topeka, I don't remember a hill, let alone a lookout. I don't even think there was a single building tall enough to provide a good town view.

After about an hour, we headed back down to Hollywood where our kind and generous driver bought us ice cream cones. Being a chatter bug (even back then), we talked the entire afternoon. I don't remember asking this all too kind woman her name, but I've always hoped it was Marilyn. That's how I remember her. And for that day, for a few hours, she made two little brown boys from Kansas feel like California kings.

I love that memory and thank God for it because just two short months after we moved to glorious Hollywood, we were told we would move again - this time to the central valley farming destination of Delano. Cesar Chavez and the UFW (United Farm Workers Union) would soon bring fame to that little town, with the help of Bobby Kennedy and his brother, President John F. Kennedy.

In a little less than a year, opportunity knocked again, leading us to Bakersfield, California, a bigger town with a better salary to meet our family's needs. My father would set type for *The Bakersfield Californian*, a newspaper that is still operating today after more than one hundred years.

I made many friends in Bakersfield. One of those friends, Jimmy Leon, was a hilarious Mexican kid whose parents owned a flower shop. They lived in a giant, two-story house near Emerson Junior High, where we attended school. My other best friend was a skinny and equally funny Black kid, Thomas Kennedy. I thought it was cool that he had the same last name as the President. Thomas' house was tiny, but that didn't stop us from going there some days for lunch. His mother was so kind, and you could spot where Thomas got his excellent sense of humor.

My family lived in a big house on Truxtun Avenue. It was rundown, but you could tell that, at its peak, it was palatial. One day after school, Thomas and I decided we'd hang out at my house for a bit until he had to head home for dinner. When we got close, I pointed and yelled, "That's my house!" I ran across the street then turned around to see Thomas staring at me like I was crazy.

"That ain't your house!" Thomas yelled nervously.

"Yes, it is!" I yelled back. Thomas couldn't believe it, and my friend wouldn't cross the street because he didn't think it was my house. His reaction completely surprised me, although, in retrospect, it probably shouldn't have. Among all my friends, many lived in beautiful homes. Their parents had new cars, they had new bicycles, and always wore new clothes! I wouldn't even think about letting them know where I lived - I was ashamed of our old house in such utter disrepair. The paint was peeling off everywhere. The yard was a patchy mess of dirt and holes without even enough grass to call it a lawn.

We had at least one family of rats we could hear stirring at night, living in the walls of our Truxtun Avenue 'mansion.' I saw one member of that rat family in our kitchen right before breakfast one morning. He was quietly sitting on the floor, enjoying a moment of solitude before the chaos of another day began. I jumped up on the counter as quickly as I could; he scurried away at my sudden movement, much to my relief. I rarely thought highly of that old battered house, but the rats certainly did.

"I'll prove it's my house," I said, yelling across the street as I ran up the stairs to the large, welcoming porch perched about five feet above the ground. The stairway had seven steps; I'd count them almost every time I climbed them.

"Get off that porch, man!" Thomas was delirious at this point, screaming with fear. "I tell you, do not go in there, Raymond! That ain't your house!"

I was getting a kick out of Thomas losing his mind and smiled at him as if his suspicions were correct. "I'm going in," I hollered through my laughter.

When I opened the door and walked in, my mother greeted me, as usual. (Most moms didn't work during that era and were almost always home.) She heard me yelling and asked what was going on. I explained the situation, then we walked together out to the porch. I had done it! I had proven to Thomas that this was my house! Mom and I waved him over. He was so relieved and now relatively calm, though very surprised his best friend lived in a 'mansion'!

Some of my childhood friends resided in mansions. Jim Brock's dad owned Brock's Department Store, and they lived in Westchester, an upscale part of town. I loved going over to his spectacular home. He never knew where I lived, and I never wanted him to know.

As beat up as that old Truxtun Avenue house was, I guess I still loved it. My brother, Danny, and I would spend hours throwing tennis balls at the steps. Those same seven steps, five feet up, about eight feet wide with a concrete walkway at the bottom, extending thirty feet to the sidewalk.

Danny and I would wear our baseball gloves and take turns throwing balls at the steps. Sometimes if the ball caught the edge just right, it would fire back like a line drive or a fly ball. We played hundreds of imaginary baseball games, always the Dodgers against the Yankees. I was responsible for the play-by-play. I'd pitch and call out, "Drysdale pitching! It's a line drive to Maury Wills!" Danny would catch the ball. "One out! Next up, Roger Maris! The pitch, a deep drive right over our heads, and into the traffic of Truxtun Avenue!"

As I continued to announce the action, cars swerved to miss the ball, honking as if there were a problem. Didn't they get it? Roger Maris just hit a home run! In Bakersfield! I announced many imaginary nine-inning baseball games from those steps.

We knew every player on the two teams. We both had good arms and could field any ball that came our way once we had played baseball on a genuine diamond. I couldn't hit a lick and transitioned to track pretty quickly. But Danny was one of the best all-around ballplayers in our family. Anything anyone asked him to do, he could do it. He would eventually become a standout shortstop for North High School in our town of Oildale, a suburb of Bakersfield.

When I turned eighty-two, we were still living on Truxtun Avenue. Well, in reality, I was only twelve, but it felt like seven decades had flashed by in a few short weeks. My dad always brought a newspaper home each evening after his typesetting shift ended. I had been reading the newspaper nearly every day since the early sixties and was old enough to understand the threat of nuclear war involving the United States and Russia. In school, horrifying films regularly exposed us to the catastrophic effects of atomic bombs. These bombs seemed imminent, having read in the newspaper an attack could happen at any moment, day or night, today or tomorrow.

During school we had drills for nuclear attacks. The fire alarm would ring, but instead of everyone filing out of class for a fire drill, our teachers instructed us to climb under our desks. In theory, this would protect us from the blast or fallout. We weren't stupid. We knew about Hiroshima and Nagasaki. I remember locking eyes with my classmates as we huddled together beneath our desks, disbelieving this was a solution. I always thought if a bombing raid happened, we might as well go out to the playground, watch the mushroom cloud, and kiss our proverbial asses goodbye!

My mother was much more realistic, if not dogmatic, about the threat. One day after another of those ridiculous safety drills, my mother sat me down to inform me the world was going to end. Her seriousness persuaded me to believe her.

"Oh well," I thought. "Perhaps twelve is the new eighty-two." I went outside to enjoy the last days of October. Inside, it scared the hell out of me, and I couldn't stop wondering what was wrong with the adults of the world who were creating an existence where a twelve-year-old boy feared for his life, even in Bakersfield, California.

An Indian in Oildale

CHAPTER 2

Photo courtesy of Raymond McDonald

IN OILDALE, PARENTS ALWAYS WELCOMED me into every home I visited with my friends. I was a minority, an actual Indian, in the midst of a sea of friendly Caucasians, otherwise known as 'white folks.' My mother was full Caucasian, so I could relate. In most of the communities where we lived, I was accustomed to minorities in the schools, with one exception - Delano, California, mostly populated by our Mexican friends. But during my eighth-grade year in Oildale, the schools were predominantly white.

Two days after school had officially begun, I walked into my home classroom at Beardsley Junior High School. All the students were sitting quietly, and when I entered the room, they all turned to look in my direction. I expected to see many different faces of color, including brown, black, white, and even an intriguing Asian kid. I froze momentarily at the sight of all those white faces staring at me and was shocked at being the only person of color, with skin a deep red with hints of brown. I was the *only* minority in the classroom. However, this did not stop me from making friends immediately. My fellow students were drawn to the funny guy who entertained everyone in the schoolyard. (A skill developed by watching comedians on television and remembering their jokes to repeat to my friends).

North High Basketball Team, the Comets
Top Row (LtoR) Mike Drennan, Glen Myers, Ray McDonald
Bottom Row (LtoR) Eddie Richards, Jack Sands,
and Coach Lloyd Williams *Photo courtesy of Raymond McDonald*

Besides my skills as a comedian, I was pretty good at sports: a better than average high jumper (all four feet six inches worth); could catch a football running; was Captain Bobby Sherrill's first pick for his all-star baseball team; could shoot hoops from any angle; *and* could run very, very fast. The reason I could run fast was that I *never* walked anywhere;

I *always* ran. Thirty years after I met Merle, he mentioned to a group of people that his first memories of me were of a little black-haired kid running all over Oildale. (Merle did some running, too. I heard he had been one of the fastest students at our rival school, Standard Junior High.)

Every day I ran to Beardsley Junior High, a distance of one and two-tenths miles each way. I even ran home for lunch, then back again to catch noontime sports. Why would I run all that way home for lunch? Because I enjoyed dining with my mom, who always had a warm, delicious meal waiting for me. I also wanted to give the impression it was uncool to bring a sack lunch to school. Have I mentioned we were poor? Having no lunch money was more than likely the reason I ran home for my meal, pretending all the way to be my hero Jim Thorpe - the incredible Native American (Sac & Fox/Potawatomi) Olympian.

In 1963 and '64, a lunch ticket cost a quarter; that's right - twenty-five cents! We didn't have that kind of money! (Keep in mind in the early sixties, a loaf of bread and a gallon of gas each cost about twenty-five cents.) I recall a stirring memory from those days when my mother handed me a quarter for lunch. I asked where she got the money, and she just laughed and kissed me goodbye (knowing that day I wouldn't have to run one and two-tenths miles home then one and two-tenths miles back again just for lunch). I very confidently strolled into school that morning, knowing I would join my friends for lunch in the cafeteria. They were pleasantly surprised! When asked where I got the twenty-five cents, the answer was easy - I proudly told them my mom gave it to me.

Lunch! I couldn't wait for that lunch bell to ring. When it rang, I was 'Joe Cool,' but not for long. Real coolness was introduced to me as a tamale pie on a warm plate. That delicacy became a lifetime favorite. It was sublime - hamburger mixed with corn, black olives, and cheese, and topped with beautifully baked cornmeal. Amen!

Not having to expend so much energy over lunch, I probably scored many touchdowns that day. But best of all, I got to spend the lunch hour with my friends. People sometimes say kids can be mean, but not these kids who knew I was poor and kindly celebrated with me! I had a quarter, and I had lunch. I don't remember ever getting another quarter for lunch again. It didn't matter - I'd already had my day.

After school that afternoon, my friend Jimmy Douglas invited me over to his house for dinner. I was concerned about getting permission from his mom, but he said she wouldn't care. We hopped a couple of backyard fences to reach his yard, where a duck immediately attempted to bite my legs! Jimmy was having a great time introducing me to the vast array of farm animals running around his backyard – there were chickens and roosters aplenty.

It was a relief to enter the house where his tired dad had just arrived home from work. I met both his parents, who were very kind and funny. They all lived in the south part of Oildale, down by the Kern River. Jimmy informed his mother that I would be staying for supper. She was delighted to have a guest and instructed him to go out back to get a chicken - I figured there'd be one in the freezer out there. (Freezer? No one in Oildale owned a freezer then!)

As soon as Jimmy entered the backyard, the chickens knew what was up and began running around, 'like chickens with their heads cut off.' Very soon, one of those chickens would meet that fate. Jimmy was moving deftly, like Rocky Balboa, as he tried to catch our dinner. Being a city boy who had never witnessed a chicken getting its head pulled off, I was horrified as that unlucky chicken joined the 'club' and quite literally began running around without its head. Jimmy knew I was horror-stricken and loved it, laughing hard from the time the chicken keeled over until he finished plucking it and delivered it to his mom. That was the best-fried chicken I'd had in a long time and certainly the freshest. My mom was a great cook, and I loved her fried chicken, but we didn't have it often, with so many mouths to feed and no chickens in our backyard!

As great as that day had been for me, a terrible day for all Americans was looming: November 22, 1963. Right before lunch, while in metal shop, I watched my teacher walk to his car, parked in the lot right next to our class. He sat in his car, listening to the radio with the door open, holding his head in despair. He got out, closed the car door, and slowly walked back to the classroom to deliver the devastating news. Our President, John F. Kennedy, had been shot and killed in Dallas, Texas. We were speechless! Kennedy was our hero. He was young and robust, with a beautiful wife and two children! He's the guy who shut the Russians down! That same afternoon, I dedicated my run home to our fallen hero - I ran it faster than ever before because it was for him. I was thirteen years old.

The following day schools closed in honor of John F. Kennedy. I remember all three television networks dedicated their programming to the events that followed, including a live broadcast of the assassination of Kennedy's alleged assassin, Lee Harvey Oswald. (Conspiracy theories began immediately and will probably never cease.) I will never forget the long procession of mourners filing past Kennedy's casket as he lay in state and the final procession with the horse-drawn carriage taking his body to Arlington National Cemetery for burial. The sound of the drums in slow cadence playing the entire route to the graveyard still haunts me. I didn't go outside to play that day - this was history in the making, and I wanted to witness it on television. I noticed during this distressing time how all the adults were comforting but unusually somber. Now, as an adult, I understand why.

About thirty years after this tragic event, I asked Merle, just once, where he was and how he felt about Kennedy's assassination. He didn't want to talk about it, nor relive it. It bothered him immensely.

Sophomore Year
at Bonnie and Merle's
CHAPTER 3

Promo photo of Bonnie Owens and Merle Haggard

IN JUNE OF 1965, BONNIE OWENS married Merle Haggard in Mexico. Subsequently, my dad accepted a job in South Gate, a suburb of Los Angeles. The thought of another transition did not make me happy, especially one month short of my fifteenth birthday. I had made so many friends, loved my school and almost all of my teachers. In short, I loved my Oildale, California existence.

We settled into Los Angeles, and I immediately felt *unsettled*. I had no friends, no money, traffic was terrible, and thick smog burned my eyes. I was unnerved by the notion I would soon be faced again with making new friends in a new school. In the morning, I'd leave the apartment and begin walking the streets alone, with tears in my eyes from the combination of smog and loneliness! I called my good friends, Buddy and Mike Owens, just about every week. I missed my life in Oildale.

August of 1965 burned hotter than blazes. The folks from our neighboring town of Watts grew unhappy with the local police force and began rioting with a vengeance. Life felt surreal as newscasters streamed the mayhem live from the streets, and helicopter crews issued reports of the calamity from above. The entire city fell under a strict curfew. Sirens and gunshots kept us on edge - we were that close! The uprising lasted five days, from August 11th through August 16th. Thirty-four people died in addition to mass destruction caused by arson and looting.

The terrible situation in Watts prompted me to call my friends, Buddy and Mike. I asked if I could live with them in Oildale for my sophomore year. (I didn't ask my parents; I was determined to go regardless of their answer.) Mike promised he would bring it up with Bonnie and Merle. He called soon with the good news that I could, indeed, move back to Oildale - back to my friends and my school. Mike shared with me many years later that Bonnie and Merle were initially reluctant to take in another teen, but Mike told Bonnie that I'd wind up in prison if they didn't. That sealed the deal with them, especially with Merle.

Merle had four children from a previous marriage, ranging in age from about two to ten years old. But those children were being raised by Merle's mother, whose house in Oildale sat in front of the old boxcar home where Merle lived as a child. The now-famous boxcar has been permanently moved to the Kern County Museum in Bakersfield, and open for public tours since April of 2017. Both homes were not far from Merle's new place on Highmoor Street.

Bonnie and Merle showed such kindness by taking me in. With Merle's career in high gear, they knew they would be on the road frequently, promoting his music. They probably thought it would be good for the boys to have a friend living there, considering they would be gone so often. It was August when I moved into Merle Haggard's home with his new wife, Bonnie Owens, her sons, Buddy and Mike, plus

Mike, Bonnie, and Buddy Owens *Photo courtesy of Buddy Owens*

Bonnie's mother, whom we all called Grandma. The house Merle and Bonnie had purchased was in a genuinely nice area of Oildale, unlike the impoverished section where Merle grew up. Now he finally had enough money to buy a charming home in a more affluent neighborhood.

Mike and I drove over to see the new house on Highmoor Street before anyone had moved any furniture in. Neither of us had ever lived in a new home, so we were extremely excited. We parked in the driveway; Mike pulled the keys from his pocket, and as we entered through the front door, his first words were, "This house comes with air-conditioning!" We were amazed at how cool it was inside. Swamp coolers offered little relief from Oildale's hot August days and nights, and we were delighted to know with this new home, those days would soon be history.

Although average in size, the new house offered a well-functioning floor plan with a two-car garage, a kitchen full of new appliances, three bedrooms, two baths - one full bath, and a master bedroom with a three-quarter bath. Merle and Bonnie chose this room, which was in the back of the house. Buddy, Mike, and I shared a bedroom across the hall from Merle and Bonnie. Grandma was in the bedroom next to ours. The living room would soon become a comfortable place to gather, with its eye-catching rock fireplace and brand-new television. From the living room, sliding glass doors exited to a large patio and backyard. I was in heaven.

The first time I dined together with my new family in their new home proved memorable, if not educational. Grandma had cooked up a fabulous Oklahoma-type meal that included a main ingredient I was not familiar with: okra. I'd never even heard of this vegetable. To be honest, it didn't make my top ten list, even though I am sure she had prepared it well!

Served along with the okra were several other vegetable dishes, including a massive bowl of mashed potatoes, loads of corn, and some green beans. I'm not a fan of vegetables, but we had plenty of iced tea to wash them down! To complete the meal, Grandma had prepared some delicious pork chops, using a lot of pepper, which I soon discovered was her method for cooking all meat, and I learned to like it that way. I was very fortunate because Grandma, who did most of the cooking, had culinary skills equal to those of my mother, who displayed a touch of genius in her cooking methods!

When the six of us sat down to dinner, Merle loved to visit and tell jokes throughout the meal. Despite his hearty appetite, he somehow remained slim (Merle stood about five feet eight inches, and I'm guessing weighed about one hundred forty pounds). While watching him closely during this first dinner, I was surprised by his *method of attack*. He piled his plate high with food, took a jar of molasses and poured a generous portion over it, then began to stir. While he was mixing this unlikely combination, he glanced up with a great big smile as if to say, "This is my way, boys." Bonnie and Grandma, who were already familiar with his unusual habit, just smiled. I remember thinking what a beautiful dinner I was sharing with my new family and how thankful I was for their graciousness.

After dinner, evenings were similar to any other American family in 1965 – it was the time to gather in front of the television. In addition to favorites *Andy Griffith* and *The Beverly Hillbillies*, it is no surprise Merle's most loved show was *The Fugitive*. This top-rated CBS series starred David Janssen, who played an innocent man running from the law. Merle and Bonnie would sit together on the floor right in front of the television to watch the latest episode. Bear in mind, we were all aware that Merle had spent time in prison not long before and had 'done time' in reform schools and jails too. We also knew that his escape from some of those institutions had, upon occasion, turned him into a fugitive. The inspiration for Merle's first number one song, "The Fugitive," requires no further explanation.

Ecstatic barely describes Merle on the day his award for recording the number one song in the nation arrived in the mail. The wooden plaque with decoupage displayed the top fifty hits in country music for one week. *Billboard*, the leading magazine that charted all modern music, awarded this honor. Who knew, at that time, another thirty-nine number one hits would follow!

Merle immediately grabbed a hammer and nail and began walking around his house, looking for a place to display his new award. His mood was cheerful, so we followed him into the living room, the bedrooms, and finally the hallway, where he suddenly stopped, deciding he'd found the perfect spot to hang the award for his first number one song. I asked him why he would display this award in the hallway, which I thought was sort of strange. Then (not being shy), I asked him why he wouldn't prefer it in the living room. He replied, "This way, every time I go down this hallway, it'll be right there; I'll see it more in the hallway than anywhere else." That made sense to me.

On a gorgeous day with intense blue skies and a hint of fall air, Merle's manager, Fuzzy Owen, pulled up in his 1953 Chrysler station wagon. I was about to witness Bonnie and Merle heading out on their first tour to promote and play their music. They were extremely excited to embark on this journey. Now, it adds interest to this story to know that Bonnie and Fuzzy had been going steady for many years, but Merle 'stole' Bonnie from Fuzzy only a few months before their tour departure. So when Fuzzy arrived to pick them up, I thought to myself, "This is a real country music story." It was unimaginable within a few short months, Fuzzy could forgive Merle and Bonnie and tour with them in his Chrysler all over America.

The Chrysler boasted a large fold-down backseat. I helped them pack up the wagon, and by the time we loaded a few amplifiers, Fuzzy's steel guitar, Merle's guitar, and all their suitcases, every square inch of that space had been filled! The vivid memory of the three of them in the front seat - Fuzzy driving, Bonnie in the middle, with Merle on the passenger side - is forever burned into my mind. They were all so happy!

Mike, Buddy, Grandma, and I delivered our farewells, and as they backed out of the driveway, we asked how long they would be gone. Merle called out through his open window, "About a month; we are going to New York and back!"

Well, I can't speak for Grandma, but we boys were delighted to hear this news. After all, part of being a teenager meant always being ready to party. However, we did attend school every day - Grandma made sure of that! But when Friday night rolled around, we'd grab some beer and head for the oil fields in Buddy's 1950 Chrysler four-door bomb. We usually brought our friend, Stuart Townsend, and the four of us would drink a six-pack. To be clear, we *shared* the six-pack. Merle's great friend, Roger Miller, had a smash hit in those days, "Chug-A-Lug-Chug-A-Lug." The song tells the story of some teenage kids' first experience with drinking. We were livin' that tune!

About two weeks before Merle and Bonnie returned from their tour, Grandma left to visit relatives in Arkansas. That meant three imaginative teenage boys had just been left alone and unsupervised for an incredible two weeks! We decided to throw a party one weekend and began inviting friends over for a few beers. Merle had a great sound system, so we loaded up our rock 'n' roll records, ready to play at maximum volume. News of our party spread quickly. Before we knew it, about twenty guys had arrived - no girls, just guys - drinking and acting like fools. (Somehow, a hearty supply of booze had emerged.) Soon the foolish behavior escalated. A couple of brief fisticuffs transpired, a few holes got punched in the walls, someone tore off the front screen door, and for good measure, ripped the screen off Grandma's bedroom window!

The next morning, we awakened to the shock of Bonnie and Merle's unannounced, early return. When they entered their home, about a half-dozen hungover teenage boys were scattered on the floor and draped over the furniture, recovering from the night's revelry. Of course, Bonnie and Merle noticed the damage inflicted on their new home, but they were incredibly calm. We thought we were in the most significant trouble imaginable. However, to our surprise, Bonnie and Merle just told the boys to go on home. Buddy, Mike, and I began cleaning up the mess as they brought their belongings inside.

Next, something happened that I will never forget. Merle told Buddy, Mike, and me to come into his bedroom; he wanted to talk to us and asked us to sit on the foot of the bed. He stood facing us and said, "Boys, boys, now you know I am responsible for you. You know that I have been in prison, and this kind of behavior could send me back. You don't want me to go back, do you?" We, of course, said no, and were extremely apologetic. Merle never raised his voice, nor was he angry. Touched (and relieved!) by his understanding and forgiveness, we knew we would never have another party in that house.

Looking back, I realize that Bonnie and Merle played barrooms and honky-tonks where everybody drank and had a lot of fun. Not that they condoned this behavior for teenage kids, but I suppose they expected it, and perhaps that's the reason they weren't so angry.

About twenty years later, Merle was performing in Phoenix, Arizona. By this time, I had settled into life in Las Vegas, now a husband and father of two children. I had kept in touch with Bonnie and Merle through the years, even though I had my career as a radio disk jockey and a surveyor in the Nevada desert. After Merle's concert, we went to his bus to visit, and I reminded him of the talk he gave us boys after the wild party at his house those many years ago. I profusely apologized again for my actions while in his home. He stopped me immediately and said, "Raymond, don't ever apologize for being a boy!" That sincere yet straightforward response was indicative of this man's soul - so forgiving, so understanding!

Merle didn't talk about many adult situations in front of us back in those days, but one instance caught my attention. It involved a new singer by the name of Dolly Parton. We knew about Dolly Parton. Her career had just begun, but it was already apparent (even to teenage boys) that she was a special lady with special talents.

One evening, Merle was talking with Mack Owen, Fuzzy's brother. He knew we were standing by Merle's car in the driveway, listening. Merle told Mack about Dolly's visit with them and described Dolly as a woman who had incredibly beautiful skin, eyes, body, and hair. Mack said he thought she wore a wig. Merle agreed but told Mack she wasn't wearing a wig when she visited them, and her hair was quite beautiful. Merle would share observations of this kind (talking about another woman's beauty), but only to his trusted friends and never in front of Bonnie. Merle was cool - he had class.

Merle loved to go fishing on the Kern River. One Saturday morning around four o'clock, he awakened Buddy, Mike, and me with a "Let's go fishing!" This early awakening was smack in the middle of the night for teenage boys, but for Merle and his fishing buddy, Fuzzy, it was probably just the end of one day and the beginning of the next.

The brand-new 1965 Pontiac station wagon Merle had bought offered plenty of room for us all. Half asleep, we got dressed as quickly as possible, then piled into the back seat. Merle was driving; Fuzzy was riding shotgun. We were on our way to a fishing spot on the Kern River that Merle called 'the rock,' about forty-five minutes from Merle's house and near a place on the river called Miracle Hot Springs. About fifteen minutes into the drive, the road widened to a four-lane divided highway as we approached Hart Park. To no one's surprise, we boys had fallen asleep in the backseat. The sun was up now when Merle suddenly slammed on the brakes. We lurched forward, tumbling into the backs of the front seats. (Seatbelts had not yet become the law!) We certainly were wide-awake from that point onward!

Merle began swearing at a crow eating his breakfast on the other side of the road - a tasty rabbit, probably early morning roadkill. Merle reached under the front seat, grabbed his .22 pistol, jumped out, and fired at the crow, which had taken flight by now. Merle cussed up a storm at that crow. I'd never seen him that angry, as he unloaded all six shots aimed in the crow's direction. He missed, returned to the car, and as he put the gun back under the front seat, exclaimed, "I hate those sons of bitches." Fuzzy laughed, and so did Merle!

We arrived at 'the rock' about half an hour later. Merle had brought fishing rods for each of us. He enjoyed sharing what he knew about fishing and, with a good deal of patience, taught us all the steps: how to take a hook and tie it to a line; how to put the weights on the line; what size hook to use; what kind of bait to use; where and how to cast the line; how to recognize a bite; how to set the hook; and if we were lucky enough to catch a fish, how to reel it in, and then begin again.

We began catching a few small rainbow trout and were excited about putting our new fishing skills into action. Fuzzy and Merle had caught plenty of fish. Merle had a strong dislike for a specific type of fish he called 'suckers' (common name, Sacramento Sucker). Just as suddenly as the crow/rabbit event occurred, a creature appeared on the end of Merle's fishing line that he was not happy to see. Merle began cussing at this ugly suckerfish, with ugly sucker lips and bony frame much larger than the trout we had been catching. He cursed at it, but in a playful yet maddening tone, as he reeled it in. We all stopped to watch Merle with his ugly catch. Angry, he threw the fish underneath a bush and pulled out his .22 pistol again. Merle shot the fish six times. Fuzzy was having a ball watching Merle's theatrics. What about us? We were stunned but amused!

Twenty or thirty years later, during another trip to see Merle, I brought up the fishing trip to 'the rock' on the Kern River. I reminisced about the dead rabbit, the 'vulture' crow, the 'vulture' fish, and the .22 pistol. I asked him if he remembered. He said, "Yes," followed with, "I guess I've always been a show-off." Then we had a big laugh. Merle's day brightened whenever the topic of fishing came up. He often spoke of his father taking him to the Kern River on many wonderful father-son fishing trips. Those were poignant memories for Merle. He so enjoyed teaching youngsters how to fish that I always believed it was an extension of his own father's spirit.

During those trips, we discovered how exhilarating it is to catch fish! Waiting one hour or more, I would completely concentrate on the line in silence and steadiness, forgetting everything else around me. When the fish began to nibble, or even better, swallowed the hook - man, what a thrill! Fishing brought such great solitude, mystery, anticipation, and finally, a reward for patience.

Merle also taught us how to clean our catch and remove the scales to prepare the fish for cooking. The first time we brought home a mess of about eighteen trout, Bonnie and Grandma knew just what to do. They cooked a most delicious dinner - perfect for my first taste of trout. To this day, trout remains my favorite!

The Kern River in Kern County became our most frequented destination. The fishing spot near 'the rock' (that unique and stunning rock) is a sacred space. We agreed to share our secret fishing hole with the boys we had invited to our beer party (remember them?). So one beautiful spring morning, about ten of us decided we would not attend school and instead loaded up a couple of cars and headed up to 'the rock.' No beer this time, but we had plenty of worms!

We stayed on the river for about eight hours, enjoying the outdoors, the camaraderie, and catching fish. We probably caught thirty or more that afternoon! When we got back to Oildale, we took our trout to Bonnie's mom and asked if she would cook them for us. (Bonnie and Merle were on the road, but we thought they would approve). Grandma, happy to do this, wasted no time coating them with cornmeal and seasoning to pan-fry them for her unexpected mob of hungry boys. She turned our impromptu trout dinner at Merle's house into the perfect ending to a perfect day.

Buck Owens happened to be Mike and Buddy's father if I haven't already mentioned it. So, between Buck and Merle, we had new electric guitars, amplifiers, and drums. Buddy played the guitar, and I sang and played drums. What else could we do but put together a little garage band? Mike did not show any interest in learning to play an instrument, so we found a great guy to play bass, Gary Guinn, and a cool guy to play rhythm, Mike Hatfield. Both were juniors in high school. I was a sophomore, and Buddy, a senior. We practiced in Merle's garage. I sang a few Rolling Stones songs, Buddy sang a couple of his dad's songs, and we both sang a few other rock songs. We called ourselves The Chosen Few, a name suggested by Buddy's cousin, Betty. She was a little younger than we were and our biggest fan.

North High School was planning a talent show, so our band decided to enter, although we had never performed in public before (or since). This talent show was it - our big chance. We were the last to perform out of about ten entries and got a rousing ovation from the student body. I sang "Satisfaction" and "Spider and the Fly" by the Rolling Stones. Buddy sang "Shapes of Things" by the Yardbirds. That crowd of teenagers went crazy. However, the judges were not as impressed.

After all the performances, the acts lined up towards the front of the stage. First, the judges called out third place. Based on the crowd's response, we thought we had won. When they announced second place, and it wasn't us, we were confident we had won. So when they finally announced first place, we began strolling over to get our trophy realizing midway they hadn't called our name. Instead, a quartet of boys who sang "The Banana Boat Song" had taken first place! The crowd booed as we stood dumbfounded! We hadn't considered that the judges were our teachers and didn't care for rock 'n' roll.

We lost! The noon-time talent show had ended. The curtains closed, and the bell rang, signaling for everyone to return to class. But we weren't finished yet! I asked the guys to pick up their guitars and play one more song for our classmates as they exited the concert hall. The Chosen Few had chosen to play another tune - another Rolling Stones song, appropriately titled, "It's All Over Now." A bright young student opened the curtains, and the kids stopped walking out as they turned to listen and cheer louder than ever for their favorite act, The Chosen Few.

Buddy and I met our first girlfriends because of the band - music is a powerful aphrodisiac! All my sophomore buddies were impressed when they learned my girlfriend was a junior. They asked my secret, and I replied, "I play drums, and I sing." The Chosen Few never played publicly again - we didn't need to. We'd had our day!

Merle Haggard was not the world's biggest rock 'n' roll fan. However, he admired many of the rock 'n' roll singers. He had a great sound system in his home, and when he wasn't there, we took full advantage of it. We played The Beatles nearly all the time, and the Rolling Stones the rest of the time - interspersed with some Beach Boys and Paul Revere and the Raiders, to name a few. Occasionally after being out for a while, Merle would return home to his stereo rocking full blast. Calmly and politely, he'd asked us to please turn down the stereo. Once, he noted the guitars were out of tune. Merle had perfect pitch, so I'm sure this bothered him. We turned off the stereo!

After that, we listened to Merle's music all the time, whether he was there or not. Even as teenagers, we recognized his incredible talent. He traveled to Capitol Records in Los Angeles, where he made master recordings, then he'd bring them home to play for us - we'd be the first to hear his new recordings! His singing and melodies were so unique and inspiring; we knew he would be a superstar.

As you will remember, Buck Owens, Mike and Buddy's dad, already enjoyed fame as a major country music superstar, and now their stepdad, Merle Haggard, was on the verge of becoming a superstar himself. We were right there at the beginning and overwhelmed by their talents.

Bonnie grew to be a significant force behind Merle Haggard's success. She sang a lovely harmony to nearly all his songs. Whenever Merle got an idea for a song, Bonnie transcribed the lyrics as Merle recited them. Sometimes she would interject her thoughts into his songs. Bonnie and Merle recorded a duet album, *Just Between the Two of Us*, for Capitol Records that did quite well. They had a great sound together, already known to a broad audience across America, which helped fill the venues when they toured.

Merle typically didn't write songs in front of us boys. Although a few times, he'd play us a new song he'd already written. That was cool. One day he brought a song home written earlier that day. It was around noon, and Bonnie, Grandma, and I were in the kitchen. Merle joined us there, sat down at the kitchen table, and immediately played for us what he'd written while fishing on the Kern River that morning.

The song "Mama Tried" became an American classic. I was standing next to Bonnie, listening intently. When he finished his new song, we all looked at one another, stunned by the storyline and the beauty of the melody. It was amazing! We knew it was a classic, and so did Merle as he sat there with a gentle smile. Once we composed ourselves enough to speak, we repeatedly told him how fantastic it was! "Mama Tried" was an incredible new song! I remember this experience so well - not like it was yesterday, but like it was a couple of minutes ago.

In June 1966, Buddy and Mike left Oildale to live with their father, Buck, at his ranch in Weedpatch, California. Bonnie and Merle drove me back to Los Angeles, in their brand-new pickup truck, to rejoin my family. The truck was a flatbed with a cab over the camper, which they were using as their new road vehicle. For me, it was a sad good-bye to a fantastic sophomore year living in Merle Haggard's household.

Merle and Bonnie invited me to a recording session at Capitol Records in Hollywood as sort of a going-away gift before putting me on a bus for South Gate, where my family lived. I had never been to a recording session before and was excited about the opportunity.

The minute we entered the studio, I had the pleasure of meeting a few men who would be involved with the recording that day. I met a fellow named Glen Campbell and a guitar player by the name of James Burton. Merle loved James Burton's guitar work and had spoken of him for months. James Burton had played in Ricky Nelson's band for years and became the lead guitarist for Elvis Presley. I had never heard of Glen Campbell but perceived him to be kind and very talented. He would later become one of the great entertainers of that era. But on this day, he would sing backup vocals on Merle's new song.

After the introductions, Merle pulled me aside to tell me I could sit in the studio, but I could not make one sound. So, I sat for hours listening to and watching take after take of his new song. They recorded at least twenty before the talented Ken Nelson, Merle's producer, called the musicians into the control room to hear what they had accomplished thus far. I observed how Mr. Nelson heard everything from each perfect note to the occasional sour one. When a sour note occurred, Mr. Nelson would point it out, and another take would begin.

Studios didn't overdub back then but played the entire song all the way through. The best of the takes is what you got; that's what wound up on the vinyl. So, perfection was imperative. After a break, Merle, Bonnie, and the band went back into the studio for another twenty or more takes. I couldn't believe what I was witnessing or that I had remained quiet and still for the entire session. When they finally got the perfect recording, Mr. Nelson called the band back into the control room. I'm pretty sure he referred to the final product as a masterpiece - and it was! The song, "The Bottle Let Me Down," written by Merle and recorded that day, has staying power over fifty years later. It is a country music classic!

We expressed our parting thank yous and farewells after the recording session. Bonnie walked me to the bus stop near the studio, bought me a ticket, and put me on a bus for the short ride back to my family in South Gate. That day will be etched in my memory forever! My mother, a huge country music fan who always had country music playing, was delighted to hear all the stories about Bonnie, Merle, and Buck. My dad preferred Sinatra, but sometimes I'd catch him humming a country tune.

Chasing Rolling Stones

CHAPTER 4

1965 seafoam green Chevrolet Super Sport (similar to Buddy's car)
Photo illustration - R. J. Shearin

BEFORE MOVING BACK TO SOUTH GATE, three former sophomores - Mike Owens, Stuart Townsend, and me - set out for Huntington Beach, California. The school year had just ended, and it was high time for girl-watching and body surfing - we body surfed because we didn't have the money to procure surfboards. Mike's older brother, Buddy, generously allowed us to drive his new car. It was a 1965 Chevrolet Super Sport with a 327 engine, mag wheels, a four-speed Hurst transmission, bucket seats, and a primo sound system. Its color was deep seafoam green, like the waves we hoped to catch later that day! This was the coolest car we had ever ridden in, without a doubt. You could say Buddy's Chevy was quite an improvement over his 1950 Chrysler he drove us to school in - when it would start.

Buddy was the recipient of these beautiful wheels as a high school graduation gift from his father, the famous country singer Buck Owens. Buddy had begun his aspiring singing career immediately following graduation, as an opening act for his dad and The Buckaroos. When Buddy was on tour, he occasionally needed someone to drive his new car to keep it in top running condition. Buddy was a warm and generous teenager and knew we'd take good care of his new car. He was also aware we'd race against the fastest cars in town. We did, and we beat every single one. There is no doubt his car was fast!

On this warm, glorious summer day, the Los Angeles beaches beckoned us. We headed out early in the morning for Huntington Beach, blasting the local rock 'n' roll station, KAFY, as we drove out of town. Before long, we switched to eight-track tapes as radio reception faded driving up the Grapevine. But once we passed through the mountains, we tuned into our favorite LA station while dropping into the greater Los Angeles basin. The energy and excitement of Los Angeles burst from the stereo speakers: KHJ!!! BOSS ANGELES!!! That radio station was the BOSS!!!

The Beatles were the brightest stars ever created by the rock gods. They were the most incredible show in the universe, and their music was unreal. They opened the door for their British compatriots, the Rolling Stones, along with so many other musicians who have entertained young and old for decades. According to many top one-hundred countdowns, the Rolling Stones had a hit song still considered the number one rock 'n' roll record of all time. In 1966, if you happened to be a teenager free of all responsibility and happened to be cruising to LA in a brand new car, and the Stone's "Satisfaction" just happened to play on your AM radio, you would have instinctively turned up the volume as loud as possible. And you also would have begun singing as loud as you possibly could. What a gift! Thank you, Rolling Stones!

After our beautiful California surf and sun-splashed day, filled with multitudes of California girls, we reluctantly began our journey back to Kern County, the home of Buck Owens and Merle Haggard. (Buck being Mike's dad, and Merle, Mike's stepdad.)

Safely back in Bakersfield, we refueled at the Chevron gas station on the corner of China Grade Loop and North Chester, where our high school friend and all-around good guy, Mike Hatcher, was pumping gas that day. Mike had some interesting information: The Rolling Stones, who would be playing in concert that night at the Bakersfield Civic Auditorium, were scheduled to land at Meadows Field any minute! Meadows Field was Bakersfield's airport and about a mile away.

Without thinking twice, we tore away from the gas station, speeding the entire distance to the airport. We parked near the fenced area on Norris Road and Airport Drive as we watched an airplane that looked like it was from a 1940s movie set, pulling off the runway to a side hangar not far from us. The plane was huge, with dual prop engines; we just knew it belonged to The Rolling Stones! We weren't dumb. We were soon to be juniors - juniors who knew every lyric to every song!

We watched as a bevy of characters rolled off the plane. It was surreal - they all had paisley-patterned shirts, colorful bell-bottom pants, and wild hair! This group had traveled from very far away to entertain their biggest fans! Us!

Minutes later, most of the group had loaded onto an old bus, but two white limousines were awaiting some extraordinary guests. Two of those guests got in the back of one limo, and a few got in the other. If we held our position, we knew the limos would have to drive by our location. We had to choose one limo to follow, and by luck, we selected the right one.

The 'chase' began as we entered the Golden State Highway, after about a three-mile casual ride directly behind the limo. The limo driver decided to lose the '65 Chevy and started to pick up speed. We caught up at about 85 mph, pulling up beside them. The driver, realizing he was speeding, slowed down to the speed limit of about 65 mph.

At that moment, we were thrilled to see Keith Richards and Mick Jagger in the back seat of the limo! We started screaming, "Keith! Mick!" as we waved and shouted, displaying the exact behavior you would expect from wild and crazy American teenagers. We were delirious with laughter and the excitement of the moment! We were in a time warp - time seemed to stand still.

Keith was smiling and waving, but Mick, who was not happy with our shenanigans, gave us the one-finger salute. We understood their individual reactions. We loved it! What else could we do now but lay back and follow them to their hotel?

The hotel was actually a motel, on the south side of town, on Union Avenue. When we pulled up behind them as they reached the motel, their driver jumped out of the limo, ran back to our car, and asked what we wanted. We replied, "We want to meet the Rolling Stones, of course!" He then relayed that bit of information to the boys, but with three crazy teenagers still lingering, they weren't about to get out of their limo. The driver, who turned out to be none other than a top DJ for our home rock radio station, KAFY, informed us they didn't want to meet at that time but said if we told no one where they were staying, they would give us a backstage pass for both shows that evening.

We enthusiastically agreed to this arrangement and left immediately to get ready for the evening, blasting an eight-track of their *Out of Our Heads* album all the way home. We kept our part of the deal and told no one. Our new friend, the KAFY disc jockey, greeted us at the backstage door at 7:00 p.m. when we arrived. The moment he let us in, our already amazing day was about to get even better. We hadn't known that the fabulous McCoys of "Hang on Sloopy" fame were the opening band that night. After their stellar performance, we could hardly wait to see the Rolling Stones! But the Stones flew right past us both upon entering and exiting the stage - we never got a chance for an autograph or a photograph (even though we had come prepared with a Kodak Instamatic, just in case). No complaints, though - both shows were fantastic in every way! We were stunned! Live! 1966!

After the shows were over, we followed the limo back to the airport, and this time all the way back to the hangar where the Stones' oversized plane was waiting. I managed to capture a photo of Bill Wyman and was able to get his autograph. What a perfect ending to our day that began with surf and sun, followed by a freeway chase of our favorite band, then an offer for backstage passes, and finally the Stones' concert itself. These events inspired a song about this unforgettable adventure. The lyrics, printed below, pretty much bring this chapter to its close.

It would be remiss not to mention here that Merle Haggard and the Rolling Stones later became friends. Merle opened for them in Little Rock, Arkansas, in 2006. Keith Richards posted a *YouTube* video describing the first time he met Merle. Keith was thrilled! Please search it out - you will enjoy it!

On the First Day of Summer
By Raymond McDonald

On the first day of summer I remember
A sunny day in '66
We were young, out of school
Acting like total fools
Driving to the beach in our Buddy's car

Now the Rolling Stones they hit like thunder
They rocked and rolled, is it any wonder
They ruled the radio
With their song
'(I Can't Get No) Satisfaction'
'(I Can't Get No) Satisfaction'

And Donavan sang about beaches and pearls
He'd do anything to get a girl
The 'Sunshine Superman' he saved the world
With his song

We drove back to Bakersfield after surfin' all day
It isn't very far to the beaches of L.A.
When we got back a friend said, listen man, hey
The Stones are gonna land, they're gonna play

So we drove to the airport
And as they were whisked away
In a pair of limousines, we picked one to chase
We caught it easy in our Buddy's Chevrolet
As we was singin'
'(I Can't Get No) Satisfaction'
'(I Can't Get No) Satisfaction'

Mick and Keith were in the back of that limousine
We waved frantically causing quite a scene
Keith waved back but Mick was a little obscene
We followed them to their motel, what a scream
And we was singin'

'(I Can't Get No) Satisfaction'
'(I Can't Get No) Satisfaction'

The DJ with 'em told us, "Forget where they are,
Don't tell anyone tonight you'll see the stars"
We begged to meet 'em but did not get very far
So we drove home blaring their song in Buddy's car
We was playin'
'(I Can't Get No) Satisfaction'
'(I Can't Get No) Satisfaction'

That night we went backstage; the DJ let us in
The Stones - they rocked Bakersfield
And we made friends
Only The Beatles rivaled them way back then
They were live! What a night!
Listening to
'(I Can't Get No) Satisfaction'
'(I Can't Get No) Satisfaction'

On the first day of summer I remember
A sunny day in '66
We were young, out of school
Mike and me and crazy Stu
And we was singin'
'(I Can't Get No) Satisfaction'
'(I Can't Get No) Satisfaction'

Ray-Baby from K-Baby

CHAPTER 5

Raymond McDonald and Merle Haggard on Merle's bus in
Bakersfield in 2005 *Photo courtesy of Raymond McDonald*

MY FIRST FORAY INTO RADIO broadcasting began in Bakersfield,
California, one September night in 1968. At age eighteen, I had followed
my best friends, Buddy and Mike Owens, sons of country music
superstar Buck Owens, into the glamorous occupation of disc jockey. I
spent time listening to them on the radio and thought: "If they can do it,
I can too." In no time, I prepared for and obtained my FCC third-class
broadcasting license.

Mike and Buddy's dad owned two radio stations in Bakersfield:
the wildly popular KUZZ, and in 1968, KBBY, one of the first FM

stations in Kern County. Buck hired me with absolutely no experience. He put me on the air from midnight till 6:00 a.m., six days a week, with Sundays off, just to play it safe. DJ's made lots of money, I was told! But my starting wage of $1.65 an hour only exceeded the federal minimum by five cents!

When KBBY was christened K-BABY, I became Ray-Baby from K-Baby. The format was rock 'n' roll. Management insisted we play current rock, no oldies such as Elvis, Chuck Berry, or Jerry Lee Lewis, already ten years past their musical prime. Due to this, we only spun records from 1965 and up. Being a disc jockey was the perfect job because I could tell from the DJs' tone of voice they were having loads of fun. Plus, I had always loved listening to the radio. It was my turn on the turntables, and I loved spinning records!

The first record I ever played on the air was by one of my favorite artists, Jimi Hendrix, singing his classic "Purple Haze." With no set format, we just played whatever we wanted (within the parameters mentioned above). It was midnight, I was nervous, and the previous DJ had already left for home. Alone with the responsibility, it was up to me, and I was game. This was it; I was on the air!

The giant studio monitors were screaming to be peaked! Thrilled, I maxed out the volume, thinking about my good fortune. About halfway through a song, I turned the volume down and reached over to turn up an old radio we had sitting next to the control board. The radio, tuned to 107.9 FM KBBY, piped "Purple Haze" into the studio! I was on the air with Jimi Hendrix and loving my 'way-out-there cool' job!

When the song ended, I flipped the microphone switch to 'on' and announced to the rockers of Kern County: "That was 'Purple Haze' by Jimi Hendrix with Ray-Baby from K-Baby! Good evening and good morning! Ray-Baby from K-Baby here with rock 'n' roll until 6:00 a.m.!"

My nerves had calmed because I'd found my groove. Friends began calling the request line. They had been waiting for the moment they would have direct access to Ray-Baby. My brother, Danny, and his gang called from Mark Mogensen's house to request their favorites. I could hear them whooping it up in the background - they were not supposed to be drinking beer, but I am pretty sure that's what they were doing. I played those wild teenagers every requested tune. In a noticeably short time, word spread about the request line at KBBY.

Soon, a vast array of Oildale friends began calling frequently. Could I say their name on the radio? Could I play some Beatles? Could I dedicate a song to someone? Certainly I could, and I did. I would announce anybody's name on the radio during that innocent time in the sixties.

Requests trickled in from all over Kern County. I enjoyed the mysterious voices and characters who called throughout my shift. One early morning, about 2:00 a.m., a young lady requested "Black Magic Woman" by Santana. She seemed very polite but sounded a little drunk and giddy. I told her I'd be happy to play her tune as soon as I had the chance, explaining I had other requests lined up ahead of hers. "Don't worry!" I said, "Ray-Baby will play 'Black Magic Woman' soon!"

About three minutes later, she called again, but her tone had changed from sweet to the street, "When are you gonna play my song, Raaay Baaaby?"

Calmly I replied, "Ma'am, you've gotta understand, other listeners are waiting for their songs, too. Stay cool and calm! I'm gonna play it soon."

She snapped, "Fine!" slamming the phone down without saying goodbye.

I played two more song requests before another call came in from my 'dedicated' listener. This time she made it clear she was through waiting and *demanded* I play her song next! I replied, "Okay!" with a tone close to a shout as I hung up the phone and began playing her tune. While the record was spinning, she called *again*, this time using uncommonly vile language - I'd heard these untamed words on the street a few times, but never with such hostility! She slammed the phone down on Ray-Baby once again, before I'd had a chance to respond.

Now Ray-Baby was angry and with emotions that were best not expressed on-air! Her song was playing; was she even listening? At that moment, it occurred to me I still had the power. Reaching over, I gently raised the arm of the turntable, releasing the needle from the grooves. The station went silent for a few moments while I casually found another record to play.

The request line lit up immediately. However, fearing a certain rabid woman who might be waiting to bark expletives, I did not answer the phone. It was my show with full control! I had the power and the music agenda. After all, I was the guy pulling down $1.65 an hour!

We at KBBY considered ourselves an underground rock station, patterned after the great KLOS-FM in Los Angeles. That meant a laid-back, low-key approach - no hyped up, wound up DJs here. Without a lot of talking, we smoothly segued from record to record all night long. Sometimes I wouldn't say a word for half an hour or more. Sometimes I'd play an entire album. FCC rules required five minutes of news each hour and a station identification (ID) at the top and bottom of the hour. I'd play an ID tape while flipping the vinyl over to hear the other side, but that was about it for rules. And like most teenagers, I didn't have an obsession with following them.

After about a month, I began inviting my friends to read news and weather reports on the air. I'm sure some rules were bent, but not broken. My penchant for ignoring rules was one reason Buck and the Owens family put me on the air from midnight until 6:00 a.m.

As an example of my light-hearted radicalism, which America's youth welcomed in the sixties, my friends and I delivered editorials on world events. This was live radio! While discussing the horrible Vietnam War or civil rights injustices, we frequently punctuated our reports with a swear word or two. The sadness of losing both Martin Luther King Jr. and the great Bobby Kennedy within months of each other inspired a few more well-placed profanities. We were angry! Bending the rules and sharing our thoughts on-air about extreme current events energized a small group, which developed into an estimated dozen faithful followers.

The radio station was housed in the Westerner Hotel's lobby on Union Avenue and Fourth Street in Bakersfield. One evening, upon arrival for work, management informed me the hotel was closed. However, the water and power utilities continued operating. As far as I was concerned, the hotel was still open for me and my friends, who soon became a regular crew. A few areas near the control room were 'appropriated' and converted to personal space. We added a refrigerator and some stereo equipment, then decorated the walls with various rock posters and black lights to complete the ambiance.

Every night turned into a party that I can only describe as a 'blast' (borrowing a sixties term). Back in the control room, I'd place another record on the turntable, announce the artist, and return to the party. (I was working, after all!) KBBY broadcast as usual, while I partied with friends all night for $1.65 an hour!

My crew of friends totaled about seven guest announcers. I pulled press off the news wires (AP and UPI) for them to read as five-minute newscasts, alone in the studio, while I returned to the party. It was hilarious - I laughed my ass off at their attempts to broadcast live, as much as they laughed at one another. They were terrible, and they knew it! The pressure of live radio was so intimidating they could hardly speak. After their five minutes of fame, I'd return to the control room to start up some music again. The management more than likely knew what I was up to but generously let me have my fun.

We didn't air many commercials in those days, so interruptions by fast-talking-heads trying to sell you something were few. It was radio bliss. However, on one occasion, I did take advantage of my underground fame. Randy Huddleston's dad, Cecil, had a barbershop in Oildale. Randy (one of my faithful followers) and his dad were funny, clever, witty souls who admired one another. Cecil Huddleston and I would become business partners for about an hour - or the total time the unauthorized commercials for his barbershop lasted!

In exchange for the commercial, I would receive a fifteen-minute hair cut from Cecil. I praised him and his barbershop throughout my six-hour shift, describing his business as the most far-out barbershop in America and Cecil as the most superb barber in California. He was quick with a quip and quick with a pair of scissors. Cecil was glad to see me when I came in for my free haircut several days later. Curious, I asked him how many customers had heard my commercials. He said none that he knew of, but he didn't care. Cecil was a cool sixties dad who treated me like Frank Sinatra when I came in for my haircut.

"Ray-Baby from K-Baby spins three at a time" is still a standard greeting amongst my friends. I earned that moniker because of another event that happened at KBBY one morning in early 1969. KBBY had switched from rock 'n' roll to a country music format a few months before. Instead of playing The Beatles, Jimi Hendrix, and my other rock heroes, we broadcast country singers like Porter Wagoner and Faron Young. And since I still had the option of playing whatever pleased me, quantities of Merle Haggard got air time, too.

Although I enjoyed the music of Buck Owens and Johnny Cash, some of the artists available for play were not to my liking, and another reason I played loads of Merle Haggard. Usually, around 5:00 a.m., Buck would call to request I play his own music. On one occasion, he asked me to play his Carnegie Hall Concert album - a live Buck Owens treasure and one of the best ever. I was more than happy to play this album for the boss! Buck never complained about my penchant for playing Merle Haggard because he loved Merle's music too.

However, one morning with about an hour left on my shift, I received a message informing me not to play any more Merle Haggard. Dorothy Owens, Buck's sister, and the radio station's general manager passed down the order, which initially came from the program director and DJ who aired immediately following my show.

This announcement did not sit well with me. My fellow DJ exited the control room after delivering the devastating message: "No more Merle Haggard!" This demand instantly activated my rebellious nature, inspiring me to quit my job in the manner of Johnny Paycheck's classic, "Take This Job and Shove It!" First, I had to confirm I wouldn't be noticed by the other DJ busy making commercials in a soundproof room. Then I quickly grabbed three Merle Haggard albums, placed them on three turntables, and played them simultaneously on the air. "Ray-Baby from K-Baby spins three at a time!"

With everything set to go, I left the station and began walking home. Friends later told me that all three records had played to the finish and ended with a few minutes of the three needles skipping as they ran out of grooves.

Dorothy wanted to kill me, so I stayed away from her for about a year. Buck, however, never said a word. Knowing him, he probably would've done something similar if faced with the same dilemma. After hearing about it, Merle was elated and kept that story close to his heart for decades, even sharing it with primary news sources in his later years. He was proud of me, and so was I.

Dorothy Owens was a tough, sweet bird of a lady. She eventually forgave me, as did all the Owens' clan, which they proved by hiring me again. I called them in 1972, asking for a DJ job, and to my astonishment and gratitude, they hired me. Since I was unemployed and getting married in a few months, the likelihood of any radical behavior was slim.

This time around, I went to work for the great country music station in Kern County, KUZZ AM and FM. My time slot was slated for 7:00 p.m. to midnight, six days a week, at a $350 monthly salary. And they gave me a new radio name: Robert E. Lee. Buck had a reason for assigning his DJs all-American names. After he explained how one of his DJs (not me!) had a minor run-in with the law, I understood why. The story appeared in the local newspaper, identifying the culprit as a DJ at KUZZ. That did it! After that, Buck assigned all-American 'radio names' to each DJ!

Buck liked the name John Paul Jones for the midnight to 6:00 a.m. shift (Misty Dawn for females). The morning DJ from 6:00 a.m. to 10:00 a.m. was allowed to use a showbiz name of his choice, providing it was not the DJ's real name. In other words, Johnny Kaye was actually Johnny Kirschner. The midday man, 10:00 a.m. to 2:00 p.m., was Bill Bailey; 2:00 p.m. to 6:00 p.m., Charlie Brown; and 7:00 p.m. to midnight, Robert E. Lee. After a year of pretending to be the Confederate General who died in 1870, I earned a promotion to the afternoon drive slot of 2:00 p.m. to 6:00 p.m. This was a prestigious move for me because now I would be on-air with the most massive audience I'd ever had. Now I would become one of America's most lovable losers, Charlie Brown.

The Owens family brought in a young pro from Arizona to boost ratings and make us a 'top forty' radio station, instead of the undisciplined lot we were. We had no real format and no real reason for playing hit records of the day in a controlled pattern. Tommy Wright changed all that. He taught me how to be a pro on the air. The Owens family so loved his enthusiasm and professionalism that they even let him use his real name while broadcasting.

Tommy took over the morning shift. Within a year, for the first time in its history, KUZZ became the number one position in the Bakersfield market. Number one had been sewn up for years by KAFY, the popular Bakersfield rock 'n' roll station. But with the implementation of Tommy's new format, KUZZ now would enjoy that honor. Luckily, I was right in the middle of all this success. Dorothy Owens and the entire family took pride in my role. One day Dorothy called me into her office and spent an hour lavishing praise on her Charlie Brown, which made it all worthwhile. Her charm and sincerity convinced me she no longer had hostile feelings toward the former Ray-Baby from K-Baby.

Not long after Tommy brought KUZZ to the number one slot, he and I both resigned abruptly, although I did so with proper notice. Both of us had similar reasons for departure, relative to the old dollar bill (or lack thereof). Despite KUZZ reaching the number one slot, in part due to our individual successes, we each learned there would be no pay raise because the station was in the red. Both of us opted to find a *greener pasture*!

My greener pasture turned out to be in the small town of St. George, Utah, where I worked for an upstanding Mormon family. I made as much money walking in the door as I had at KUZZ in three years! However, I quit that job in 1975, after about nine months. I was required to play too much Andy Williams music, and I'd had my fill!

In San Luis Obispo, California, a local radio station advertised a nationwide essay contest in *Billboard* magazine. They asked us to describe what we liked about being a DJ and why we wanted to move to San Luis Obispo. The prize was a DJ job at the local radio station KATY. News of winning the essay contest came as a big surprise! Shocked but delighted, my pretty young wife and I soon moved to the lovely California coastal town of San Luis Obispo, just a short ten miles from the beach.

The station KATY was a low watt AM station with a rock 'n' roll format. It was exhilarating to be again playing the music that suited me most, despite the fact this was a 'six days a week with no holidays' job. Reluctantly, I had come to accept this as the standard for DJ work.

The program director's method of programming was most unusual. Each day, he wrote down every song to be played for each shift. We were supposed to stick to the number system he had developed, but I found myself deviating from it occasionally. I had to! His program was driving me nuts! However, I did persuade him once to let me play a country song on our rock 'n' roll station. Surprise! It was Merle Haggard's "It's All in the Movies."

During my late shift, one lonely Saturday evening, a listener called asking if I'd like his two tickets to an Elton John concert in Los Angeles the following weekend. "Sure!" I said, asking if he could bring them to the station. With tickets in hand, the idea came to me to completely ignore the music list and play nothing but Elton John for an hour, with a ticket give-away right after. So, I played Elton John for a solid hour as the phone lines lit up with requests for his different tunes. I chose the forty-fourth caller as the winner, and a delighted KATY listener soon picked up the tickets from the station.

Monday morning turned interesting. The owner and furious program director called me into the office. They were not happy with my deviation from the number system, nor the solid hour of Elton John with the contest following. Secretly hoping they'd fire me, so I'd have a little break from the six-day per week grind, I didn't feel nervous in the least. They began their wild accusations: How *dare* I endanger the integrity of KATY; KATY *never* plays one artist for an entire hour! KATY *never* holds contests! How *dare* I conduct myself in such a manner!

The rant continued for several minutes. It ended when I interrupted and told them calmly that if they didn't like what I had done, it would be fine with me if they fired me immediately. They both tilted their heads one way and then the other, kind of like a confused puppy. I told them I thought the hour had been successful, evidenced by the phones lighting up like Christmas trees from listeners showing excitement and enthusiasm. Their respective eyebrows danced up and down as they contemplated this and realized maybe I was making sense! I was making sense out of complete nonsense – an action The Three Stooges had made me a believer in years before.

As fate would have it, Tommy Wright called with a job offer a few days after the meeting. He asked if I'd like to move to Las Vegas and become the midday DJ and music director for KLUC FM and AM, starting at $750 a month! I accepted immediately and gave them my one week notice at KATY. The owner wasn't pleased, saying two weeks is the normal advance notice time. I told him he should have known by then I wasn't normal! He settled for one week and proceeded to brag all over town about his DJ, who had landed a coveted position at KLUC in Las Vegas. We parted ways with no animosity.

KLUC was a blast! We brought ratings to number one within a year. I followed Tommy Wright's programming ploys while, in addition to Las Vegas, he programmed our sister station in Tucson, Arizona. Having received a promotion after a few months, I was now his acting program director. Tommy let me experiment using The Beatles as a staple for our station, so I promoted playing a Beatles record every hour of every day. And why not? Their music had changed the world. Even after their famous breakup in the spring of 1970, by 1976 (the year I ran the promotion), their music was still fresh, and they still had many fans.

KLUC asked their DJs to pick any Beatles song they wanted from any Beatles album with one caveat: they must check in with other staff to ensure no one repeated any songs throughout the day. We used short, live, on-air promos, sometimes with a teaser. For example: "I'll be playing a cut from *Sergeant Peppers* soon, stay tuned!" The response to the Beatles promo was so successful that we doubled the Beatles song play from one to two per hour. I passionately believe this promotion helped move KLUC to its number one position - that and the fact we gave away cash frequently during the Arbitron ratings! (Arbitron ratings are to radio as Neilson ratings are to television.)

In addition to the Beatles promo at KLUC, I had permission to broadcast the extended version of popular tunes during the 5:00 p.m. time slot. "Stairway to Heaven," by Led Zeppelin, "Voodoo Chile," by Jimmie Hendrix, "Light My Fire," by The Doors, "I'm Your Captain," by Grand Funk Railroad, "In-A-Gadda-Da-Vida," by Iron Butterfly, and of course, "A Day in the Life," by The Beatles are classic examples.

Some say all good things must come to an end, and my job at KLUC was no exception. While enjoying our 'Number One' celebration party, it came to my attention the man I replaced as acting program director had been paid a higher wage during his employment with KLUC. When I expressed this unfairness to the owner, he explained his reasons using profanity I did not appreciate. In return, I used a few choice words that promptly got me fired. I never regretted my actions. The man had it coming.

Las Vegas had numerous radio stations. I wound up working for KFM and then the crazy KDWN. KDWN called themselves KDAWN. (I called them K-R-A-Z-Y.) The owner was a peculiar soul. He phoned one Saturday night, asking why I was playing weird music on his station. The bizarre music he referred to was The Steve Miller Band. I wanted to explain how his music preferences had nothing to do with who or what the listeners wanted to hear, but it slipped out as, "So what!" He responded by firing me and told me to turn the station off and go home. We hung up as I was telling him what a ridiculous suggestion that was.

While waiting for reinforcements, I entertained the audience with the story of the crazy owner who wanted me to turn off a 50,000-watt station and go home as if I were turning off the lights at a sandwich shop. I delighted in playing "Purple Haze," and some Beatles songs we were not allowed to play on his station. When my replacement DJ arrived, that was it: I was officially retired. My radio DJ career ended that day at the age of twenty-seven.

Same Train, A Different Time

CHAPTER 6

Same Train, A Different Time: Merle Haggard Sings the Great
Songs of Jimmie Rodgers - Album released May 1, 1969

IN 1968, MERLE HAD JUST recorded an album called *Same Train, a
Different Time*. The album paid tribute to the great Jimmie Rodgers'
music of the 1930s. Merle recorded twenty-five songs – all Jimmie
Rodgers – in a two record set. I was eighteen years old and playing
country music on Buck Owens' radio station, KBBY FM (the precursor
to KUZZ FM). One night, my midnight till 6:00 a.m. shift was most
pleasantly interrupted by Merle Haggard, tapping on the window to
catch my attention.

KBBY had its radio station set up in the Westerner Hotel lobby on Fourth Street and Union Avenue in Bakersfield. A glass partition divided the lobby and the radio station. You could walk up close to the window and watch the DJ playing his records, which was pretty cool. But looking up from the turntable to see Merle Haggard knocking on the window at 2:00 a.m., waving a new record in his hand, was the best! Visitors were rare on my late-night shift, except for several of my friends who I'd let read five-minute news clips or choose some music to play (as you read in chapter five). I was pretty confident not many people listened to the midnight shift but hoped if they did, they'd get a kick out of my programming. Anyone listening in the night Merle paid his surprise visit was definitely in for a treat.

The album Merle Haggard was waving at me happened to be *Same Train, a Different Time*, in dubbed form. Dubbed form means pressed on vinyl but not yet available in any store. Merle's copy didn't have an album cover, but the songs' names were written on all four sides of the two sleeves. He had stopped by to see if I would like to be the first DJ in the world to play his new album on the air. "Of course!" I said, trying to contain my excitement.

Merle took a seat at the guest microphone while I hosted him from the main mic. We played every song on all four sides of the album - all twenty-five. We talked about his arrangements and the musicians who played on each recording. One selection titled "Down the Old Road to Home" featured Merle solo, singing and playing his acoustic guitar - the only song to my knowledge he ever recorded that way. Merle mentioned that the song "Down the Old Road to Home" was a favorite of Dean Holloway, who'd been his best friend since sixth grade and his first tour bus driver.

The album was destined to be one of the most historical albums in the genre. To followers of country music in the 1960s, this album helped re-introduce Jimmie Rodgers as the father of country music. In 1968 when Merle decided to record this album, he explained why he was doing it. At thirty years old and with several number one hits under his belt, he could have easily made more money working on recordings of his own songs (royalties, etc.). But out of respect for Jimmie Rodgers and considering how the song royalties would go to Jimmie's heirs, Merle felt compelled to do it. It was his tribute to Jimmie Rodgers, someone he admired greatly!

For this occasion, Merle brought Glen Campbell and James Burton into the studio band. (He had worked with them on "Tonight the Bottle Let Me Down," two years prior.) He also enlisted Norman Hamlet and Roy Nichols, who became stalwarts of Merle's band, The Strangers. Merle sang all the songs with such authenticity, delivering some of the topmost vocals of his career. To promote the album, he released "California Blues" as a single. The album is remarkable and still one of my favorites.

Once again, I was fortunate to be invited to Capitol Records to watch and listen to Merle during a recording session. This time it was for one of the songs included on *Same Train, a Different Time*. Now I knew about the new album in progress! A friend from high school, Steve Woods, who also loved Merle's music, drove to Los Angeles with me for the recording session. Merle was gentle but firm, telling us we could sit in the studio but could not make a sound. We sat for hours watching this great man and his band make history. The song we were privy to that day was "Peach Pickin' Time in Georgia." It's a classic!

After the session, we thanked everyone involved, then headed down Hollywood's Sunset Boulevard, on our way to Interstate 5, and the short trip back to Bakersfield. I was driving Steve's 1960-something Volkswagen coupe. Around midnight we stopped at a red light. While waiting for the light to change, a guy came bopping across the street, followed by a little boy, maybe eight or nine years old. Both of them were barefoot. We watched at first in amusement but then realized it was unusual to see a child that age crossing the street so late at night, without an adult holding his hand. But we soon discovered this was not an ordinary situation! The adult was none other than Jim Morrison, lead vocalist for one of the world's best-known rock bands, The Doors!

Steve noticed Jim Morrison first and jumped out of the car, yelling, "Jim! Jim!" We were both startled to see a superstar crossing the street in front of us. Hadn't we been lucky enough for one day? Jim acknowledged the kids from Oildale with a smile and a wave. I've always wondered about the little boy.

The next time I saw Merle, I told him of our brush with the famous Jim Morrison, but Merle had no idea who Jim Morrison was. The Doors? Merle was so focused on his own recording career and monitoring what was going on in country music that he didn't pay much attention to other genres, especially rock 'n' roll.

Merle vs. Buck

CHAPTER 7

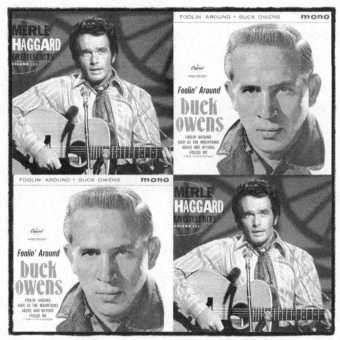

Two country albums by two country superstars!

MERLE HAGGARD AND BUCK OWENS were huge fans of each other's talent, and I was fortunate to often witness firsthand their mutual admiration. The first time Merle and his Strangers played at Buck's Crystal Palace, I listened as Buck introduced Merle by saying, "This man has no peers; he's the greatest singer-songwriter in the history of country music." In a *Bakersfield Californian* interview, Merle stated, "Buck was one of the greatest entertainers of the century. He influenced everybody, from me to The Beatles."

Buck and Merle inspired one another (like the mutual inspiration between The Beatles and the Beach Boys), but they were rivals in the business of country music. Buck had nineteen number one hits; Merle totaled forty by the end of his career. In 2005, Buck asked me how many times Merle had topped the charts with a number one hit. When I stated the number, his response was insightful and sincere. Buck felt he could have had more hits if Don Rich had not died so young. The multi-talented Don Rich was the ultimate sideman with his brilliant harmonies, guitar playing, fiddling, and in essence, imperative to the success of Buck Owens.

In July of 1974, Don Rich was only thirty-three when a motorcycle accident in Morro Bay, California, cut his life short. Everyone was devastated, not only for the loss of his talent but also for losing such a warm, caring man. I'm sure Buck was correct in his assessment of how Don's passing affected his career. He didn't just lose his sideman; Buck lost a friend he'd known and worked with for around seventeen years. Professionally, he never quite recovered from that loss. (However, Buck shared a number one hit, "Streets of Bakersfield," with Dwight Yoakum in 1988.)

Merle and Buck had so much in common, but they were different spirits. Buck would rather play golf; Merle preferred fishing. Buck would rather watch golf on television; Merle would choose to watch a program on fishing. Buck excelled at all his business ventures, including real estate, country music, radio stations, and television shows (remember *Hee Haw*?). Merle excelled at his country music business but wasn't inclined to let other business commitments tie him down - he'd rather go fishing.

Here's an example of Merle's reluctance to commit. In 2001, while working as his personal assistant/office manager at his ranch in Palo Cedro, Merle was besieged by a startup radio venture from Sirius

XM. They repeatedly called, asking him to lend his name to one of their stations featuring country music, but Merle just as often turned them down. They couldn't understand his reluctance to commit, but I did. Even though he had a marvelous opportunity for inclusion into a significant worldwide venture, he made it clear he didn't want to be *controlled* by any corporation - even if it proved to be a sound and profitable business venture. Merle was a curious soul.

Although a digression, this paragraph illustrates a mischievous aspect of Merle's personality. During negotiations with Sirius XM, he had told me that he occasionally answered the office phone by impersonating my voice. He even went so far as to make a verbal deal with Sirius, which he knew wasn't binding since 'Ray' had made the deal, and Merle had no intention of signing it. Merle asked if I'd like to hear his impersonation of me, and of course, I said yes! Hearing my voice coming from Merle was mind-boggling. He was a master at impersonations – check "Merle Doing Impersonations" on *YouTube* – you will be impressed by this unique talent of his.

Merle and Buck were both athletic. In his youth, Merle was a fast runner and good at baseball. Buck could throw a mean football when he played quarterback for both our practice teams, comprised of Buddy, Mike, myself, and many of our high school friends. And Buck, who was above average at the sport of golf, taught Buddy, Mike, and me how to play – I still play golf and appreciate Buck for teaching me the game.

Both men were great at singing and playing guitar - world-class at their profession. How do these skills equate with athleticism? It has been my observation that most great guitarists are incredibly coordinated. The addition of voice adds another layer of complexity. It takes years of practice and toil to perfect rhythm, timing, and phrasing, even though men like Haggard and Owens made it look easy.

Merle and Buck were musical athletes. Just as superstar sports heroes aren't born that way, and must spend years of hard work and dedication developing their talents, so do superstar musicians as they perfect their gifts. And like athletes, it takes physical endurance to perform: imagine standing, sometimes jumping (think Mick Jagger), under hot lights in a stuffy atmosphere, concentrating on making music in front of a large crowd for several hours at a time. To say performing is demanding and exhausting is an understatement.

Merle and Buck each were generous souls. Buck had a strong, sweet brother named Mel, who died of cancer in the early seventies - a devastating loss for the entire family. Buck channeled his sorrow by starting the Buck Owens Invitational to help raise research money for the Cancer Society. He invited some of the biggest names in stardom to participate: John Wayne of movie fame; Willie Shoemaker, a celebrity jockey; Mickey Mantle, Steve Garvey, and Johnny Bench - all giants of the baseball world. Countless other big-name actors, singers, and athletes contributed their time and talent to his fundraising efforts. Buck was a noble man, always willing to help a good cause or someone in need.

Now that I played golf and enjoyed a good game, and knowing the tournament was a worthwhile cause (not to mention the celebrities in attendance), I desperately wanted to play in the tournament. Feeling disappointed because I didn't have the $300 entry fee, a friend with a generous soul and kind heart saved the day. Merle Haggard paid my fee that year and several years after.

Merle was not a golfer and was usually busy working during the annual tournament. One day, while paired with country singer Charlie Pride (who claimed he'd be better if he played more!) and television star Johnny Crawford (*The Rifleman*), Merle suddenly appeared. It was cause for wonder how Merle knew precisely where to find us at that particular moment. I learned later he had telepathic powers. He must have channeled them that day!

As we walked up to a putting green not far from the nearby road, a brand new Lincoln Continental slowed, then stopped close to the fence. A man got out, hopped the fence, and began walking toward us. As soon as Merle was recognized, Charlie rushed to him with a warm greeting and big hug as he exclaimed how happy he was to see him. Merle had recently won Entertainer, Vocalist, and Song of the Year Awards from the Country Music Awards (CMAs). Merle was the biggest star in country music and Charlie Pride's hero.

Charlie asked Merle to hop in and ride in his golf cart, and Merle obliged. When Charlie hit a terrible drive into the trees, Merle laughed and continued to chuckle as Charlie chopped away, trying to help the ball find its way back to civilization. (Charlie came close to becoming a major league baseball player - more proof of the connection between music and athletic ability. I am sure he would have been better at golf if he'd had the time to practice.)

Merle accompanied us until the ninth hole - a few beyond where he joined us - then turned to walk back to his car. I think he left the golf course for fear of creating a stir among the crowds, or he may have had an appointment. Whatever his reason for departure, the time he spent with us was the highlight of the tournament.

One morning, Merle and Buck teamed up against Buddy and me at the Kern City Golf Course. This was the first time I had seen them play golf together, and I was quite surprised that Merle had joined the game. He played well for a guy who didn't play much! They rode around in their cart, laughing and thoroughly enjoying each other's company. Buddy was a lucky guy to have two dads – especially two dads who got along so well as friends. (If you've forgotten, Merle was Buddy's step-dad.)

Buddy and I enjoyed playing golf with Merle and Buck. Merle had a long putt and rolled the ball a good fifteen feet past the hole. He took his next shot and purposely sent the ball about thirty feet beyond the hole. Buck found Merle's shenanigans hilarious. Buddy and I finally caught on that the golf match was over. It wasn't too surprising we didn't finish all eighteen holes. Merle yelled to Buck, "Let's go, man!" They got in their cart and drove off laughing, leaving us there with a great memory. I loved days like these.

One of my warmest memories of these two great men is from the year 2005. Merle was opening for Bob Dylan, and both Bob and Merle had invited Buck to the concert. Buck called to see if I'd like to fly to Portland, Oregon, for their performance. We asked our girlfriends to join us, and we all headed out together on Buck's private jet. Buck brought along a special gift for Bob Dylan - a red, white, and blue, custom Buck Owens, Fender Telecaster guitar. Buck and Bob had not met yet but had become huge fans of each other..

Our girlfriends sat out front while Buck and I were on the side-stage watching Merle perform. Buck asked me to find Bob's crew to ask if he and Bob could meet before Bob went on stage. I delivered the news, but they said Bob always sleeps before his show. So I went back to the venue to let Buck know that they probably wouldn't be meeting before Bob's performance.

As I walked back into the venue, a mighty roar came from the crowd. When I arrived, Buck was descending the stairs from the stage. I surmised that Merle had called Buck onto the stage. The audience was still elated and continued to roar! My guess was right; Merle *had* introduced Buck to the crowd – it was a total surprise! Buck, so overwhelmed by the audience's response, began crying. I'd known Buck for forty years and had never seen such pure emotion pour from his soul. Buck grabbed me by my shoulders and said, "Raymond! You don't know how happy I am to have experienced this moment!" I will admit he moved me to tears. Buck was overjoyed, as was I to see him so happy. We were two grown men shedding tears of joy!

After Merle's performance, we went backstage to see if Bob Dylan had awakened from his nap. He was standing there, as majestic as I ever could have imagined. I was awestruck being in his presence. When Buck handed him his new guitar - the look on Dylan's face was that of a ten-year-old who had just been given a brand new bike for his birthday. He was delighted to meet Buck Owens. All this was happening as Merle looked on with the biggest smile I'd ever seen from him.

Merle and Buck were elected to the Country Music Hall of Fame in Nashville, Tennessee. Merle in 1994 and Buck in 1996. Merle informed me of his honor by phone. It was August of 1994, but the ceremony wasn't until October in Nashville. He sounded melancholy, but I was elated! I gave him short but sincere congratulations, telling him they were about twenty years late with their election.

Merle asked if I would call Buck with the news. This was an honor, and I called him immediately at his home in Bakersfield. Buck was warm in his praise, absolute in his assessment, and firm in his belief that Merle Haggard was the greatest all-around country music artist ever. Buck told me a 'cold chill' had run down his spine! He thanked me profusely for calling with the great news.

Two years later, I received a call from Buck Owens in August of 1996. Buck had just been elected to the Hall of Fame! After hearty congratulations from one Raymond McDonald, his former pass-catching DJ, and golfing partner, Buck asked if I'd call Merle with his good news. I'd had another honor bestowed on me, so I called Merle immediately. He was home relaxing in his favorite easy chair when he answered the phone. Merle loved the news! He gave me a ten-minute dissertation on why Buck Owens deserved the honor. He said a 'cold chill' had run down his back. Merle and Buck's reactions were so similar it was uncanny! This gave *me* a cold chill!

I'd watched the CMA awards for nearly thirty years, and every year I wondered why Merle and Buck had not yet won the award. Buck titled on of his classic songs "My Heart Skips a Beat." I imagine that's what both of these great artists experienced when they were finally elected to the Country Music Hall of Fame!

Buck and Merle at the Palace

CHAPTER 8

Backstage pass – Grand Opening: Buck Owen's Crystal Palace
Photo courtesy of Raymond McDonald

BUCK OWENS AND MERLE HAGGARD, both one-in-a-trillion type characters, were two of the coolest cats I have ever known. I loved it when they got together, which wasn't often enough.

Around 1996, Buck Owens opened a nightclub in Bakersfield, California, called the Crystal Palace. The Palace resembled a museum and nightclub rolled into one superb venue. Buck wanted Merle to perform at the Palace, but somehow in the two years since the doors opened, this had never happened. So Buck called me in Las Vegas (where I'd moved to work with KLUC) and asked if I could get in touch with Merle about performing at his nightclub. Surprised by Buck's call but always willing to help him with anything he asked, I agreed to contact Merle. I caught Merle at home and passed on Buck's request.

"When?" asked Merle.

"As soon as you can; Buck mentioned something about two weeks from now," I responded, hoping he wasn't already booked.

"Alright, tell him I'll play two nights down there. We're not booked right now anyway," said Merle.

I called Buck right away with the good news. On a Friday or Saturday evening, a week later, Buck said, "Thank you, Raymond!" Then he invited me to be his guest at the show. I brought my wife, Kathleen, my high school sweetheart and all-time love. Our evening at the Palace, watching Merle Haggard and Buck Owens, could not have been more gratifying.

In those days, like most bands, Merle didn't have a formal introduction. His band, The Strangers, usually played a theme song then cranked it up when Merle walked on stage. However, Buck wanted to introduce him, so Merle agreed. When Merle walked onto the stage (without his theme song), Buck put his arm around him and said, "This man has no peers. He is the greatest country music singer/songwriter in history." Merle humbly accepted this glowing introduction as the crowd gave him a roaring ovation.

Later in the set, Merle called Buck to the stage to sing harmony on a Haggard classic, "Swingin' Doors." The following night they would do the same: Buck would introduce Merle, then Buck would leave the stage and wait for Merle to call him back right before "Swingin' Doors." The song kicked off, but Merle had not yet invited Buck to sing with him. Buck had been sitting in the audience with his girlfriend, and the second it became clear Merle was not calling him back on stage, they jumped up and quickly left the Crystal Palace.

I called Buck the next day and said, "I'll bet you a million dollars, Buck, that Merle forgot to have you join him on stage. He doesn't use a set-list; he wings everything, and I think he just plain forgot!" Buck said, "Well, Raymond, I'm so glad you called me about this, and I hope you're right because it did hurt." Merle and I never had a conversation about it, but I am sure he really did forget. Merle wouldn't do something like that intentionally, especially to Buck. He was a huge fan of his music and held Buck and his music in the highest esteem. Not many know or remember, but Merle played in Buck's band for a few weeks in the early sixties and was the person who gave the Buckaroos their name.

Merle called me the morning Buck died, March 25, 2006. He said, "Buck Owens may have been the best ever." I think Merle was referring both to Buck as his friend and to Buck's incredible legacy. Those were some poignant days…

Trip to Kansas

CHAPTER 9

Merle's 'Super Chief' bus – 14 feet tall, 45 feet long, 48,000 lbs.
Photo courtesy of Raymond McDonald

AFTER MERLE DIED ON HIS birthday, April 6, 2016, I retired from commercial driving. Taking a road trip in a standard vehicle sounded relaxing compared to driving a monster tour bus with the weight of responsibility for others' safety - particularly a friend and 'national treasure' like Merle.

About ten months after his passing, I decided to visit my roots back on the Prairie Band Potawatomi Reservation. It was over fifteen hundred miles from Las Vegas to Mayetta, Kansas, a relatively short journey for a well-seasoned, retired tour bus driver. The distance gave me substantial time to recollect the many trips I made on the road with Merle. The act of recalling and ruminating would also help keep me awake! Recording my memories while driving seemed the obvious solution - I could transcribe them later. This chapter tells a few of those recollections of the myriad adventures I had the privilege and good fortune to experience as Merle's friend and tour bus driver.

Merle had some strong opinions of what he liked and disliked about traveling in America. He didn't like bumpy roads, and there are many bumpy roads in these United States. Some of these rough roads go on for hundreds of miles and even continue into neighboring states. Some states, such as Arkansas and Louisiana, don't have a smooth road anywhere.

A million-dollar-plus-tour-bus, such as 'The Super Chief,' doesn't ensure a smooth ride. Merle used to say, "A bus is still a bus. It is going to be bumpy. Your drinks will go flying, you will go flying, and everything that isn't tied down will go flying." If you happen to be walking in the back when the bus takes a tight curve, you may get knocked down or slammed against a wall. This is true – I know because I have experienced it with other drivers at the wheel.

Having toured for more than fifty years, Merle had more than a few stories to share about the perils of 'living' in a moving bus, but if I ever caused him to hit the floor, he never mentioned it. Merle was like a great football coach: he knew when and how to chew you out. I told him he was the country music equivalent of Vince Lombardi, the great Green Bay Packers' coach. He asked, "Who in the hell is Vince Lombardi?" The point here is that even if I did inadvertently cause him to fall, he knew it was not intentional nor a result of reckless driving and wisely never mentioned it. If a road were particularly rough, sometimes Merle would carefully work his way to the front to ask how fast I was driving. I'd say 65 mph, for example, and he'd tell me to go 50 mph. So I'd turn on the flashers and slow to the requested speed, knowing that despite a slightly smoother ride, the dangers of moving so slowly among legions of big rigs are many.

Forty tons of steel moving at 70 to 85 mph can appear suddenly from nowhere to create 'terror in the rearview mirror,' like Dennis Weaver in Spielberg's action thriller, *Fuel*. Then with horns blaring as they bolt past, generating enough force to rock a 24-ton tour bus, I'd wipe the sweat from my brow and thank God we were still rolling down the pavement. This stress intensified with time and imagination, not knowing if the semi closing the gap behind us included a driver reading a book, watching a movie, texting, or doing all three simultaneously. After suffering a few hours of this, conditions permitting, and with the hope that Merle was fast asleep, my speed would climb back to 60 mph!

Typically we drove three to four hundred miles every night, leaving after the end of a show around 11:00 p.m. Merle needed to sleep well during this travel time. However, sleeping on a bus is not easy, and it's one of the less glamorous aspects of touring. Of course, a lot depends on the road and the driver. Still, generally, as a passenger, you will experience a fair amount of bouncing, gravity shifts from up and downhill grades, and a few surprise curves with enough centrifugal force to roll you out of bed.

Also, especially during night driving, circumstances can cause a sudden down-shift and/or use of brakes. A few of these sleep-disruptors include, but are not limited to: an unexpected wreck around a blind curve; an extremely slow vehicle with no taillights; a deer leaping out of the darkness; or one of many ill-fated critters from west to east coast waltzing onto the road for a leisurely late-night stroll. Unfortunately, most of these nocturnal amblers end up as roadkill because the risk of braking or swerving to avoid them is too dangerous.

One night, Merle watched the road with me from the passenger seat before heading off to sleep. An armadillo (you guessed - we were in Texas!) was perfectly aligned with the 48,000-pound behemoth heading his direction. I had no choice but to squash him. Merle remained calm and commented, "Well, I guess it was his time to go."

Bridge abutments were definitely not a favorite. With no exception, in every state, the transition over the abutment from smooth road to bridge was as rough as driving over a railroad track when you catch a little air then land with a jolt – not great for sleeping!

FOG! Merle and I shared a mutual disdain for this hazardous natural phenomenon. Give me ice, sleet, snow, wind, driving rain, or heck, even a tornado! Out of all the elements that negatively affect driving conditions, fog is the worst because you literally cannot see what's coming! You may as well put on a blindfold and begin heading down the road. Fog waits for you, looming heavily with its devious purpose.

I have driven through the fog in just about every state: North Carolina, Oklahoma, and especially in California's central valley, where Haggard grew up and where I had lived long enough to develop my distaste for it. They call it Tule fog - it is the thickest fog I have ever encountered. What's unfathomable is how some people, once enveloped, continue driving the speed limit or even faster. Frequent multi-car pileups along foggy segments of Interstate 5 are a testament to this foolishness.

Merle often sat up front to help calm my nerves. He advised me to stay focused on the vehicle directly in front of us, keeping the maximum distance before the fog entirely swallowed their already dim taillights. Sometimes they'd pull off, and without those guiding lights, I'd be forced to slow down again.

After returning from Texas, we drove Interstate 5 amid this formidable fog for hundreds of miles. Once black, my hair had turned multiple shades of gray, compliments of my nemesis, the fog! Praying constantly, I'd watch for front running taillights like a hawk watching for breakfast. Not soon enough, we arrived safely in San Luis Obispo just off highway 101. Three other drivers on board, all great at driving, shared the stress of that leg of the journey: Biff Adams, Merle's drummer; Joe Manuel, his guitarist; and Ben Haggard, Merle's son and guitarist. They had all mentored me during my rookie days of driving.

The next and last show of the tour was scheduled for Santa Barbara, California, about one hundred miles from San Luis Obispo. I needed a break. My nerves were shot - I felt I'd have to be committed if required to drive one more mile in the fog! The three other drivers on board could easily maneuver the bus back to Palo Cedro. I mustered up the courage to ask Merle if I could go home to Bakersfield, explaining my rationale. He calmly looked at me and said, "Get the hell out of here!" Thinking he was angry, I told him I was sorry, but this tour had freaked me out after driving in so much fog and explained how my nerves were shot, and I didn't feel up to anymore driving. He repeated himself, laughing but serious, "It's okay, Ray, now get the hell out of here!" Those were beautiful words!

That was the only time I bailed on Merle out of fear. We had been fortunate no one had ever stalled in front of us. And we had been lucky not to end up sandwiched in one of those fifty car pileups mentioned above, happening religiously every year on Interstate 5 and Highway 99 during the foggy season. The other three drivers got Merle safely back to Palo Cedro; while I recovered, nursing a bottle of whiskey at home in Bakersfield. Good old Coach Haggard knew when to bench me, even though I had asked for it.

Most everyone knows of Donner Pass, named after the doomed souls who tried to cross the Sierra Nevada mountain range from Reno, Nevada, to California's Sacramento Valley during the winter of 1846 and 1847. Some of those ill-fated pioneers resorted to cannibalism to survive. At a total of 7056 feet elevation, the pass is one of the few routes crossing the Sierra Nevada from the east to the west side. The drive from Reno is very steep and often closes during heavy winter snowstorms. Donner Pass is where I nearly let us slip into the pages of history.

In the winter of 2011, Merle had just performed another successful concert for the folks in Reno. Snow had begun to fall, and as we left town, I was ready to postpone the drive over Donner Pass. However, not having the authority to make that decision, we proceeded towards the summit. Merle put on his co-pilot hat and began advising me on controlling the bus in such dangerous conditions. He made it clear that once the bus was driving uphill, I should not use the brakes, or we'd slide backward uncontrollably.

We stopped where required by California Highway Patrol and paid to have our chains installed. Only one lane was open now due to stalled vehicles clogging the inside lane. After driving about 15 mph for a few miles, both lanes were at a complete standstill. Merle had instructed me only to use my gears to keep the bus in check, never the brakes. We had come to a stop but had started sliding backward, which caused me to hit the brakes instinctively. We began sliding more when I suddenly remembered to use the gears as instructed. The bus grabbed, and we now had traction! Thankfully, a lane had opened, allowing us to miss a big rig by inches as we passed it and continued on our way.

To avoid further potential fiascos, Merle wisely continued giving me instruction from the back. We could have ended up at the bottom of the mountain, and Ray McDonald would have gone down in country music history as the infamous Donner driver who met his doom. I still shiver at the thought of us sliding off that mountain. Merle, along with good fortune, and in part, my skill (I'd like to think), prevented us from increasing the number of Donner Pass victims that day. I was sixty-one years old when we started up the mountain and one hundred and twenty-one years old when we reached the other side. Thank God it wasn't the other 'other' side!

Thick fog and a snowy mountain pass were not the only situations Merle helped me navigate. Once in Canada, we had to traverse five hundred miles up and around a mountain to get to our next venue. Merle must have been exhausted, having worked all day and night, but came up front to help guide me through a snowstorm. He told me not to drive faster than 10 mph and then sat in the passenger seat for four hours, keeping me company (and keeping an eye on everything, I am sure). He grew tired and told me to pull over to get some rest as he headed back to finally do the same. Fortunately, the only rest stop for many miles appeared minutes later. After resting a few hours, we continued the journey, arriving safely after a very long winter's night.

After the Canadian tour, Merle mentioned we had another tour there in a few months. I immediately told him I didn't want to go. He asked, "Now, Raymond, why wouldn't you go help us when we need you the most?"

I said, "Because Canada has the worst roads in America!" He laughed as I continued, "Canada calls one of their main highways a superhighway. But superhighway it is not! It is more like a two-lane road with no lights for thousands of miles. I have never seen a warning sign, 'Caution; Moose Kills' in America! It is a dangerous road, and I do not want to go!" Merle did not reply. He had a variety of facial expressions that did not require words. His expression was inquisitive – the 'I wonder what this guy is thinking?' look. Merle often tried to decipher why people thought and acted as they did. Well, we did go to Canada one more time, and I drove, but it was another close call with insanity. Thank God for home and whiskey!

Merle appreciated 100% honesty, 100% of the time. He may not be 100% happy with you initially, not even 1%, but he always tried to understand. So I tried to be at least 99% honest, 100% of the time. This next situation demanded 100% honesty.

We had a few weeks of downtime, and I was playing some golf and relaxing at home while listening to The Beatles and Merle Haggard and the Strangers. Merle called in a good mood and asked if I could pick him up in a few days and drive him to San Quentin to perform for the inmates. San Quentin prison is maybe two hundred miles from Merle's house, so not far...a comfortable trip. Nevertheless, I immediately responded, "Can I pass on that?"

Merle asked, "Now, why would you ask that? Why would you not want to go to San Quentin?"

I said, "Because I've visited people in prison before, and I did not like the rules for the visitors such as: sit up straight; don't put your hands in your pockets; don't touch each other; don't do this; don't do that. The guards watch you like a hawk, and you don't dare annoy them, or they'll kick you out. You cannot wear certain clothing, and basically, the guards are in total control of you. I didn't like that, and I don't want to be in that position ever again. I don't want to go inside those gates - I don't want to go to San Quentin. Can you please find someone else to drive instead?"

He paused a moment, then said, "Hell! I'm not going either! Merle canceled the show. Did I feel sorry for the inmates? Yep! But I thought Merle had steel balls ever to go back inside, even as a visiting musician - and he had performed a few times in prisons already! He had spent nearly three years as an inmate in San Quentin when he was very young and knew how the inmates felt. He hoped to brighten their day, but after being reminded of that environment, he chose not to subject himself to all the rules and the guards' unpleasant behavior.

The Weather Radio

CHAPTER 10

Photo illustration - R.J. Shearin

MERLE WAS A STICKLER FOR safety. He'd been on the road in some capacity in various vehicles for around fifty years and millions of miles. So with great confidence, I followed every bit of advice he gave me. Merle enjoyed driving his buses, from the first in 1965 to the last in 2015 - his Prevost beauty and Rolls Royce of the bus world. And on the matter of safety, Merle became adamant about one thing: the weather radio channel.

At his request, he had a weather radio installed in his trusted 2005 MCI (Motor Coach Industries), the next to last bus he owned and one of several over the decades. While still daylight, we had just left his ranch in northern California, headed to Oklahoma on Interstate 5. He instructed me to pull into the next truck stop to purchase a weather radio. My co-driver was a mechanic and well trained in all sorts of applications. I knew he could install it as soon as time allowed. Merle made it clear he wanted the radio operational as quickly as possible before heading into areas of the country that nearly always experienced severe weather. This inclement weather included ferocious winds, rainstorms so intense you literally couldn't see past the windshield, and frankly, just about any concoction brewed up by Mother Nature.

The radio was now up and running. Merle wanted us to leave it on twenty-four hours a day, seven days a week. Each state had constant updates, particularly if severe weather was predicted. We relied on these predictions, which brought relief by aiding our decisions in driving routes and patterns. There were warnings for tornados, rains, floods, ice, snow, fog, and high winds, with the wind's direction, speed, and location. Access to all this information was new to me. I quickly became a huge fan of the weather radio even though the announcers sounded like computer-generated weather radio robots.

The weather had been good all day but surprised us by changing quickly. It had become a dark and stormy night, and we had turned the weather radio volume up loud as we listened intently. We were leaving Tulsa, Oklahoma, heading home to California after a two-week tour of Middle America. Now heading west on Interstate 40, massive thunder and lightning storms raged from Tulsa to Oklahoma City.

Tornado warnings were issued near our path but not directly in it, so we forged ahead. The weather radio announced a severe wind warning for Interstate 40 West from Oklahoma City to Amarillo, Texas, with 70 mph winds heading straight down from the north, cutting across our path. Merle was in his private quarters in the back of the bus, so I informed him of the situation and asked if we should pull over somewhere. Calmly he instructed me to slow down to 45 mph and turn on the flashers until we were out of the windstorm. He then left again for the back of the bus.

Some truck drivers seem oblivious to any road dangers. A few had blown past me at 70 to 80 mph as if the road conditions were perfect with no wind or rain. I felt nervous driving at 45 mph because of their recklessness but had promised Merle I'd follow his advice. So as we traveled west at 45 mph down Interstate 40, the winds began their assault - just as the weather radio had predicted. They hit the side of Merle's fourteen-foot tall, forty-five-foot long, 48,000-pound bus with relentless force. The 'mortal' (as I called it) MCI handled the conditions well, but I definitely had to keep a tight hold!

After about fifteen minutes of constant, strong side winds, three semi-trucks blew past us in the fast lane. Those trucks are fifty-six to seventy feet long and can weigh up to 70,000 pounds. I thought, "Man, those guys are crazy!" About five minutes later, all three were flipped on their sides, laying in the median of Interstate 40 like beached whales. The winds had swept them up and toppled them like toys! Maybe they were unaware of the warnings; maybe they didn't care. If nothing else, common sense should have kicked in, but it didn't, and it cost them.

The winds receded as we pulled into a truck stop in Amarillo about fifteen minutes later. I went to the back of the bus and told Merle about the three trucks blown over by the high winds. He said, "Good job Raymond! You were listening to the weather radio! Let that be a lesson to you!" It was a lesson. I had learned to respect Merle's wisdom even more. Thanks to Merle, I'm convinced the weather radio saved us!

His Music

CHAPTER 11

Monument at the Harley Davidson store on Merle Haggard
Drive in Oildale, California *Photo courtesy of Raymond McDonald*

THE VOICE IS THE VERY first thing you notice when you hear a Merle
Haggard song. Pure, strong, soft, emotional, sincere, smooth, rough -
whatever the lyrics called for, he answered with a style all his own. Merle
was a natural-born vocalist, unsurpassable.

I was fourteen years old in 1964 and listening to music at
the home of my good friends, Mike and Buddy Owens, who had a
record player! The first record album I ever heard by Merle was titled,
Strangers. The album covered a wide variety of country music, and each
song deserved a standing ovation.

Bonnie Owens was Mike and Buddy's mother and a wonderful lady previously married to Buck Owens, long before Buck became a big star. She was a great singer, too. Bonnie and Merle had recorded a duet album for Capitol Records, so she happened to have a brand new copy of Merle's latest solo album at their house. The vinyl was shiny without a scratch on it, and when we played that album, it blew our teenage minds!

One song that stood out above others and melted my young heart was "Falling for You." It is the most beautiful song, and Merle sang it with every ounce of his soul. The arrangement, full of violins, was as lush as anything I'd ever heard. Ralph Mooney, the great steel guitarist, wrote this ballad. It deserves mention here because, without Ralph, there is no song!

Growing up, we never owned a record player because we couldn't afford one. We listened to the radio, which my mother always had tuned to country music. In 1955, I was five years old and shared a room with my fourteen-year-old brother (poor guy!). He acquired a radio of his own, so I was very soon exposed to a new kind of music called rock 'n' roll, and I loved it! Elvis Presley, a young singer who was among my favorites, would, in time, become known as the king of rock 'n' roll. He was simply the best - until I heard Merle Haggard.

Willie Nelson once told Merle and me as we sat on his bus one California evening, "Everyone has an opinion, and they will gladly give it to you!" I'm giving you my opinion now: Merle is the king of country music and the best singer from any genre, period.

I had the pleasure of driving Merle all over America for the last six years of his career. During those long bus rides, we had the opportunity for conversations that were just as long. We talked about everything under the sun. I was so curious about his songs and was happy to be able to inquire about my favorites. He'd always respond to my inquiries and appreciated that his works meant something to so many people, including me. Here are a few recollections of some of those conversations and experiences.

KERN RIVER

It took me thirty years to ask. After another long tour, we had stopped for fuel at a truck stop in Bakersfield on our way home to Redding. The sun was just rising on a beautiful California morning. In a great mood after a good night's sleep, Merle had walked up to join me in the front of the bus. It was quiet, so I seized the moment to ask questions that I had wanted to ask for decades: "Did you really lose your girl, your best friend, in the Kern River? Did she die in the moonlight? Did she drown?" I asked these questions using a tender tone, a little nervous about bringing up bad memories. What a surprise when he answered, "No, I made that one up, Ray."

Merle wrote "Kern River" one morning on his tour bus, just around sunrise, and possibly from the same truck stop where we were now discussing his tragic ballad. Many theories of its inspiration had surfaced over the years, and I shared a few with him. Some believed it was because his horse had drowned, and others thought it had been his dog, and I didn't know, but always hoped someday I'd learn the truth. He just laughed his unique Merle Haggard laugh as he repeated, "No, I made that one up, Ray."

IF WE MAKE IT THROUGH DECEMBER

The story behind this heartfelt song begins with the title. Merle's hero and former guitarist, the great Roy Nichols, had suffered a stroke, so Merle decided to hold a benefit concert on his behalf at North High School in Oildale. North High was my alma mater and provider of four years of sweet memories, which were about to become even sweeter.

Halfway through the setlist, the band started playing "If We Make It Through December," Merle stopped the band about twelve seconds into the song. He shouted, "Hold it! Hold it!" The band stopped abruptly; the audience laughed. Merle continued, "I've got something to tell you! I think I owe Roy Nichols some money! He explained that a few years back on an early December day, he had asked, "How're you doing, Roy?" Roy simply answered, "If we can just make it through December..."

Roy's answer stuck with Merle until he recognized the remark as an excellent title for a song and promptly wrote lyrics and music to go with it. Merle never gave Roy credit for the title and thought now was the right time to settle up. What a warm moment - Merle, honest and unabashed, confessing this omission to his hometown audience. The next day, my wife and I delivered $16,000 in cash proceeds from the concert to an astonished and grateful Roy Nichols and his wife.

Once Merle asked, out of all his songs, which was my favorite. Without taking any time to think, I replied, "If We Make It Through December," and explained how the melody, together with the melancholy message, made it my favorite for all time.

I THINK I'LL JUST STAY HERE AND DRINK

Merle told me he'd been writing songs one evening at home in California with his third wife, Leona Williams. They were working for hours on several songs. She grew tired and fell asleep around midnight, but Merle continued working. He said this song only took about ten minutes to write and just came to him out of nowhere as if the phone had rung and someone on the other end was telling him what to write. When Leona woke up about an hour later, he sang it for her. She asked, "Why didn't you let me help you?" He replied, "I didn't need your help."

WORKIN' MAN BLUES

I had to ask! What about this song released in 1969, with a timeless theme that became not only an anthem for the American working man but a world-wide anthem for all working men. Merle didn't remember where he wrote "Workin' Man Blues," but said Johnny Cash's upbeat tempo in "Folsom Prison Blues" had inspired it. He felt he needed to explore this tempo. He was also hoping to capture a little bit of a Chuck Berry feel.

Merle requested they play this particular song in the key of A-flat, a rarely used key in country music. He felt it would give the song a different sound. James Burton played the sensational guitar riffs, making them up on the spot. His guitar solo is a classic, and in fact, so good that the Country Music Hall of Fame guitarist, Grady Martin, had to call Merle from Nashville after hearing it. He was driving down the road when "Workin' Man Blues" played on the radio. Grady nearly wrecked his car and had to pull over to the side of the road to listen. That's the kind of impact a great song can have on you. Merle must have told this story nine hundred times, at least!

MAMA TRIED

In the spring of 1966, I was still living with Bonnie and Merle, serving out my sophomore year of high school. It was about 11:00 in the morning and a beautiful day. Mike and Buddy were not home, but Bonnie, her mother, and I were in the kitchen when Merle entered from the garage. He immediately sat down at the table and magically pulled a guitar out of thin air as he exclaimed, "I just wrote this song on the river this morning!" He began singing his new song. We were stunned and momentarily speechless, looking at one another as if to ask, "What just happened?"

Merle was always excited to immediately share what he'd composed, so this was not the first time we had been privy to something new. But this was different. After he finished the entire song, Merle just sat in the kitchen chair with the contented smile of a gentle genius.

He had done it! He had created a masterpiece! He knew it, and so did we, and indeed it was a masterpiece. "Mama Tried" became a Country Music Hall of Fame classic.

About fifty-four years ago, at age fifteen, I knew I was very fortunate to witness something like this, and looking back, I appreciate these experiences all the more. Now, with great pleasure, I can share memories of my good fortune with others.

The Language of Music

CHAPTER 12

State Street School second grade class photo, Topeka, Kansas.
I'm sitting in the 2nd row from the right, four seats back.
Photo courtesy of Raymond McDonald

I BELIEVE WHEN YOU ARE a child, you begin listening to music that's around you in any form: a lullaby sung by your mother, church hymns at Sunday school, or music on television, radio, and records. You start listening to it immediately. How could you not? Some studies show that a healthy fetus, nearing the third trimester, will react differently to various beats and music styles. So, it's plausible that your musical tastes, assuming you had parents who listened to music, were already forming before you were even born. As a child, exposure to a catchy tune that was pretty or even somewhat unusual grabbed your attention, whether you liked it or not.

Right around 1955, when I was in kindergarten, I began listening to music more intently. I started hearing the arrangements, in addition to being impacted by the lyrics. You could say it was the very beginning of my understanding and enjoyment of music. My mother influenced me by playing country music on the radio ALL THE TIME. I'm sure that's where I first heard Hank Williams, Bob Wills and his Texas Playboys, Tommy Duncan, Lefty Frizzell, and similar artists. Later came the next generation of that genre: Patsy Cline, Jim Reeves, and Willie Nelson.

Very soon, the new invention, rock 'n' roll, was introduced to me via my older brother with whom I shared a bedroom. Bobby was a bona fide American teenager when the world took this giant musical step into the future. It was as though electricity had a greater purpose. Imagine attending high school dances when the whole vibe of popular music changed from Bing Crosby and dozens of orchestral ensembles to Elvis, Ricky Nelson, Chuck Berry, Jerry Lee Lewis, Carl Perkins, and all the legendary doo-wop groups. It was absolutely fantastic!

I remember this time so well, and much of what I remember has to do with that particular period's musical evolution. As you begin developing the ability to listen before you're born, even music you heard from the womb stays with you throughout your life. All music you hear can mold you and, over time, create bookmarks in your brain that help you remember events and inconsequential moments. I believe that humans are emotionally and psychologically tied to music. Thousands of years of history bear this out. We have an entire academic field of study surrounding musical anthropology. Music is how we relate to others, to nature, and even to ourselves. However, as a kid in Topeka, Kansas, who knew nothing about anthropology or history, I sensed the importance of music and how it was becoming a dominant theme in my life.

My dad decided to move our family to Hollywood, and we arrived on my ninth birthday in July of 1959. From the moment we got there, I enjoyed hearing the variety of music piped out into the streets from every store, every car, and every apartment window. The streets were alive in sunny California, and it was cool. And I thought I was cool just being there. You can understand why certain songs were imprinted in my memory, such as the catchy tune "Itsy Bitsy Teeny Weenie Yellow Polka Dot Bikini," by Brian Hyland, or another great one, "Personality," by a fellow named Lloyd Price. The list could continue for pages because musicians produced truckloads of good music during this era of rock 'n' roll.

Looking back at the sixties, I think many would agree it was one of the greatest music eras.. It included so many different genres: rock 'n' roll, country, folk, Motown, easy listening, and to a degree, they were all impacting each other. What better example than Motown, who influenced one of the most predominant groups in the history of music, The Beatles!

This era was the perfect time for music. In addition to The Beatles, the British 'invasion' brought The Rolling Stones, The Animals, The Dave Clark Five, Donovan, The Who, Dusty Springfield, The Yardbirds, and The Zombies! In America, we had Chubby Checker, The Beach Boys, Bob Dylan, Joni Mitchell, Jimi Hendrix, Janis Joplin, Creedence Clearwater Revival, and of course, all sorts of crossover artists like Emmylou Harris and Johnny Cash! It would be impossible to list all the significant contributors to '60s music. This short paragraph is not even the tip of the massive music iceberg formed during this inventive and prolific era.

Radio playlists were forever fresh with all this new talent (musicians, singers, songwriters, and both). Young people were amazed. Songs about changing times influenced attitudes - revolution was in the air! Clothing styles transformed, hairstyles morphed from crewcuts to unruly mops, and parents were appalled! Squares (including myself) were still hanging on to Perry Como and Patti Page. Yet, this avalanche of new music and the impending Cultural Revolution caught up nearly everyone I knew.

But always for me, it was about the music! I enjoyed every facet of guitar work, listening closely to the variety of melodies and harmonies. Even though I only played the guitar, I loved violins, the piano, and, well, just about every instrument! The production value of the records had become phenomenal. If you were lucky enough to attend a concert, you might think, "Wow! They can do that in person, too, huh?" But going to concerts was a rare treat, so instead, I jumped at the chance each day to listen to the radio, or better yet, visit a friend at his home where we could play a record on a phonograph. That was truly magical!

Because I have followed music so closely, looking back, I can confidently say good music has emerged from each decade since the sixties - the era I became so obsessed with music. It might be music from new artists or some from the old guard, whose talents keep them relevant. It might be music geared toward the younger crowd: rock, pop, EDM, hip-hop, rap, country rock, alternative rock, etc., but I try to take something from everything I hear and enjoy it for what it's worth, even if I only listen to it once or twice.

I will admit I was never a big fan of classical music but have many fond memories of watching *The Nutcracker* on television during the sixties. Tchaikovsky's *The Nutcracker Suite* was perhaps the most beautiful and magical music I'd ever heard. That experience left me believing good music is good music, regardless of genre.

Music has been a catalyst for happiness my entire life. If I had the blues, I'd play some blues. If the blues didn't help, then fine – I'd just go with it, try to feel it. If you get down low enough, the only way to go is up. That's what it's all about, right? Somebody else has it worse, so you try to find the joy by pulling yourself back up through the tales of hardship and slide guitar! You feel the pain, so happiness means something on the other side.

To make music myself, I learned to play the guitar and sing the songs I loved. At one point, I must have known about a hundred or more by heart. Many were written by my talented friend Merle Haggard whom I had the honor of knowing for so many years. I played mostly dive bars in Southern California and probably played mostly Merle Haggard songs. Why not impersonate the best? By the time I began performing, I had concluded and still believe that Merle is the ultimate country music artist of all time. His talents included singing, songwriting, playing guitar and fiddle, leading the band, and captivating audiences with his cool and collected stage presence. He was an incredible all-around musician, and everybody tried to emulate the best.

As a musician, singer, or just someone driving down the road with the radio blaring, it's fun to sing along with favorite tunes that make us feel happy, sad, or indifferent. We are all so unique; we undoubtedly find different emotional connections with the same song – it might be the lyrics, the vocals, a guitar riff, a sax solo, a key change, or a B string that bends and moans. Whatever the nature of the connection, speaking for myself, I couldn't be happy without the music that has shaped me, my relationships, and my memories throughout life. Music has been a steady companion – one that never calls to say it's sorry and never texts to say it can't show up.

Music can bring people together and help heal wounds. It is a therapy for the soul and a language with the potential to connect people who may not even understand its meaning. Music is a lot like love. The world might do well to make more music.

Johnny Cash, Johnny Cash

CHAPTER 13

Photo by Olga Popova / Shutterstock.com

MERLE LISTENED TO JUST ABOUT everything pertaining to music, so he knew of Johnny Cash from the radio back in the 1950s. When he first saw Johnny Cash in person, it is no secret Merle was in California's San Quentin Prison. Johnny had brought his band to the prison to perform for the men on New Year's Day. According to Merle, it was during this show he decided what he wanted to do with his life once released from prison. He wanted to be an entertainer who played the guitar and sang songs.

Merle was twenty-three upon his release from San Quinten in 1960. Still eager to be like Johnny Cash, who had so inspired him, Merle set out to turn his life around. Within seven short years, he had several number one hit albums on the country charts. Johnny, who had an American television music variety show running on ABC from 1969 to '71, would frequently invite the former prisoner he had inspired to appear as a guest performer on *The Johnny Cash Show*. It is worth the time to look up a few episodes on *YouTube* not only to enjoy the music but to witness the genuine camaraderie between these two gifted men.

Right around 1968, Johnny Cash recorded a live album at Folsom Prison. It was to become one of the greatest selling albums in country music history. The feature song was "Folsom Prison Blues," which Cash had recorded in 1955. Merle, impressed by this song's upbeat tempo as well as a little Chuck Berry, combined the two influences to write "Workin' Man's Blues." Not long after its release in 1969, it became a number one hit and a worldwide anthem for the working man.

Whenever I got the chance, I scoured *YouTube* to find videos Merle might enjoy. My efforts paid off one afternoon when a golden nugget surfaced – *The Johnny Cash Show* opening with Merle's song "Workin' Man Blues." I couldn't wait to show it to him! When viewed on my iPhone, Merle was astonished, having never seen it before. He was so pleased; he asked me to play it for everyone on the bus. Johnny sang it with the classic Cash tempo, similar to "I Walk the Line." In his opening remarks, Johnny said something like: "I hope Merle Haggard doesn't mind if I borrow one of his songs tonight." Merle got the biggest kick out of this video.

My first encounter with Johnny Cash, or John, as Merle used to call him, came in the early 1990s. Merle had a mobile phone with him on the road, so while he was touring America, I'd call him nearly every day, and we'd talk about everything. One day, Merle mentioned that John was playing at the Hilton Hotel in Las Vegas, and he needed to speak with him. Knowing I lived in Las Vegas, he asked me to call the hotel and give John his contact number. I asked Merle what I should say to get past the front desk, and he said, "Tell them you're calling for me...use my name." I made the call and got right through to his room. Johnny answered, "Hello" in that rich, mellow baritone. (He didn't answer "Hello, I'm Johnny Cash.") He thanked me for the information and said he'd give Merle a call. I did take a second to tell him how much I admired his music. He thanked me, and that was it.

Merle knew Johnny would be calling, so he answered using his best Johnny Cash impersonation: "Hello, I'm Johnny Cash," and Johnny said, "That's pretty good, Haggard!"

You don't have to be blood-related to be brothers, Merle told me, referring to John. Marty Stuart shared a poignant story with a few of us one day in the back of Merle's bus about Merle and his brother, Johnny Cash, several years after it happened. I listened intently as Marty reminded Merle of that day.

Johnny Cash knew Merle was in Nashville and asked Marty to find him and have him cancel any plans so that he could come to John's estate the next morning. He wanted to see Merle but didn't tell Marty why. John was waiting in the kitchen when they arrived and asked everyone to leave so he could speak privately with Merle and Marty.

Not too long before this meeting, Johnny Cash had been deathly ill in a Nashville hospital. Frank Mull and I had taken Merle to the hospital so that he could cheer John up. We waited down the hall during Merle's visit due to 'family only' restrictions. After about ten minutes, we watched as Merle slowly walked down the long hospital corridor toward us. When asked about his visit, he described how he'd put on a doctor's smock as a disguise to walk into John's room.

John's eyes were closed, so Merle leaned down to whisper a soft hello. He opened his eyes and said, "I thought you were a doctor!"

Merle replied, "I am, now don't you check out on us, man!"

"I've got some more pickin' to do!" said Johnny Cash.

Back at the breakfast table, John revealed the reason he invited Merle to his estate. It was important for John to relate to him, in person, how Merle's hospital visit had inspired him to get well and get well he did! He praised Merle warmly for his kindness, concern, and support when he needed it the most. Marty's recollection of this day brought back heartfelt memories for both Marty and Merle.

On September 12, 2003, Johnny Cash died only a few months after his wife, June Carter Cash. It had been several years since Merle's visit with his brother Johnny in that Nashville hospital room - the visit that inspired John to keep on pickin' a little while longer.

Merle and I were living not far from one another when I got the sad news, via national television, that Johnny Cash had passed away. I immediately drove to Merle's ranch to support him in his grief. He was sitting alone in his pickup truck, parked among some peaceful oak trees on his property. Doug Colosio, Merle's pianist, arrived about the same time. I walked over to Merle and said, "I'm sorry about your friend, Merle." He was peaceful but pained. Merle told us he believed Johnny Cash would be sitting next to Jesus now. Soon after, Merle called his band and asked them to come to the ranch's studio to honor Johnny by recording his music. Music was Merle's way of dealing with grief.

Merle asked Doug and me if he should just stay home now or continue to tour and record to carry the flag for country music now that Johnny was gone. We agreed that he should continue playing and singing. Surely, Johnny would have wanted that.

Six years later, I would begin as Merle's tour bus driver, traveling all over America. During each tour, often totaling thousands of miles

and hundreds of hours on the bus, Merle was vulnerable to the travelin'
blues. He enjoyed conversations with anyone on the bus, especially
his horn man, Don Markham. He loved to watch his favorite religious
programs or lose track of time by reading a book or magazine. I realized
if I could find a book or two of interest, it might help him pass the road
time more quickly and pleasantly. In a thrift store in Redding, California,
I found Johnny Cash's autobiography, *Man in Black,* published in the
1960s. As we headed out on another long tour across America, I gave
Merle the book as a gift.

Merle loved the book and read it all the time, sometimes out
loud when we stopped for a break. One day, sometime around noon,
we pulled in for lunch at a Cracker Barrel. Whenever we stopped for a
meal or a break, I'd always walk back to check on Merle, day or night.
On this day, he was reading the Johnny Cash book and quietly crying.
If you have the opportunity to grab a copy of *Man in Black,* read pages
138 and 139 to discover why. Copyright laws prevent me from printing
those pages here, or I would do so.

Cry, Cry, Cry, Third Eye Blind

CHAPTER 14

Stephan Jenkins, lead vocalist-songwriter for Third Eye Blind
Photo by Tony Norkus / Shutterstock.com

WHILE WORKING IN MERLE'S HOME office in Palo Cedro, California, in 2001, a fascinating proposal was introduced to Merle. Stephan Jenkins, lead vocalist-songwriter for the rock band Third Eye Blind, called the office with a request. I answered and immediately recognized the band's name as they had recently had a very successful tune, "The Jumper." I heard this impressive song on the radio frequently while driving a taxicab in Las Vegas sometime before going to work for Merle. I liked their latest hit!

Stephan explained how Atlantic Records was to release a tribute album to Johnny Cash and invited Third Eye Blind to appear on the album along with an array of popular artists. They had chosen the classic Cash tune, "Cry, Cry, Cry," as their tribute song. They asked if Merle would consider lending his voice to the project for a spoken word intro/outro Stephan had written as an addition to the original song. They also wanted Merle to sing one of the song's verses.

While on the phone from their studio two hundred miles away in San Francisco, I repeated what Stephan was telling me so Merle could hear the rocker's proposal as he sat in his living room rocker, smoking his pipe. Merle appeared intrigued. Stephan offered to send the band's recorded tracks to Merle's studio, along with the added spoken words. I reiterated what Stephan said in the form of a question, looking to Merle for approval. He nodded, "yes," and we received the tracks the following day!

Merle was impressed. Third Eye Blind had a most unusual approach to the song, but it was good. Stephan's vocals backed by rock 'n' roll drums, electric guitar riffs, and a premier bassline gave the tune a creative new feel. But Merle needed to ponder his decision. This band of rockers, thrilled that Merle would even consider sharing his name and talents on their tribute tune, called each day hoping for a positive answer.

Finally, after an excruciating waiting period of only several days, Merle decided to join the band for this music adventure. One morning, I had just arrived at work when he immediately had me sit down and listen to what he'd recorded the night before. Merle's decision took me completely by surprise because he had expressed reservations and seemed to distance himself from the proposal every time I mentioned it. But he was pleased with his part and felt honored being included on the tribute album.

Merle's vocals on the tracks astonished me. His spoken words were haunting and an excellent addition to the original tune. He instructed me to take the finished tapes directly to Third Eye Blind in San Francisco. When I arrived, they were waiting out on the sidewalk with the Rolling Stones blaring from their studio. One of the band members sat perched on top of a stack of wooden milk crates, on the lookout for the hand-carried precious cargo I was about to deliver.

Once in hand, they bee-lined for the studio, where the band played the tape loud and proud. They became immersed in Merle's additions while Stephan listened in disbelief as Merle spoke his written words to perfection. The band was blown away! They graciously treated me to an herb well known in the San Francisco area. The bassman walked me into a local bar and insisted I try his favorite drink, 90 proof Maker's Mark Kentucky Straight Bourbon Whisky. He threw down three celebratory shots; I nursed one on ice. I've always been a might intimidated by whiskey, and this stuff was proof. But it sure hit the mark as we celebrated this tribute version of "Cry, Cry, Cry."

So, it came as a huge shock and disappointment a few weeks later to learn the producer had decided not to include Third Eye Blind's song featuring Merle on the tribute album. To listen to Stephan Jenkins' remarkable written intro/outro, with Merle's haunting spoken word and the verse he sang so beautifully, we must again rely on our friend *YouTube*. For your entertainment and listening pleasure, please search and enjoy Third Eye Blind's "Cry, Cry, Cry," featuring Merle Haggard!

I'd like to thank my good friend Chuck Seaton, one of the greatest guitarists to come out of Bakersfield, for reminding me of this closing anecdote. Chuck and I had met at Fishlips in Bakersfield while playing a gig there. I had gone to listen to the band play and asked if they'd like to hear the latest Third Eye Blind/Merle Haggard tune. At least they didn't give me that "what the heck did you just say?" kind of look. They followed me to my car parked in a dark alley during their break. We were not far from the local jail Merle had occupied a few times very long ago. When they heard "Cry, Cry, Cry," they were speechless. I repeated what I had told Third Eye Blind: "This song could rise to the top of the country music charts if given a chance." When I mentioned this to Stephan Jenkins, he replied loudly, "Yeah! 'F' rock 'n' roll!"

Almost Stuck in Folsom Prison

CHAPTER 15

Merle and Scott Joss perform at Folsom Community College.
Photo courtesy of Dannie Ray Spiess

IN APRIL 2013, MERLE PERFORMED two consecutive shows (sold out months in advance) at a community college in Folsom, California. The community college had built a state of the art concert theater, which was brand new. Folsom is known worldwide as home to many prisoners. Johnny Cash's classic, "Folsom Prison Blues," placed both the town and the prison on the map.

Merle played his first show to a wildly enthusiastic crowd, then lingered to sign a few autographs. Typically after a show, we would drive three to five hundred miles to our next venue, but this time we could relax a little since we were staying in Folsom for the second concert.

After a good night's rest, Merle called around 10:00 a.m. the next morning to ask if I would drive him (in the bus) over to Folsom

Prison. He had invited his sons, Benny and Noel, to ride with us along with his valet. We fired up the bus and headed to the prison, which was only about twelve miles from our motel. When we arrived at the prison parking lot, I quickly surmised the design could not accommodate a forty-five-foot tour bus - most parking lots can't. But after a few deft maneuvers, I managed to find enough space for the 'Super Chief' in a field next to the parking lot.

When we finally got parked, the coach was facing the freeway. Merle jokingly said he had seen the freeway but had never seen Folsom Prison. Then he asked if I could turn the bus around to face the prison. Remaining calm and taking my time, I successfully positioned the 'Super Chief' to face the state's second-oldest penitentiary. I had initially parked facing away from the prison because I'd thought Merle was going in for a visit.

After sitting on the bus for a few moments, Merle's son said, "Let's go in!" Merle let us all know he had no intention of stepping one foot inside those prison walls. The boys left to find the prison gift shop, while Merle and I stayed put. I in my driver's seat, and Merle in his jump seat. Merle and I began visiting when he shared a little story about his last days in the Bakersfield jail before transferring to a state correctional institution.

It's a well-known fact Merle Haggard spent time in California's San Quentin Prison back in the late 1950s. Someone in the Bakersfield jail system had delivered a message that he was transferring to Folsom Prison. However, instead of Folsom, when he received his official prison assignment, the paper stated San Quentin. At this point, Merle paused - as though he had just received the official assignment. He then continued to describe the reason for his dismay. San Quentin was the harsher prison of the two institutions, but he had heard that the cells in Folsom had no windows. When Johnny Cash sang his line about not seeing the sunshine, it reverberated. Now with eyes locked on the prison, Merle exclaimed, "Look at those walls! Look how gray and big they are!"

Suddenly a pickup with two guys in the cab and one in the back with hands atop the cab drove onto the field, stopping on the driver's side of the bus. Merle said the guys were trustees. When I asked how he knew, he said you could tell by their clothing and the prison license plate. The guy in the passenger seat yelled, "Is there somebody famous on that bus?"

Looking at Merle, I asked, "Is there somebody famous on this bus?" Merle said, "Yeah! Tell them it's Merle Haggard."

I yelled back to those young men, "Yeah, it's Merle Haggard! Pull up a little so you can wave to him!" They pulled up about five feet, far enough to be able to see their hero: the man who had spent time in prison, the man who had sung about prison, the man who, for decades, had given hope to prisoners with his music.

The three men were ecstatic and began shouting, "Hi Merle! Hi Merle! Glad to see you, Merle!" Merle waved back and called out, "Hi, men!" Three delighted Merle Haggard fans then vanished as quickly as they had appeared, as if they might get in trouble for circling the bus.

I turned to Merle and said, "Merle, in the next few minutes, the entire prison is going to know you're out here in the parking lot! Just knowing you're here must raise the inmates' spirits, if even for one day, and I'm sure the prisoners understand why you aren't going inside to visit." I never quite knew how Merle would react to my comments, such as those made that day to affirm his positive impact on the inmates. But this time, he merely smiled, knowing what I said must be true.

A few minutes later, Merle's sons came back on board with an assortment of Folsom Prison T-shirts, key chains, bumper stickers, hats, and the like. Apparently, while in the gift shop, the news had spread that they were Merle Haggard's sons. Benny and Noel told Merle they had spoken with the warden who knew Merle was outside in his bus observing the prison, and that the warden had invited Merle and his entourage for a private tour. Merle politely told the boys, "Go tell the warden thank you, but no thank you." The boys seemed a bit disappointed, and I believe I was, too. However, we all understood, so we boarded the 'Super Chief' and headed back to the motel for some rest and preparation for Merle's performance later that evening.

Merle played "Folsom Prison Blues" at nearly every concert. That song was his tribute to Johnny Cash and Johnny's timeless song that had resonated with so many prisoners and had brought notoriety to Folsom Prison and the city of Folsom.

Daddy Sang Bass

CHAPTER 16

Merle sitting in the driver's seat of the 'Chief'
Photo courtesy of Curly Jones

ONE BEAUTIFUL AFTERNOON, MERLE AND I were waiting in the parking lot of a hotel on Rosedale Highway in Bakersfield. A relative of Merle's with the requisite skills was configuring a combination pickup truck/camper-on-the-back contraption; he was due to return with it at any moment. Merle was growing more anxious by the minute. He wanted to go home, and home was 450 miles away. I had learned, through observation and experience, how to alter Merle's mood if need be. Music! Good music was always the answer!

While Merle watched for his 'contraption,' I climbed in my car to play a Johnny Cash classic, "Daddy Sang Bass," knowing it was the perfect tune to pull him out of his 'mood.' Immediately, like a pelican diving for fish, Merle plunged into the music. With kamikaze-like intentions, ears folded back, he dove straight down into the sound, instantly rewarded by the delicious morsel, "Daddy Sang Bass." He devoured it, laughing throughout the song. When it was over, he exclaimed, "I quit!" This was Merle's way of saying in two words that Johnny Cash was so good he couldn't possibly match him. I understood. He made me play it again and I was happy to do just that.

As the song was nearing its end, his pickup came rolling into the parking lot. Merle, whose attention was entirely on the music, hadn't even noticed. He asked me to play "Daddy Sang Bass" yet again! He finally became aware his truck had arrived when the driver, who was his relative, ask him what was going on. Merle answered, "Raymond is entertaining me with his Johnny Cash music." With that, he climbed aboard his newly configured camper truck, and with a hearty thank you to all, he said his goodbyes and headed north for the Interstate 5 to Palo Cedro. All I can say is, "Thank God for Johnny Cash and his captivating, mind-altering music!"

Honky-Tonk Night Time Man

CHAPTER 17

Merle and Roy Nichols *Photo courtesy of Raymond McDonald*

"HONKY-TONK NIGHT TIME MAN" could be Merle's most important song in terms of any rock 'n' roll undercurrents. Some might ask, "What rock 'n' roll?" Well, Merle was a rocker at heart and mentioned more than once he wanted to be in the Rock and Roll Hall of Fame. In 1977, Merle's twenty-seventh studio album was his tribute to the music of Elvis Presley. *My Farewell to Elvis* reached number six on the country album charts. You can't get much closer to rock 'n' roll than the King, right?

Merle wrote "Honky-Tonk Night Time Man" based on his own experience playing honky-tonks, but he had never experienced what was about to take place on the first studio take recorded in 1974. He enjoyed telling the story of the unpredicted successful recording of this song many times. Merle's incredible guitarist, Roy Nichols, started burning it up with his blazing guitar solo, of which mere mortals can only be envious! Then the next man up, Norman Hamlet, perhaps the greatest Dobro guitar player on the planet, pretty much sealed the fate of "Honky-Tonk Night Time Man" to immortality. It is worth a listen if you get the chance.

Merle enjoyed telling another story about how Roy stepped up during a live recording in Bakersfield. Roy Nichols could lay these inimitable riffs down because he was always up to the challenge and could always nail it, no matter what the music. You may have never heard of it, but there is another song titled "Silver Bells" - not the Christmas tune you've heard a zillion times - but the instrumental "Silver Bells," and it rocks! Merle explained how the steel guitar was the preferred instrument for the difficult lead on this double-timing up-tempo tune. The steel guitarist made the mistake of mentioning this to Roy, just as the announcer introduced the song. Well, with perfect timing when the moment arrived, Roy jumped in to take the lead and led the band in a most rousing rendition of "Silver Bells," the instrumental. I'd say that was more than a challenge well met!

Lynyrd Skynyrd, a rock band, covered Merle's song "Honky-Tonk Night Time Man" on their album Street Survivors and sent Merle a check for $25,000. Merle was very proud that a significant force in rock 'n' roll would cover his song. Forty years or so later, I found the Lynyrd Skynyrd version on *YouTube* and played it for Merle. You can hear the singer call out in the middle of the guitar solo, "Sounds like Roy!" Haggard smiled and winked as if to say, "No, it doesn't sound like Roy, but it's pretty damn good!"

Merle held a benefit concert for Roy Nichols in 1996. Roy had suffered a stroke that left him confined to a wheelchair and unable to play his guitar. I was honored to arrange the event for Roy and had gone to his home to discuss the project. He met me at the door in his wheelchair and, after a quick hello, instructed me to play song number twenty-two on his *Haggard's Greatest Hits* CD. It was "Honky-Tonk Night Time Man," the original first-take classic. Roy smiled through the entire song, but especially during his incredible guitar solo. What a gift this world-class guitarist shared with everyone!

Merle in Oildale for Roy Nichols

CHAPTER 18

Mark Kendrick presents Merle with his new 'Tuff Dog Tele'
Photo courtesy of Raymond McDonald

THE PRINCIPAL OF NORTH HIGH introduced Merle at the Roy Nichols Benefit Concert in Oildale, California. Then Merle sang "Workin' Man Blues," "Big City," "Twinkle Twinkle Lucky Star," and "If I Could Only Fly." The following dialog is Merle's, verbatim - taken from the video we filmed March 30, 1996.

Over here on the right, we have a gentleman who's been allowed to come home from prison. We're proud to say that Junior Fite is with us tonight. He was up here in Tehachapi in prison doing time. They give him less than six months to live with terminal cancer. He's here with us tonight through the grace of God and some help from some judges and

Ray McDonald, and a bunch of people. We got the man out of prison. (Junior stood up and waved to Merle. He was in his pajamas.) I want to especially thank Mayor, Ex-Mayor Hart, and Ray McDonald. They did a wonderful job and just wouldn't take no for an answer. Otherwise, you wouldn't be out.

We had a terrible thing happen for a guy like me. I wanted this to be one of the greatest evenings of my life, and it very well may be. Anyway, but two of the most important members of my band - they're quite the comedians - they got themselves in trouble in St. Louis. They're two of the soberest, (crowd laughter) upright citizens I think I've ever met in my life, and they detained them for singin'. Security wouldn't let them on the airplane in St. Louis cause they sang! And I thought, since all this security started, since Pan Am 303 - I think it was. They haven't found one bomb, and all we can manage to do is arrest people for singin'. (crowd laughter) They offered to take blood tests to prove they weren't intoxicated. They said surely no one can have fun like that in America, the way it is, unless they're intoxicated.

I don't know if there's anyone within the sound of my voice who can do anything about it, but I've asked these friends that are here tonight, judges, and anybody with any influence at all, to call somebody in St. Louis and shame them for the terrible thing they've done... for holding up a beautiful time this evening. If I was them, I'd be ashamed of Branson! Johnny Cash. I've never heard Johnny Cash never say a bad word about nobody in my life, and Johnny Cash said, "I'm never playing Branson again." He put it in print and, "I'm going to do some serious thinking before I go through Missouri again. They have really made me mad. I'm gonna talk to everybody, and if I can get on Larry King, I'm gonna tell him about it." (crowd laughs and cheers)

Everybody knows you have to go through security at the airport. Everybody knows you have to go through that gate. But now there's another deal, do you believe that? Now there's another gate, now they have another gate, they have their own set of people that come out there, and they wave the wand, and they have to inspect you, too. That means it doesn't make any difference if you're flying their direction or not. If you're flying from San Francisco to Lubbock, Texas, they have still got to look up your, you know what!

I want to tell you that there's been a lot of things change since I ran around Oildale. Sure nice to be back here. I tell you there's a lot of love here this evening. (enthusiastic applause) I want to tell you a little bit, I don't talk a lot on my shows, but this is a special show. When I was about twelve years old, my brother, (Lowell) who is here tonight... I don't know if he's brought his wife or not. I didn't see her. He's probably slipped off! But in 1949, I was twelve years old, and this lady standing back here fillin' in for Bonnie - she's having foot surgery. I want to tell you a little story. This lady back here is one of the greatest that ever lived. She's in the category of Bob Wills and Bill Monroe, Ernest Tubb, and those people. This is Rose Maddox! (much applause).

One night in 1949, Lowell, my brother, talked to me about this little guy that played the guitar that he heard, and he said he was really good. He was from Fresno. He said he's only fifteen or sixteen, somethin' like that, and he's workin' for The Brothers Maddox and Rose. And I'd learned a few chords on guitar. He knew I was interested in guitar. But he took me out to see The Maddox Brothers and Rose at the Pumpkin' Center Ballroom! There they were! And the first thing I seen when we got to the bandstand, where I could see good, was a little-black-headed guy named Roy Nichols, playin' guitar. He was playin' a big yellow Epiphone, and it changed my life. I said, "Look at that guy! He's not much older than I am. He's not in school!" (laughter) And he's makin' a living, and people is talkin' about him all over the southern part of the state. I said something's goin' on, and I wanna be like that. And it wasn't just a short time later I heard a guy named Lefty Frizzell singin'. The two of them inspired me to do what I've done. Those two people were the most inspirational to me than anyone I've ever met.

I didn't get to meet Roy that night. I met him sometime later, about 1953. He came to town with the hottest band in the nation, who was Lefty Frizzell. Roy was on the stage that evening. Here I was again; I was sixteen. That night they got me onstage out here at the Rainbow Garden. First time I'd ever been on-stage in my life, holdin' Lefty Frizzell's guitar and playin' with Roy Nichols (points to Roy - loud applause) in the middle of Lefty's show. Nobody could've drug me except Bob Teague, a boy I couldn't whip. He got me out there, and I sang about three songs. After the show, I remember asking Roy, "How is it workin' with Lefty?" He said, "Not worth a shit." (crowd laughs) I didn't jump right on the next question. I said, "What are you gonna do?" He said, "This is my last night, and I'm going to work for Herb Henson."

Buck Owens took me over here today to see a thing he's building, a museum. He talked to me and said, I think you and me oughta be the first ones in there. I thought, well, that'd be nice, but what about Herb Henson, you know, and what about ole Lewis Talley? What about Don Rich? And Roy Nichols! Then you've got Bill Woods. Then you've got Billy Mize. Then we might talk about me and you. I think those are the people that Buck should consider to be in the foundation of the business that we've fell into." (loud cheering for all mentioned - Bill Woods was backstage that night)

I was born and raised here. I guess you could call it that. Anybody that lives in Oildale and says they was born and raised is a liar! (crowd laughter)

I love Roy Nichols a lot. I always have, since 1949. I want everybody to know that! (loud cheering)

Fender guitar has been kind enough to make us a guitar. A couple of things happened tonight. I'm very proud of Mark. Where's Mark at? One of the finest guitar craftsmen in the world - one of the most famous in the world has made me a series of the 'Tuff-Dog tele.' (Telecaster guitars) I wanted Roy to see this. I'm going to suggest that they get on the ball and make a signature guitar for Roy Nichols, before somebody else does. (loud cheering) It might be interesting to see what Mark and Roy come up with. I met a lot of people that worked on guitars, everyone from Semi Mosely to Fuzzy Owens (laughter) - but this guy is actually...where you at, Mark? I want you to come out here and take a bow. I want folks to see the man that made this guitar. He's a neat guy. I've spent some time with him. Listen folks...let me tell you something, (Mark makes his way to the stage and shakes hands with Merle - nice applause - then Merle holds up the guitar) this is a work of art, and he did it the first time. I don't understand how he did it, but it needs to be shown and bragged about, and I'm very proud of it. Thank you, Mark!

Now we gonna get on with some music. I don't know what we intend to play, but we've got a lot of it to do. (BOB WILLS! Loudly from Billy Joe Sheets then Merle repeats) BOB WILLS! (loud laughter) Well, we've had a problem with my fiddle, somethings wrong with the adapter. Did they get it fixed? They did! Well, what about "Ida Red," is she ready? Rose? Are you ready? Don? Are you boys ready? Well, let's see if you are: 1, 2, 3, 4. (They play "Ida Red," "Milk Cow Blues," "Kern River," "I Think I'll Just Stay Here and Drink," and "Place to Fall Apart")

We had a request for a song tonight...read that. There's a doctor here that has volunteered to give Roy Nichols free therapy, orthopedic therapy. What's the doctor's name? Well, we'll find out his name afterwards. (Barry Townsend) Roy, he's volunteered to give you lifetime orthopedic therapy. (loud applause) Now, Roy, he's asked me to do something, and I've never done anything like that in my life! NO! (laughter) No, all he wants me to do is to sing "Roses in the Winter." Now, it's been a long time since we've sang this, so if somebody will hold these words out here - way out there. (laughter) The best I remember, we did this in D. (Merle sings it beautifully)

Sometime back there was some people, mostly on the west coast, got together and did a tribute album to do some of the old songs that we did. They called it Tulare Dust. (applause) Some of those songs we completely forgot about. They've sort of revived them for me. One of em' I wrote comin' home from, uh... up North. (San Quentin prison - crowd laughs) Anyway, about nineteen, oh I forgot where I was at... (laughter) Anyway, about nineteen somethin' or other when they took off the steam engines, they took off things like mannerisms, (laughter) but there was a lot of things had changed while I was gone. A few of em' I jotted down on the way back on an old Greyhound bus.

Abe (Manuel) has the kickoff on this. I guess I could hum his part, you know I'm really sorry that you guys didn't get to see Abe and Eddie Curtis. (bassman) They're two of the funniest, greatest players I've ever seen, and they're the only guys that would miss a job, and you'd still like 'em. (laughter) I know damn well at this moment, as I speak, they're on their way. (laughter) Did I hear you say, "Merle, smile"? (to an audience member) Why would you say that? (The audience yells: Merle, please smile! Merle laughs and gives a big smile – the crowd loves it! A man yells out: Thank you, sir!)

A man born in Oildale learns he doesn't smile unless he means it! (laughter) That's one of the first things I learned out here on Norris Road. (Merle hums the beginning to the next song, and they segue into "Tearin' the Labor Camps Down," then play "My Favorite Memory" and "Mama Tried." Just into the song, Merle says) Hold it! (band stops, audience groans and laughs) There's somethin' I gotta tell ya. This lick that Roy Nichols played on…this was first played on "Branded Man." This lick caused a lot of people to go crazy. (Hobo Bill) Roy Nichols… (interrupted by the crowd yelling) Wait a minute, I'm still runnin' the show here! (crowd cheers and laughs) Let me say somethin' to ya. This is important to me. Roy Nichols has been married and divorced five times. (laughter) That's nothin' to laugh at! (more laughter) Wait till I say somethin' funny! That's serious! My God, man's been married five times. Seems like the problems arose towards the end of the year. That was Roy's history. One time I asked Roy, "How's things goin'?" He said, "If we… if I can just make it through December. Seems like I never can make it through," and I thought, man, that's great. I knew there was somethin' there. If we make it through December! And I never did give Roy his part. (laughter) I think I owe you some money, Roy! (laughter, then Merle kicks off the song "If We Make It Through December.")

There's a couple of songs we want to do off our new album. This is a song we did for the truck drivers. We call it "The Truck Driver's Blues." We got to thank ole' Tracy Barton; he's sittin' in over here. (nice applause) He missed about fourteen or fifteen hundred chords on that, but he'd never heard it. But boy, I'll tell you what, things are hard if you don't know 'em. Thank you, Tracy, for comin' up and helpin' us. He's from Portland now. He used to live in Bakersfield, and he used to be a 'Stranger.'

One of the big reasons that I am in this business is because of a lady named Bonnie Owens, and she was unable to be here because she had foot surgery and just got her cast off. She's still on crutches. She couldn't be here, Roy, but she's written a personal thing that… being the bad reader that I am, I'm gonna have a man over here step forward and read this to you. It's so nice for Bonnie to write this to you. She's a special lady, and when you see her, she's always the same, and she greets everybody with the same beautiful personality. I'm proud to have her on stage, and she's been a great, great asset in my life, my stage life especially. Joe, I want you to read what she wrote to Roy. (Joe Manuel reads Bonnie's letter to Roy and Quita, Roy's wife.)

Dear Roy and Quita,

Sincerely, I wish I was there to hold your hand. But please know my heart is with you as always. Beginning with the first time I ever saw you, it was Mesa, Arizona, 1947 with The Maddox Brothers and Rose show. Roy Nichols was playing guitar. Buck Owens and I standing in front of the stage, with our elbows resting on the stage. We stood there for four hours, never taking our eyes off the great guitar player, Roy Nichols. Then, Bakersfield, 1953 or 54 at The Clover Club nightclub on Edison Highway. I was a cocktail waitress. You and the band, with Fuzzy Owen, Louie Tally, and I thanked you guys for letting me sing a song once in a while. Then in 1955, Cousin Herb Henson TV show on KERO-TV, living next door to you, me bumming a ride to the TV station because I didn't have a car and you did. Your kids playing with my kids, and Merle Haggard's story beginning in 1963, the great recording sessions (all night), Merle Haggard roadshows, memories nobody can take away, Roy. We needed you then, and we need you now!

Always love and good wishes!

Your friend,
Bonnie Owens

(Obviously moved by the content of the letter, Merle immediately picks up his guitar and sings, "Ain't got no time to cry.")

This is a new song. I think we're all kids at heart; that's what this song is about. (They play "Kids Get Lonesome Too," then the last song "Goodnight Little Sweetheart." Merle gets a standing ovation, then tells the crowd,) I Love you all, and I hope you love me too. Goodnight.

◈ ◈ ◈

NOTE: My wife and I took $16,000 in cash to Roy and his wife the next day. They were so appreciative.

Photo courtesy of Raymond McDonald

Frank Sinatra Party

CHAPTER 19

Photo by Kraft74 / Shutterstock.com

FROM THE TIME HE WAS a child, Merle Haggard knew he wanted to be a singer and had the confidence he could do it. It was a kind of magic. He once said he knew he would play the fiddle someday, just by looking at the dynamics of the instrument and observing others play it. He also knew he was a good singer.

Merle loved the stylings of Bing Crosby, Elvis Presley, and Frank Sinatra. Of course, he loved Jimmie Rodgers, Hank Williams, Tommy Duncan, Lefty Frizzell, and all the greats from that era. But to Merle, Frank Sinatra was an absolute superstar, and he knew a lot about him.

One day in the early 1980s, Frank Sinatra called Merle while at his ranch near Redding, California. Merle was just finishing his day of work or solitude or both and had informed his manager, Lewis

Talley, that he was through for the day. He walked out the door to drive back up the hill to his home, which was on the same property. As Merle started up his truck, Talley's lanky frame lumbered toward him. Merle was agitated by the news of one more phone call. "Man, I thought I said I didn't wanna take another call," Merle said calmly yet accusingly. Lewis replied, "I think you wanna take this one, Hoss." Knowing his manager well, as they'd been together in one way or another since the fifties, Merle knew this was likely a meaningful call, and one he'd damn sure better take. Merle slipped out of his Ford truck, shuffled into the house, and picked up the phone. It was Old Blue Eyes himself, Frank Sinatra.

As Merle would tell the story, Frank said, "Merle, the President wants me to put together some music and entertainment for a show at the White House, and he told me to get the best. So, I called you first."

Merle was giddy, which is a word I would not often use to define his demeanor. What an honor that President Reagan wanted him to perform at the White House! Of course, Merle was also pleased Frank Sinatra wanted him to be a party to the celebration organized by Sinatra for the President of the United States of America. Out of all the entertainers in the world, Frank called Merle first. But to his great disappointment, Merle's prior tour obligations required him to decline the most high-profile proposal he would ever receive. He was a showman and a professional.

Due to illness, Merle missed quite a few shows during his later years and possibly many more early in his career for other reasons. But when he was well, he was a man of his word and a man of honor, as he had proved by declining Frank Sinatra's invitation to perform at the White House. Ultimately, he did play a few shows for the Reagans. Merle was a great American, and he was proud to entertain the president.

For at least the last seven years, when we were on the road, not much Sinatra played on Merle's tour bus despite the fact I enjoyed his music and owned *Frank Sinatra's Greatest Hits* CD. The album has about twenty-five or twenty-six songs – each of them fabulous!

While driving, Merle typically allowed me to play whatever music I preferred, unless he came to the front with a CD in hand or wanted to listen to Willie's Roadhouse on Sirius XM. This station aired mostly what Merle liked to listen to - current songs back to the 1940s with a lot of Bob Wills, Willie, Waylon, and Johnny Paycheck, not to mention loads of Merle Haggard.

Now and again, when Merle couldn't sleep, he would visit me in the front, sit in his jump seat and listen to whatever I had playing. Once on tour during 2013, we were barreling through the Mojave Desert eastbound on Interstate 40. The sun had just set as we were leaving Barstow, and I was thinking about the Sinatra story and asked Merle if he'd like to listen to Frank. He obliged. I popped in my *Frank Sinatra's Greatest Hits* CD and turned up the volume. Merle commanded me to "turn it up louder!"

When on the bus, Merle always preferred music to be loud so he could hear every detail of the arrangement of whatever song was playing. His MCI bus was custom built, and Merle had not held back on the stereo system, as you can well imagine. Nothing bothered the kids on the bus - Bennie and, well, the big kid, Don Markham - who both usually had headphones on even when sleeping. So Merle knew the music wasn't keeping them awake, and honestly, they probably would not have complained even if it was.

We were blasting Sinatra's classics, heading east toward Arizona. Ervin Drake's "It Was a Very Good Year" filled our ears as Merle sat, nearly frozen, listening intently. He would do this often – sit motionlessly as a song seemed to take over his very being. Merle was deeply spiritual, and I would describe his relationship with music as the same. Like a monk, he would slip into a meditative state where were collecting it for his consciousness. Merle had such an incredible memory and strong emotional attachment to music; when something touched him, it became a part of him.

Merle had probably heard "It Was a Very Good Year" many, many times since its release by Sinatra in 1966. Still, in over fifty years of listening to this song, it moved him into that meditative, introspective trance, which nearly always ended in tears. And this evening was no exception.

As impactful as this song was, it seemed to rank only second on Merle's 'top Sinatra tunes playlist.' The song that completely grabbed him was "Strangers in the Night," written by Bert Kaempfert, Charles Singleton, and Eddie Snyder. Any music fan should be able to tell you that "Strangers in the Night," sung by Frank Sinatra, is one of the smoothest, most beautiful love songs ever recorded. Two strangers meet and fall in love almost immediately. The song is a testament to the human condition: our frailty, impulsiveness, and ability to love without restraint. When "Strangers in the Night" ended, Merle scrunched his shoulders and leaned slightly to his left, as if he were going to tell me a painful secret. Then in a raspy, labored tone, fighting back the tears, he quipped, "That may have been his best!"

We had a long way to go. We were all on that bus, and we weren't getting off any time soon. Merle sat in his jumpseat, atop the stairs, and near the bus's only door. He sat there for about an hour-and-a-half and listened to the entire album of *Frank Sinatra's Greatest Hits*.

Gene Autry Is God

CHAPTER 20

Jackie Autry and Merle at a Los Angeles Angels game
Photo courtesy of Raymond McDonald

MERLE HAGGARD THOUGHT COWBOY MOVIE star, singing star, radio star, television star, and business mogul, Gene Autry was GOD. I found that out via a telephone conversation with Merle, sometime back in the early nineties, when we were discussing the incredible talent of Gene Autry. Merle had been a superstar in country music for over thirty years. I asked him if he'd ever met Gene Autry. He said no, they'd never been introduced nor had he ever spoken with Gene. This was unacceptable!

As soon as possible, I called Gene Autry's business office in Los Angeles and asked if I could speak with Gene. The secretary asked who was calling. I said, "Raymond McDonald, a friend of Merle Haggard." Mr. Autry was not available at the moment, so they asked if they could take a message. I told them Merle and Gene had never spoken to one another, and it would be a pleasant surprise if Gene would call Merle. I gave the secretary Merle's home number and asked if they could have Gene call at his convenience.

About two hours later, Merle called. He asked if I'd given his phone number to Gene. "Yeah!" I said, proud of my accomplishment!

Merle was incredulous but not mad - annoyed would probably be a better description. He said, with a noticeable change in his voice, "Raymond! Don't you know you just don't call GOD?!"

I answered, "No," a little sheepishly, explaining how I had felt it would be a pleasant surprise.

Merle happened to be downtown, getting a haircut at the local barbershop when Gene called, so he didn't speak with him that day. Merle asked me to let him know if I was planning any more surprises, and if so, please ask first. I apologized, then, curious, I asked if he had returned Gene's call. I'm sure he had, although he wasn't willing to share anything about the conversation with me. But Merle did tease me, telling me they'd had a delightful conversation. Gene Autry was a world-renown star in the forties. He had a personal friendship with Merle's idol, Jimmie Rodgers! I am sure they would have had plenty to discuss. Haggard never did reveal what they talked about when they spoke - I suppose that was my punishment.

Gene Autry owned an American League baseball team, the Los Angeles Angels, for thirty-six years from its inception in 1961. During Gene's ownership, the team made the playoffs three times but never won the pennant. (They finally won a World Series Championship in 2002.) The Angels aired their games on KPMC, a radio station Gene Autry owned.

Merle loved baseball. He played the game when he was young, like most Americans. He frequently spoke of the times spent with his dad at Bakersfield's Sam Lynn baseball field, where they'd watch the minor league games together. The primary television sport Merle watched with interest was baseball - golf and Tiger Woods were a distant second.

Gene Autry died in 1998, but his widow, Jackie, in addition to eight seats behind home plate, still owned the Autry suite for her personal use at every home game. She invited Merle and his entourage to join her for a game; each of us could not have enjoyed it more. Merle, decked out in an Angels jacket and hat, courtesy of Mrs. Autry, sat next to Jackie the entire nine innings - they were so animated! When Merle's face appeared on the big centerfield screen, the crowd went crazy, knowing their California neighbor and superstar singer from Bakersfield had joined them to cheer on the Angels!

We met Mrs. Autry when she and the Autry Museum chose Merle to receive their most prestigious honor: the Spirit of the West Award, given to those who had made significant contributions to the American West's culture. Merle notified me he was to receive this grand award and that I should plan, with the Autry staff, for his attendance at the awards ceremony. I would definitely be driving his private bus.

This lavish extravaganza took place at The Autry Museum in Los Angeles, California, in early October 2010. Under the roof of a large tent, guests enjoyed formal dining with an incredible array of food and drink and a variety of entertainment. Merle sat at Jackie Autry's table, with Dwight Yoakum and their guests. At Merle's request, I was seated at a table next to his, with some of Merle's family and my friend Torie Queen, famously of the Glen Queen legacy. Merle appeared to be enjoying himself - talking, laughing, and so graciously speaking to all the well-wishers who approached him.

Before the award presentation, an excellent short but pithy film on Merle's extraordinary career entertained and enlightened the guests. Finally, Jackie Autry appeared on the podium to present Merle his prestigious honor. Merle was never one to string out an acceptance speech. I'd watched him on television and before a live audience many times; he was always short and sweet but with eloquence and warmth. This night was no exception. After Merle received a rousing ovation from the large crowd, he simply said, "Thank You."

Merle surprised me, though, by announcing, "Today is Jackie Autry's birthday! Let's all sing her a happy birthday!" Everyone sang along with Merle, who led over the microphone with a robust version of this familiar tune. Caught completely by surprise, Jackie was both astonished and flattered by the acknowledgment of her birthday... by the honoree. Who does this sort of thing if not a humble and gracious man! Merle's actions were fractionally indicative of his spirit.

Merle and his retinue stayed for about a half-hour after the presentation. Soon he motioned me to his table and quietly asked me to warm up the bus. He was ready to travel the 550 miles back to his home in Palo Cedro.

I rounded everyone up while Merle was saying his goodbyes. A considerable crowd remained in the giant tent, noisily enjoying themselves. Merle had installed two train horns on his bus, one on the passenger side and one next to the driver. These super loud air horns were installed so he could push the lever up and blast the horns anytime he chose. As we were pulling out but still very near the tents, Merle pushed the lever. The shock wave from the horns shook the tents and the crowds inside. A returning wave of surprise and laughter mingled with the blaring horns and barely remained audible as the horns continued blasting for a city block.

Not long after the party, I spoke by phone with Maxine Hansen, who worked for the Autry organization for years. Maxine organized all sorts of things, including Angels tickets (at Jackie's invitation) for Merle's friends and family; arrangements, once, for Merle to throw out the first pitch; and if anyone needed an authentic major league jacket and hat, Maxine took care of it. She was a professional, marvelous, and caring soul.

Maxine wanted me to tell Merle how much she enjoyed the wonderful and surprising train-horn goodbye. She asked me to find out if Merle always says goodbye to everyone, no matter where, with the same charming, unique, long, and rousing horn blast. I did, and he did. Merle blew those horns almost every time we left a concert. And now, every time we'd leave an Angels game, he'd deliver the expected long and loud blast from his train horns, much to the delight of the fans and Maxine Hansen.

Cher Infused Christmas

CHAPTER 21

Photo illustration - R.J. Shearin

MY FAMILY ARRIVED AT MERLE'S ranch a few days before Christmas to spend the holiday with me and Merle's family. At that time, I was Merle's personal assistant/office manager and living in one of the houses on his property. We gave Merle and his family plenty of privacy; however, we were thrilled to join them for Christmas dinner at Merle's request. Merle and his family knew my family well. For nearly thirty years, he'd known my wife, Kathy, and had known my children since they were born. My son, Benjamin, was eighteen, and my daughter, Alison, twenty-two when we spent this memorable Christmas together in Palo Cedro.

Merle had informed me that Cher had called him a few weeks before Christmas. She had asked Merle if he would consider indulging her boyfriend's Christmas wish: to speak with Merle by phone on

Christmas Day. Merle and I both found this very cool, and Merle was pleased to grant the Christmas wish. Beyond what Cher had requested, Merle signed a boxed set of his music and asked me to mail the gift to their home - they received it just before Christmas.

At the appointed time on Christmas Day, Cher called right on the minute. Merle answered the phone, knowing it was Cher. Immediately, both families became hushed, so Merle could focus on fulfilling the Christmas wish. Merle's normal speaking voice was powerful and resonant. But upon entering a recording studio to sing, he'd unveil an even clearer, deeper tone. That tone is what he used when he began speaking to Cher and her boyfriend. He picked up the receiver, looked at all of us, paused for a moment, and in that Haggard voice, boomed, "Hi Cher!"

They exchanged warm Christmas greetings, even though we couldn't hear details of what was said. Then Cher handed the phone to her boyfriend, whose Christmas wish was about to become a reality. Merle said, "Merry Christmas, man!" Merle enjoyed talking with him, humbled by the knowledge that a few simple moments of conversation with Merle - out of all the people in the world - was the only thing this grown man desired for Christmas. They spoke for a few minutes, then Merle bade Cher's boyfriend a merry goodbye, no doubt leaving them both very happy. Merle proceeded to entertain us with his powerful presence - he had an aura about him. Merle Haggard was a gifted man, also humble and kind, particularly around Christmas.

All Merle's band members and his staff were gifted a nice cash bonus that Christmas. Bonnie Owens once told me he had always been generous like that. A few years later, Merle tried to buy a house for me sometime around the holiday season. It would be the first house I could purchase since my divorce about ten years earlier, and essential I do it independently. Merle asked me about the purchase price. "$90,000," I told him and then tried to explain how buying the house unassisted had something to do with personal integrity. He wanted to buy that house for me, "Right now!" he said! I so appreciated his bighearted offer but could not accept it. He understood and didn't press me further. By this time, I was driving his tour bus for $450 a day, so he was indeed helping me buy that house!

It was time for my family to return home after the Cher infused holiday - one I'm sure they will always remember. Not only did they enjoy the time spent at Merle's ranch, but they had the thrill of witnessing Merle grant Cher's boyfriend his wish. My kids were familiar with Cher and appreciated her many talents, even though from a different era. They had heard Sonny and Cher's song, "The Beat Goes On," and they knew of the duo's fame as television and recording stars.

Now it was back to work for me and all too quiet after my family departed for Las Vegas. Fortunately, one of my first assignments got me out of an empty house to scout the area around Palo Cedro, looking for old cabins. I was to photograph the cabins for potential use as cover art for a new gospel album Merle had been working on, *Cabin in the Hills*.

Back in October, when I first arrived at Merle's ranch, he described his vision for the album cover: he wanted a painting depicting Jesus looking down on a cabin, with him looking up at Jesus in gratitude. I was sitting on the couch beneath a portrait of Jesus with his head surrounded in a beautiful halo. I pointed to the painting above me as an example, and he said, "That will do fine." I found a professional photographer from Redding willing to drive out to the ranch for the photoshoot.

Merle chose his front yard high with wheat-like grass as the setting. He described to the photographer how he wanted the poses of himself with one of his favorite guitars - the photographer shot around a hundred photos. They used one to compile the final image for the album cover; another they selected as the cover for an upcoming autobiography, *My House of Memories*. Both the album and book cover turned out wonderfully. I imagined Cher's boyfriend eager to own both. He probably camped outside the night before the book's release, anxiously waiting for the bookstore to open. I imagined Cher was there with him.

Natalie Cole: Sister to History

CHAPTER 22

One of many terrazzo stars from the Hollywood Walk of
Fame in Hollywood, California *Photo courtesy of R.J. Shearin*

MERLE ALWAYS SURPRISED ME. Every day he'd say or do something
unexpected, so naturally, I grew to expect the unexpected. The year was
2001. I worked as his office manager and personal assistant at his home
in Palo Cedro, about seventeen miles outside of Redding, California.
We'd usually take his Ford Expedition for trips into town. Merle enjoyed
driving and always had music playing - usually Bob Wills, Lefty Frizzell,
or the like.

One day he asked me to drive him into town; his car was low
on gas, and he didn't want to risk a potential hitchhiking episode. Merle
always trusted my driving, so we hopped in my little 1999 Mercury

Cougar and headed down the hill. Music always played in my car, too, and today's selection happened to be Natalie Cole's *Greatest Hits* CD. I absolutely love Natalie Cole – yes, the late great singer from the legendary Nat King Cole family.

Merle listened intently to every song. One of her very best is a song titled "Angel on My Shoulder." It is beautiful, and she sings it so brilliantly! Merle was trembling with eyes transfixed on the road ahead and welled with emotion. He confided in me that the angel on his shoulder would be his father. He explained that he was aware of Nat King Cole's early death, leaving his wonderful daughter, Natalie, without her hero. Merle could relate, having lost his father when he was only nine years old. He surmised Natalie's dad had inspired her powerful performance.

"Natalie Cole is my favorite female vocalist," he said melodically. He always spoke with a subtle rhythm, but I remember that line as if he were singing it. He may have said 'girl singer,' which for a country boy would seem more apropos, but regardless, it was surprising news to me.

I always thought Merle's favorite was Connie Smith or I imagined it might be Patsy Cline because whenever her voice came over the sound system, he would just laugh, utterly amused by her incredible voice. His laughing was a high compliment. Never easily impressed, if Merle laughed at a performance, you knew he was really enjoying it. "That was great," was not something Merle would say. He'd always just say 'good,' unless it was bad, then it was 'terrible.' If he said it was good, that meant it was great. His indifference was generally observed without comment. I came to understand his lingo.

How do you respond to a man like Merle when he reveals something so quietly personal? I always learned to tell the truth or just listen and not say anything. Merle was good at reading a person's eyes. When you talked to Merle Haggard, you'd better be sincere. It seemed like he could see right through your eyes and into your mind. Sometimes he would stare into my eyes so forcefully I would hear his voice in my head and wonder whether he was projecting his thoughts. Situations were always intense around him. He was a very kind man, but he liked to keep me on my toes.

I left Merle's employment near the end of 2001. I wanted to take the money from my divorce and do nothing for two years or until the money ran out, whichever came first. It was a virtual tie! The money ran out in about two years, as expected, but I enjoyed not having to answer to anyone.

At fifty-one years old and semi-retired, a lady came along, heard me singing in a bar, and took me into her home. That woman saved me. She was fine with me singing in a bar twice a week for $60 a night, as long as I went to church with her. I believe in God, so I went to church. After a year or so, she got a job in San Diego. I was all for that, so we loaded up and moved to southern California. I remember driving up to Merle's ranch to say goodbye. He was sitting alone in his pickup truck. I climbed in to say goodbye and tell him we were on our way to San Diego. He responded simply, "When it doesn't work out, come on back."

Now, how did he know it wasn't going to work out? I think he saw it in my eyes. Our relationship lasted just two weeks after we arrived in San Diego. So I wound up a straggler again, this time showing up at my brother's house in Corona, California. I stayed for about a month with my brother Bob, then moved on to good ole Bakersfield, my favorite town. My brother-in-law, Donny, was very receptive. He told me I could stay as long as I wanted, providing it was only for the next two weeks. I lived with him for a year - he was a good friend, and we laughed all the time.

Bakersfield became home again, and I survived with the help of great friends, odd jobs, and singing in a nightclub a few times a week for $50 a night, plus dinner and cocktails. I found another girlfriend who liked my singing, too, and asked me to move in with her. We stayed together for about a year. She kept nagging me to get a job - I'd sing her songs to quiet her down. This girlfriend was enamored with famous people and knew of my friendships with Buck Owens and Merle Haggard - in Bakersfield, you don't get much above those two in the fame department. I sang as a guest many times on Buck's live shows at his diamond nightclub, the Crystal Palace. We visited Merle, on occasion, when he'd come to town. I didn't mind inviting her to meet and get to know these men, and of course, she loved it.

It was a very lucky day when my friend Kip Sullivan who owned a nightclub in Bakersfield, gave me two tickets for a Merle Haggard/Bob Dylan concert in Los Angeles. My girlfriend was as eager as I was to attend. My niece, Brianne, was working in Hollywood then and was able to join us for the show. After an incredible performance by Bob Dylan and Merle Haggard, we decided not to go to Merle's bus. A tour bus is a chaotic scene at the close of the show. There are instruments and equipment to pack, safety precautions to observe, and even the calmest moments are tainted with the understanding that it's time to get on the road with likely another show to play in less than twenty-four hours. Merle was always very kind to receive as many friends and fans as possible, but it could get jam-packed on the bus. So, we steered clear of the bus and decided to make our way to the front of the Pantages Theatre.

There stood Natalie Cole. Natalie Cole! Merle's favorite 'girl singer.' I *had* to talk to her! We approached Natalie and her entourage, which included her sister and other family members and friends. I introduced my niece and girlfriend and then told her that Merle had proclaimed her his favorite female vocalist. She was stunned and took a step back as she placed her hand on her heart and told us she had been a fan of Merle's forever. Natalie gave me her manager's phone number, telling me she wanted to speak with Merle and maybe even work on a project with him.

Weeks later, I received a phone call from Merle. His tone indicated he was upset. He seemed guarded, hesitant, and seemingly more deliberate than usual with his word choice. He told me that he and Natalie Cole were scheduled to perform a duet together at the upcoming Academy of Country Music awards show, but something was wrong. He wanted me to call Natalie's manager and tell him that he would not be able to perform with her. He was canceling on one of his favorite singers, and canceling was something he never did. They were supposed to sing the Nat King Cole classic, "Unforgettable." Merle had recorded it on his album of classic songs, and Natalie, with the help of modern technology, had a big hit with her late father. They simply took Nat's version and added Natalie's voice to blend with his, and it was so good!

Merle told me that he was backing out for a variety of reasons, but the main one was, "Who do I think I am to try and take the place of the great Nat King Cole?" He was as superstitious as he was spiritual, and he refused to tempt fate.

I made the call to Natalie's manager, and he was livid. He said she would be devastated - she'd even bought a beautiful dress for the occasion. He demanded to speak with Merle's manager. There's more to this story with hurtful and lasting ramifications, but it's more than is appropriate to share. The show did not go on.

It did turn out that I was able to attend the awards ceremony that year in Las Vegas. I flew there on Buck Owen's private jet with Buck and our respective girlfriends. We had great seats at the ceremony, four rows back. As soon as I sat down, I thumbed through the beautiful informational packet for the 2005 ACM Awards out of curiosity. On the program was Merle Haggard and Natalie Cole singing a duet,

"Unforgettable." I wondered aloud why, with two weeks' notice, the people who made the program insisted on inserting this portion of the show, knowing it wasn't happening. It sure looked good on paper, though. It truly would have been "Unforgettable."

Brother George Jones

CHAPTER 23

George Jones with Merle Haggard, June 1997

Photo courtesy of Raymond McDonald

I HEARD THE VOICE OF George Jones in the 1950s, on my mother's radio. We lived in Topeka, Kansas, at the time, and my mom had that radio tuned to her favorite country music station regularly. Whenever George sang, it was as if his voice was making the little radio dance. It seemed like the window shades all rolled up and started spinning around. I swear the sun came out from behind the clouds for a listen, birds flew in, landed on the windowsill, and sat still in fascination! Was that my imagination? No! It happened! He was that amazing! I followed his career through the years. When we moved to California in 1959, my mom found the local country music station, and George Jones's music was there. In 1968, I became a professional radio DJ. I played records on KUZZ Bakersfield, California, and was happy to play his music. Sometimes I dedicated his songs to my mother.

I first met George around 1990, when he came to Las Vegas to perform with Merle and Conway Twitty. These great musicians were touring America and stirring things around in every town from coast to coast. I was backstage in the greenroom visiting with Merle and some members of the show when George came into the room. He walked over to the couch Merle was sitting on, gingerly put his hand on Merle's shoulder, leaned down, and kissed his forehead at the peak of his receding hairline. George said, "I Love you." It was such a tender, humorous moment. Everyone in the room laughed with delight at his wonderful entrance. Merle said, "Man! You don't have to kiss me!" George replied, "Yes, I do!"

I didn't have a chance to shake his hand or say hello, but I didn't need to. He solidified everything I'd heard about him in that display of affection for his friend, Merle Haggard. George immediately left the room and went to work on stage at the sold-out MGM Hotel Concert Hall. George opened, with Conway up next, then Merle closed the shows. Merle told me initially he was to open, but that only happened one time. After that first show, George and Conway pulled him aside and told him moving forward, Merle would always close. He asked them why they told him, "We ain't never gonna follow you again!" That's a high compliment, and Merle was honored and humbled to comply. I watched the show in Las Vegas, and it was fabulous!

About seven years later, I ran into George in Nashville. We were backstage at an awards event that Merle and George were attending as presenters. George always had a unique knack for making Merle laugh. They had so much fun together!

During that same awards show, I was walking backstage with Merle when the duo of Brooks & Dunn approached Merle and started walking with us to the dressing room. Ronnie Dunn asked Merle if he was a NASCAR fan. Merle kind of went, "hmmm, well I..." Ronnie pointed to a man standing about twenty feet away, waiting to meet Merle. Ronnie explained, "Merle, I'm asking because that's Dale Earnhardt standing over there. He's a big fan of yours, and he wants to meet you!" Dale was kind of coy as we approached. He glanced at Merle, shyly looked away, shuffled his feet, put his head down, then put his head up. Merle was more than happy to meet Dale. Dale Earnhardt gave Haggard a warm, wonderful greeting. Dale said, "Man! I've been a fan of your music all my life! It's great to meet you!" I noticed that Dale's hands were huge as he shook hands with Merle. Would it be fair to state that 'the intimidator' was intimidated? Yes! Merle was quite impressed with Mr. Earnhardt, and they spent a few minutes talking. I took a photo of Johnny Paycheck, Dale, Merle, and Brooks & Dunn together a few moments after their meeting.

A few years later, in 2001, Merle was home in California, where I worked in his living room/office. On a Monday morning, when I walked into work, I noticed his mood was despondent. He was watching the news and quietly crying. He told me that Dale Earnhardt had died at Daytona on Sunday. He said, "Dale Earnhardt was my friend. My God, he was a fan of mine!" I was shocked by the news. After a few minutes, I asked him if he'd like to send condolences to his family - to his son, Dale Jr. Merle said, "Not right now, everyone in the world will do that, and we might get lost in the shuffle. I'll wait until the time is right." He was so upset about losing a friend and America losing an icon.

I presented Merle with a framed photograph of Dale and his musical friends several years later. He'd never seen the picture and was quite appreciative. He asked if I'd taken the photo, and I told him that I had. He was impressed but mostly thankful that I'd captured the moment.

Not long after that, I got a phone call from Merle. I was in Bakersfield, about 450 miles from his home in Palo Cedro, California. He asked me if I'd like to come up to his house and take photos at a recording session he had planned with George Jones. He said, "You can be my professional photographer!" I said, "Thanks!" Then I was on my way! I took my trusty 35mm camera and captured a few moments of Merle and George in the studio. I felt like I was imposing, so I didn't take a hundred photos. My camera only had room for twenty-five photos anyway.

Fast forward another few years. Merle called and asked if I'd bring his good friend, Sonny Langley, up to his home to visit. George Jones had a concert in nearby Redding and would be visiting Merle's at his home. So Merle wanted Sonny and me to share in his friendship with George. When Sonny and I arrived the next day, George was sitting on the couch talking with Merle. George was so friendly! He rose and gave us both a warm greeting. He was so happy to be at Merle's house! Merle was all smiles and enjoyed the social scene that he'd arranged. As we sat around Merle's living room discussing country music, George suddenly blurted out, "Merle is my favorite 'living' singer. Hank Williams was my favorite singer too, but he's gone."

With that, Merle stood up and told George he wanted him to see the new addition to his house. Merle had a beautiful master bedroom and bath just completed. George said, "Fine." Merle stopped in the kitchen and told Sonny and me to show George the way. As soon as we entered Merle's new bedroom, George noticed a Merle Haggard model Martin guitar standing in the corner. He grabbed it, without a word about the now-forgotten new bedroom. He started playing and then began singing a Hank Williams gospel song about 'mama.' Merle came walking down the hall, listening to George singing and playing his guitar. George stood there and sang the entire song for us. When he finished, Merle could hardly speak. Merle's eyes were softly glistening with tears when Merle said, "Thank you, George! You've christened my bedroom." The moment was so tender.

Why Me? Kris Kristofferson

CHAPTER 24

Jamie, Kris, Willie, and Merle at The Kennedy Center Honors, December 2010 *Photo courtesy of Jim Haggard*

KRIS KRISTOFFERSON, WILLIE NELSON, AND Merle Haggard played at an enormous Indian casino/hotel complex in Oklahoma in April of 2015. Willie had finished his set, and it was time for Merle and Kris, backed by The Strangers, to begin theirs. During a brief discussion with Merle before the show, Kris said, "Look, Merle, this is your show, and I want you to call out whatever you'd like to play. When you want me to sing something, just ask – we don't need a setlist." That's how Merle preferred playing his solo concerts, and Kris wanted Merle to have that option, so that's what they did.

Kris and Merle had been on tour a few times together, playing many shows per year. This evening was near the end of their tour and, in retrospect, an incredibly poignant evening, because unbeknownst to all, the 'live performance' part of Merle's long and successful career was nearing an end. Merle always closed the show with his number one song, and the one he was well known for, "Okie from Muskogee." He'd finish the song, thank everyone, walk off the stage, and that was it.

But this particular night, at the end of their extraordinary ninety-minute set, Kris Kristofferson sang "Why Me Lord," the stirring gospel song he had written in the 1970s and had become a standard, especially in the gospel country music genre. Merle helped Kris sing this beautiful song, and when they finished, Merle said, "That's it, goodnight everybody!" Both the band and Kris looked at him as if to ask, "Wait, aren't you going to end with 'Okie from Muskogee?'" Then Merle repeated, "That's it, thank you and good night," as he set his guitar down and walked off the stage.

At the end of just about every show, I would greet Merle and accompany him to his bus, helping fend off aggressive fans or do whatever he needed at the moment. As soon as I saw him, I commented he hadn't ended with his usual, "Okie from Muskogee." He said, "Ray, there was no way any song I've got could follow "Why Me Lord," and I wasn't gonna do it. That was the end of the show!"

I had watched hundreds of shows over the years, and "Okie from Muskogee" was always the last song. No one who followed Merle regularly had ever seen him close the show any other way, but he surprised everyone that night. Kris Kristofferson's stirring classic had *moved* him. Merle was humble and selfless enough to let that tender moment be as meaningful to his fans as it was to him.

For the curious, the following is a little backstory about this from-the-heart song by Kris Kristofferson. Ralph Emery, of Nashville television and DJ fame, hosted a weekly program, called Ralph Emery Live, from 2007 to 2015, always with a panel of celebrities. Willie Nelson was seated next to Kris; each, in turn, would sing then discuss their well-known song. It was Kris' turn, and Ralph asked about his song, "Why Me Lord," and could he talk about when he wrote it, what inspired it, etc. Kris explained how one morning in Nashville, he had gone to church with Connie Smith (a multiple Grammy-nominated country singer). The preacher was Hank Snow's son, Jimmy Snow - Hank was a huge country music star from the 1950s into the 1980s. Larry Gatlin was on stage, singing his heartfelt song, "Help Me."

Merle wasn't a big fan of Larry Gatlin after Larry had sent a note backstage (with his phone number included) that read, "I came to see a legend tonight, and all I saw was an old man. If you need help, give me a call." Merle was not pleased with this mean-spirited note. He mentioned that he had 'analyzed Larry Gatlin's credentials,' and if he ever saw him again, he'd have a few questions for him, along with a kick in the shins. I know this incident bothered Merle because he spoke of it often.

In December 2015, when Merle was ill enough to be hospitalized in Palm Springs, we watched Ralph Emery's interview with Kris about his song "Why Me Lord." During the interview, Kris relates, "I'd had a profound religious experience during the sermon, something that had never happened to me before. Jimmy asked if anybody was lost, to please raise their hand." Kris, who wasn't a regular churchgoer, said the notion of raising his hand was entirely out of the question…when suddenly he felt his hand begin to lift. Feeling self-conscious, he hoped no one was watching. As Jimmy Snow wound down the service, Larry Gatlin was singing his song, "Help Me." Larry's song deeply moved Kris.

Pastor Jimmy said, "If you need to accept Jesus, come down to the front of the church." Kris thought to himself, "That's not going to happen!" About that same moment, he found himself walking down to the front of the church, with many other people. Pastor Jimmy asked Kris if he was ready to accept Jesus Christ as his savior. Kris responded, "I don't know! I'm not sure what I'm doing here!"

Jimmy asked Kris to kneel. Then, as Kris tells it, he doesn't remember what Jimmy said, but he found himself weeping and felt forgiveness that he wasn't even aware he needed. The song, "Help Me," and the humbling moments that morning inspired Kris to write his song, "Why Me Lord." I encourage the reader to find the *Ralph Emery Live* interview with Kris about his song, "Why Me Lord," on *YouTube*.

Merle had already been in the hospital for two weeks. His cancer had returned, his pneumonia was not improving, but he was well enough to get out of bed and sit on the couch in his robe and baseball cap. I thought he would enjoy watching the interview with Kris and appreciate the story behind the song.

We watched the video, and he wept. Merle loved Kris' song, "Why Me Lord." He had recorded it, and they had performed it multiple times together, in many different venues. When he learned that Larry Gatlin's song "Help Me" had inspired "Why Me Lord," Merle asked me to have a heartfelt note written and sent to Larry Gatlin, explaining how Merle hadn't known that Larry inspired Kris' song, and to tell Larry he loved him and forgave him. He asked for Larry's forgiveness for anything he may have said against him over the years.

I had never seen Merle weep as he did during the video, but maybe once. The interview touched him in ways I can't describe. The profound lyrics had always resonated with Merle, but now, with his terminal illness and all the emotions he must have been feeling, he was overwhelmed when he learned the story behind Kris' song. That one song, "Why Me Lord," out of all the great songs Kris Kristofferson has written, meant the world to Merle.

Fishlips - Bakersfield's Downtown Bar

CHAPTER 25

At Bakersfield's honky-tonk, Fishlips, Merle Haggard helps
celebrate the birthday of his friend, Dr. MC Barnard!
Photo courtesy of Kim Barrett

TWO YEARS AFTER MY DIVORCE, I moved back to Bakersfield. I
had been married to my childhood sweetheart for twenty-eight out of
the thirty-two years we had been together. This move was not an easy
transition. My brother-in-law, divorced for some time, said I could stay
with him for a few weeks while deciding what to do. Somehow a few
weeks turned into a couple of years. So there we were - two bachelors
in Bakersfield.

One day I headed downtown, looking for an old high school
friend, Kipp Sullivan. I'd heard he had a bar/restaurant called Fishlips,

and I hoped to play some music there. Kipp, I understood, was in the middle of moving his establishment down the street from the Padre Hotel to the corner of 18th and Eye.

I caught up with Kipp at the Padre Hotel. Kipp was one funny guy - his given name was Francis, a name that got him teased relentlessly in grade school. In the second grade, he changed his name to Kipp, saving himself years of torment. (We all know how grade school kids can be brutal but act like perfect angels at home in front of their parents!) So, I lovingly called my friend Francis in private and Kipp in public.

Kipp and I, along with Steve Woods, Mike Owens, Glenn Queen, and a host of other teenage radicals, spent a couple of years in 'prison' together during high school. The course that felt a bit like prison was called Boys Glee Club. But, as confining as it was, we had a marvelous time for one hour a day.

Despite his penchant for visits to the principal's office, Steve Woods was the best singer I'd ever heard in high school. I would always stand next to Steve to hear how songs were supposed to sound. Kipp was also a fabulous singer and wound up providing sweet harmonies for me at Open-Mic Wednesdays. Yes, I had landed the job I wanted at Fishlips!

My gig at Fishlips lasted about three years. I performed solo acoustic sets and was privileged to play with some of Bakersfield's best musicians on occasion. Kipp introduced me to all these musicians - I hardly knew anyone, having not lived there for so many years. I was honored to play with guitarist Chuck Seaton and bassman Ron Mitchell, from Big House. It seems like I had every great drummer in town at one time or another, including Tanner Byrom, also from Big House, and Dave Wulfkeler from Buck Owens' Buckaroos. These players were pros and knew all the music I did and more.

Mark Yeary, the former pianist for Merle Haggard's Strangers, often helped me immensely. We never rehearsed - I'd just tell them the song title and the key, then we'd count it off and play it through. These musicians loved playing Merle Haggard's music, and that's what I played about fifty percent of the time. The rest was a mix of 1960s rock: Rolling Stones, The Beatles, Donovan, Del Shannon, etc. Mark Yeary could play and sing any Ray Charles tune, so we often cut him loose on the patrons with his renditions of Ray Charles' excellent music.

We had Kipp's place jumpin' on the weekends with a bigger crowd than Buck Owens had over at his Crystal Palace, three times the size of Fishlips. In fact, we pulled a lot of our regular guests from the Palace, including nearly everyone who worked there. Waitstaff and even managers came to Fishlips because we were rocking it with our country and rock mix.

Fishlips became a haven for the youngsters in town that hadn't been a part of the sixties scene. They were there nearly every night, having a great time! Many from this crowd worked in downtown Bakersfield most nights but slipped over to Fishlips to be with their friends. They were predominantly waitstaff from the other bar/restaurants downtown.

Kipp was an excellent host; he was there every night with a warm, sincere greeting - everyone received a big hug, and the girls got a kiss on the cheek. Fishlips was a phenomenal scene. Every night was a party! I never witnessed any fights - the atmosphere simply would not allow it. In fact, it was quite the opposite, with an ambiance that fueled romances, followed by quite a few marriages. Consequently, a large number of children owe their existence, in part, to Fishlips.

Because of this incredible 'scene' consistent with its lively atmosphere, fun music, and friendly people, the blues brought on by my divorce got left behind somewhere in downtown Bakersfield. This had been an excellent time for me, a young guy in his fifties! My age group and the folks I had grown up with were well represented among the Fishlips crowd, so evenings there often felt pleasantly like a class reunion.

Opening day at the "Haggard House" in Bakersfield, now part of Pioneer Village at the Kern County Museum. Tour Merle's childhood home while enjoying an exhibit of heirlooms provided by the Haggard family. Learn more at *kerncountymuseum.org* *Photos courtesy of Michele McClure*

Side view of Merle's childhood home restored and moved from Yosemite Drive in Oildale to the Kern County Museum in 2017. In 1935, Merle's family moved from Oklahoma into the renovated 1910 refrigerator boxcar. Two years later Merle was born and lived there until his family moved into their permanent home built on the same property in the early 1950s.

Merle with one of many pets he would own over his lifetime. *Photo courtesy of Jim Haggard and Lillian Haggard Rea*

Family portrait: James, Flossie, and Merle Haggard
Photo courtesy of Jim Haggard and Lillian Haggard Rea

Haggard family portrait: L to R James, Flossie, Merle's
brother Lowell, sister Lillian, with Merle in front
Photo courtesy of Jim Haggard and Lillian Haggard Rea

A young boy and his dog - Merle truly loved his animals! *Photos
courtesy of Jim Haggard and Lillian Haggard Rea*

Afternoon picnic with Merle's Uncle Bill Rea and his mother, Flossie
Photo courtesy of Jim Haggard and Lillian Haggard Rea

Portrait of a 50s teenager *Photo courtesy of Jim Haggard and Lillian Haggard Rea*

'The Oildale Kid' *Photo courtesy of Jim Haggard and Lillian Haggard Rea*

Portrait of Merle with his siblings, Lillian and Lowell Haggard

Photo courtesy of Jim Haggard and Lillian Haggard Rea

Bonnie and Merle circa 1965, Capitol Records promo photo

Frisco at his birthday party in New Braunfels, Texas. Note Merle and band on stage. *Photo courtesy of Loren Stumbaugh*

At home in Palo Cedro, CA, Merle poses for photo reference shots for his bronze statue to be placed in Buck Owens' Crystal Palace in Bakersfield.
Photo courtesy of Raymond McDonald

Merle signing guitars for charity *Photo courtesy of Raymond McDonald*

Candid photo of Merle in Bakersfield - note Kip Sullivan in the background!
Photo courtesy of Kim Barrett

Merle thanking the crowd at Folsom Community College,
Folsom, CA *Photo courtesy of Dannie Ray Spiess*

Merle with Kim Barret (Sheriff Youngblood's girlfriend)
in Bakersfield, CA *Photo courtesy of Kim Barrett*

Ben Haggard performs with his dad at the 2011 Hardly
Strictly Bluegrass Festival in San Francisco, CA. Below:
Merle and Kris Kristofferson share the stage at HSBG.
Photos courtesy of R.J. Shearin

Merle's talented band, the Strangers. From left to right: Scott Joss, Norman Hamlet, Kevin Williams (behind Merle), Doug Colosio, Johnny Drummer and Norm Stevens with Merle and George Jones, taken in the parking lot at Merle's recording studio in Palo Cedro, CA *Photo courtesy of Raymond McDonald*

Lee Roy Parnell on stage with Merle *Photo courtesy of Lee Roy Parnell*

Brooks and Dunn with Merle, backstage in Nashville, TN in June 1997
Photo courtesy of Raymond McDonald

Left to Right: Johnny Paycheck ("Take This Job and Shove It"), Nascar legendary driver Dale (The Intimidator) Earnhardt, Merle, Ronnie Dunn and Kix Brooks, taken backstage in Nashville, TN in June, 1997
Photo courtesy of Raymond McDonald

J.D. Crowe, Merle and Ricky Wasson *Photo courtesy of Raymond McDonald*

Merle and legendary Billy Mize, celebrate Billy's 80th birthday, April 29, 2009, at the Buck Owens' Crystal Palace in Bakersfield
Photo courtesy of Raymond McDonald

Miranda Lambert visits Merle at his dinner table after the Kennedy Center Honors gala held in Washington D.C., December 2010. Miranda performed a Merle Haggard classic during the CBS broadcast of the event. *Photo courtesy of Raymond McDonald*

Two of my favorite Strangers, left to right: the multi-talented Scott Joss and multi-talented Doug Colosio, backstage at Bass Hall, Fort Worth, TX *Photo courtesy of Raymond McDonald*

Left to right: Johnny Paycheck, Randy Travis, George Jones and Merle *Photo courtesy of Raymond McDonald*

George Jones and Merle on the band bus at the Legends of Bronze event held at Buck Owens' Crystal Palace in Bakersfield *Photo courtesy of Raymond McDonald*

Dierks Bently, George Jones and Merle at the Legends of Bronze event in Bakersfield *Photo courtesy of Raymond McDonald*

Youngsters Buddy Owens and his brother Mike Owens in Las Vegas at the Bonanza Hotel Casino *Photo courtesy of Buddy Owens*

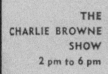

THE CHARLIE BROWNE SHOW 2 pm to 6 pm

Charlie Browne, a native of Bakersfield, brings the motorist home with his special brand of chatter and loads of his youthful approach to the modern sounds of country music

Promo photo from KUZZ radio archives circa 1973. My shift was in the afternoon - They gave me the DJ name of Charlie Brown

Buck Owens gave me this Buck Owens model signature guitar, custom made by Fender guitar master builder, Mark Kendrick. Please note the tender inscription to me: To Ray McDonald "A FRIEND TO RIDE THE RIVER WITH," your friend, Buck Owens, February 1, 2005

Left: Merle on his bus with the local newspaper *The Bakersfield Californian* he had just signed for a boy whose story on the front page saluted him for alerting a family their house was on fire. The boy was from Merle's childhood alma mater, Standard Elementary School in Oildale, CA. *Photo courtesy of Raymond McDonald*

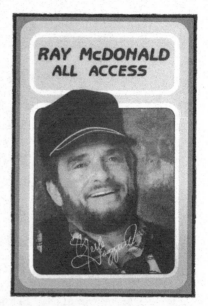

This plaque hangs in Bakersfield's downtown post office. Members of Merle's family, including his 98 year old sister, Lillian, attended the dedication.

Merle's new Prevost parked at a private compound outside Palm Springs, CA, December 2015. After two weeks with pneumonia, Merle was on an outpatient basis from Eisenhower Medical Center   *Photo courtesy of Raymond McDonald*

Above left: My son Benjamin McDonald, Merle, and my sister Connie McDonald **Above right:** My daughter Alison with Merle and his little dog, Fannie Mae, in Primm, NV **Below:** My son Benjamin, daughter Alison (McDonald) Marsh, and me, in Las Vegas, NV, during Christmas 2014

Photos courtesy of Raymond McDonald

Shipshee family portrait: My paternal great grandfather, John Shipshee, and wife Sophia with their children Mary and Rosie, taken in 1889 before my grandmother, Alice Shipshee, was born. The photo below is of a bronze plaque attached to a marble monument in Shipshewana, Indiana, included here in honor of my Native American heritage.

Photos courtesy of Raymond McDonald

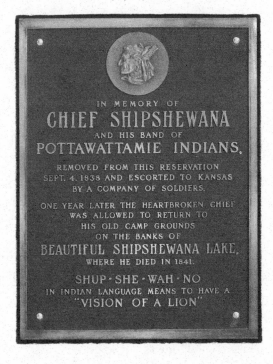

IN MEMORY OF
CHIEF SHIPSHEWANA
AND HIS BAND OF
POTTAWATTAMIE INDIANS,
REMOVED FROM THIS RESERVATION
SEPT. 4, 1838 AND ESCORTED TO KANSAS
BY A COMPANY OF SOLDIERS.

ONE YEAR LATER THE HEARTBROKEN CHIEF
WAS ALLOWED TO RETURN TO
HIS OLD CAMP GROUNDS
ON THE BANKS OF
BEAUTIFUL SHIPSHEWANA LAKE,
WHERE HE DIED IN 1841.

SHUP·SHE·WAH·NO
IN INDIAN LANGUAGE MEANS TO HAVE A
"VISION OF A LION"

213 in a Dream with Haggard, Dylan, and Starr

CHAPTER 26

Photo illustration - R.J. Shearin

IN MARCH OF 2005, I was living in Bakersfield with a California woman. I was nearing fifty-five, she was a young fifty years old. I had the perfect job as the open mic host at Fishlips, Bakersfield's honky-tonk. As you probably know, open mic is a live show where audience members perform onstage, often for the first time.

I only worked on Wednesdays and sang solo for the first hour. My compensation was $50 in cash, dinner, and all I could drink, which which turned out to be mostly whiskey, with the occasional rum from the top shelf. After my set, I'd call up the open micers (pronounced 'mikers'). Some were good, others not so good - many were trying the live mic for the first time and were intimidated and frightened by the situation. I gave them my guitar to play and told them to relax!

My friend, Francis (Kipp), who ran Fishlips, was an enormous help introducing me to the finer points of interest, such as Zaya, a rum from Trinidad, that initiated the best dreams one could hope to have. I usually requested a shot or two.

One night during a most intense dream, the numbers **2-1-3** appeared and lit up my dreamscape; these numbers would not go away! They appeared in the clouds, on the sides of boxcars rolling down railroad tracks, on the sides and tops of buildings; they were everywhere! I woke up around 3:00 a.m. and felt I had to wake up my girlfriend – a pretty little woman but ornery when provoked. Irritated by my actions because she had to work in the morning, she wanted to know why I had awakened her. I explained that I needed to tell her about my dream so she could help me remember the numbers **2-1-3**. She was intrigued and promised not to let me forget as we drifted off to sleep.

I got a call from 'Fishlips Francis' later that day. He had purchased two tickets to see Bob Dylan and Merle Haggard in concert at the Pantages Theatre in Hollywood. He was unable to use them and asked if I'd like to go. "Sure, man," I told him, then quickly called my girlfriend to see if she was interested. Of course, she was thrilled! LA is only about one hundred twenty miles from Bakersfield - we could leave directly after work.

Francis had given me the tickets, but I hadn't looked at them until we walked up to the Pantages door that night. I handed my girlfriend her ticket - number 212, mine was **213**! Our minds were blown! (The Rum! Zaya! It brought me the numbers **2-1-3**!) After we found our seats, we left to find Merle's bus and say hello. He was surprised to see us. The show didn't start for an hour, so he was relaxed about our visit. We had seen Merle with Bob Dylan in Portland, Oregon, just a few days before (compliments of Buck Owens, who had treated us to his private jet and all the accommodations for the show). I told him about the dream and the numbers **2-1-3** and then how I'd scored the tickets for his performance - he was amused and intrigued. Merle often mentioned that I was a lucky guy. That was one of the reasons he hired me to drive his bus.

We were sitting on Merle's bus when his phone rang. The call was from a guy named "Ringo" who wondered if he could come to visit. "Ringo who?" Merle asked with a wink and a loud laugh. "Of course," he said warmly.

I had never met or seen the Beatles' drummer in person, but in the next two minutes, I would be shaking his hand as he boarded the 'Super Chief.' I remember telling Ringo, "I grew up in Merle Haggard's house listening to The Beatles!" He responded with an amiable smile. My girlfriend melted when she met him.

During most of their visit, Merle and Ringo talked about sound systems. Ringo told Merle that the promoters of one of his shows in Denver wanted to cancel because the stage monitors weren't working. Ringo told them to turn the main speakers in just a little bit, and they'd be fine - something the promoters should have handled. Ringo went on to tell Merle that when he was a member of The Beatles, he had only one microphone over his entire drum set; now, each drum and cymbal has its own mic. Ringo confided he missed the simplicity of those days.

Merle knew I was mesmerized. They visited for a few minutes more then I walked Ringo outside; I had to tell him something! What? I didn't know! What do you say to your idol? All I could think of was, "God bless you!" He sincerely replied, "Thank you so much."

My girlfriend and I then returned to our seats to watch Bob Dylan and Merle Haggard's fantastic show for the second time in one week! It seemed like every star in Hollywood attended this concert.

They were enjoying themselves like ordinary people with no one bothering them for autographs or photographs. We saw Meg Ryan and Jack Nicholson but didn't approach them. We just stood there watching everyone with a bewildered look!

After the show, we were visiting with my niece, Brianne, near the theater entrance. I noticed a beautiful Black woman nearby; it was Natalie Cole, Merle's favorite female singer - but you may have already read about our encounter in a previous chapter.

The numbers 2-1-3 weren't through with me yet. About two months after the dream, I was approached by my friend, Buck Owens. He asked if I'd like to fly with him and his girlfriend to Las Vegas for the Academy of Country Music Awards. He told me to invite my girlfriend and said he'd pay for everything, including our room and tickets to the show. Who wouldn't answer with a resounding YES?! We flew to the show and took a limo from the airport to the hotel - a hotel with four thousand rooms. When we stopped at the front desk to pick up the keys, my room number was 2-1-3, of course!

That number was still not ready to let me go. In Merle's honor, his hometown of Bakersfield, California, had named a street after him - "Merle Haggard Drive." Merle asked me to transport his doctor and friend, the esteemed Dr. M.C. Barnard, Sonny Langley, and their respective ladies to the ribbon-cutting ceremony. The doctor insisted I drive his personal limousine for this special occasion. When Merle told me the upcoming event's date, I was not surprised when he said, "February 13th." Oh! Of course! 02/13/08! Merle cut the ribbon at the new Ronald McDonald House in Bakersfield. He was honored to do so on the same date of 02/13/08.

Not long after the Bakersfield ceremony for the street sign, I visited my son, Benjamin, and his family in Reno, Nevada. We went to the Peppermill Casino to play some KENO. I noticed they were running a special: choose three numbers, hit all three with one of the numbers as the last ball, and win $213! My three most favorite numbers and pick for the special ticket were thirteen, fourteen, and fifteen (my birthday, our wedding anniversary, and my wife's birthday). Of course, these three numbers these three numbers popped up, and I won $213 clams on a two-dollar bet! Sweet 2-1-3! You can bet I ordered a shot of Zaya to celebrate!

The Beatles at Merle's House

CHAPTER 27

Photo by Brad Aaron / Shutterstock.com

THE BEATLES PLAYED ON MERLE'S fabulous modern stereo system every time we teenagers got the chance. It was 1965-66. We had about six albums: four Beatles, one Rolling Stones, and one Paul Revere and the Raiders. With Merle and Bonnie on tour for weeks at a time, we mostly played (loudly) our favorite group, THE BEATLES. We played many Merle Haggard songs, too, and not just because we lived under his roof. It was because they were and still are beautiful and meaningful songs! They were heart-wrenching songs of lost love, broken homes, and drinking problems brought on by lost love and broken homes. Merle sang better than anyone else in country music about these sad life situations. He also sang and wrote songs relating to the time he served in prison.

But The Beatles sang about new love, holding hands, dancing together, a sweet innocent kiss, and trusting one another. They sang beautiful melodies, and when they rocked, they were unmatched. As teenagers in the 1960s, in Oildale, California, we were delighted to ingest each music type. We mostly listened to hardcore country music supplied by Merle, mixed in with the most extraordinary rock and roll group ever, The Beatles.

Merle understood our infatuation with this incredible group - he'd been a teenager at one time, too. His heroes were Jimmie Rodgers, Bob Wills, and his Texas Playboys (with Tommy Duncan on lead vocals). It would be safe to say he was probably more infatuated with them than we were with The Beatles. Bob Wills and his Texas Playboys were the most remarkable country band ever. They had the best songs, fiddlers, horns, drums, guitarists, and singers around. So here's a young kid named Merle Haggard, living in Oildale in the 1940s and 1950s, just soaking it all in. That's why he never complained when he'd come home to The Beatles at maximum volume. Smiling, he'd politely ask us to let him have his stereo back - believe me, he understood.

The Beatles and Merle had some things in common: they both came along in the early 1960s, both were young and fresh, and both were signed by Capitol Records. I remember Merle commenting back in those days that it wasn't fair! He elaborated: The Beatles were selling so many records, so fast, all the other artists signed with Capitol weren't getting their records pressed. The only way to buy music in the early '60s was on a vinyl record, and the majority of records Capitol pressed for Beatles fans. The record company placed limits on Merle and the rest, including artists like Frank Sinatra and Buck Owens. Merle mentioned once that The Beatles had another advantage over him. "There's four Beatles and only one Merle Haggard," he said.

In 2001, we were talking about the Beatles and what a worldwide sensation they had become. John Lennon's death was a tragic loss - imagine how much more The Beatles could have achieved if they could have reunited as a band. Merle was sitting in his favorite chair at this point in the conversation. He rose, started to walk out of the room, and with his back to me, stopped and said, "A cold chill just went up my spine!"

In the early 1990s, Merle welcomed two men named Ringo Starr and Don Was up to his house for a visit. The Beatles drummer was a fan of Haggard - a huge fan! Merle was Ringo's hero! They recorded a song that Merle wrote called "Set My Chickens Free" while they were in Palo Cedro. So I missed Ringo and Was by one week while preparing for my move and then driving the seven-hundred miles from Las Vegas, Nevada, to Merle's ranch. When I arrived and walked in the door, the first thing Merle said was, "You missed Ringo by a week!"

"What?" I repeated at least nine times. He heartily laughed at my reaction. I wanted to know everything since I had missed this once in a lifetime opportunity and asked Merle what he thought of Ringo. He said Ringo came into his house (which was very humble), looked around, and said, "You're just like I thought you'd be."

Years later, when Merle's children reached school age, I lived in a house on his property, employed as his office manager. One of my jobs was to take the kids to school each day. I was to take Merle's Ford Expedition - that's what he wanted me to use for safety's sake. One morning, Merle told me to drive my car because his Ford was low on gas. When the kids got in my car, a flurry of Beatles songs greeted them. His daughter, Janessa, was about eight, and his son, Benny, was five, I'd guess. Clapping and singing along, they were immediately captivated! I had the music turned up loud, of course!

When the first song was over, they asked who these guys were, and I said, "The Beatles!" They had never heard of The Beatles or listened to them. After about fifteen minutes, I dropped them off at school. Benny ran around to my window and tapped on it, motioning me to roll the window down.

He asked, "What's the name of those guys again?"

"The Beatles," I answered.

Then he asked, "Do they know my dad?

They were pretty excited when I replied, "Yes, the drummer, Ringo, has actually been to your house."

Benny yelled, "YAY!" Then he sprinted onto the playground waving his arms and shouting, "The Beatles! The Beatles!"

After that day, when I picked them up from school, the first thing they wanted was to hear more Beatles! When we arrived back at Merle's house, Merle was sitting in his favorite easy chair. Benny and Nessa ran inside to tell him all about The Beatles and how great they are.

Merle looked at me and said, "Ray, you didn't play The Beatles for my children, did you?"

I said, "Yes, Merle. You asked me to drive my car, and you know I play The Beatles all the time."

He said, "Okay, but in the future when you take your car, I want you to play fifty percent Bob Wills and fifty percent Beatles. I should fine you $500, but I'll let it pass this time."

The Beatles had even reached the home of Merle's idol, Bob Wills, the most superb fiddler in the world. Merle asked Bob his opinion of The Beatles. Bob's response was, "They's entertainin' the folks, ain't they?"

Garth Brooks - Another Okie

CHAPTER 28

Garth Brooks Boulevard exit sign on Interstate 40 in Yukon, Oklahoma, the hometown of Garth Brooks. *Stock photo*

MERLE WAS ALWAYS A LITTLE taken aback by the new country music. He'd been at it since the 1940s, so when George Strait, Vince Gill, Randy Travis, Alan Jackson, and others came along, he was flattered when they recorded his songs and idolized him. Some said Merle was the main reason they wanted to perform country music. In my opinion, they were all good, and country music in the 1980s and 1990s was well represented with solid songs and new voices.

Then along came Garth Brooks. Garth changed the scene. His songs were great, and his stage act was so outrageous that any rock group in the world would be hard-pressed to follow. Garth sold records at an astounding rate. He became what's known as a crossover artist, appealing to all ages and genres. It's a fact that he's sold over one hundred million records and counting. Not bad for a country boy - an Okie from Oklahoma. He was a damn good singer and live performer.

The first time I had the pleasure of watching Garth was in Las Vegas, where I lived with my wife and two kids. Sometime in the early '90s, Garth was headlining a show at the old Desert Inn. Carlene Carter (June Carter's daughter) was his opening act. The theatre filled up fast, with about two thousand attendees. Buddy Owens had invited my wife and me to the concert and to meet Garth after the show.

Waiting for the opening act, we were sitting in the balcony with a perfect view of the people filing in. Suddenly something or somebody was causing a loud buzz below. Scanning the audience, we spotted Johnny Cash and June Carter making their way through the crowd, apparently looking for the backstage door. Every eye was on them as they stood at a side entrance, with their backs to the crowd. I suddenly remembered something Merle shared with me about his long-time friend and idol, Johnny Cash. He said of all the celebrities he had met, Johnny Cash had the most remarkable presence, and I quote: "Johnny Cash could stand facing a wall, with his back to an entire room filled with people, and still command and dominate the room." As soon as I saw Cash dominating the room, not facing the crowd, I fully understood what Merle had told me. Everything Merle had said was true!

Johnny Cash was a stepfather to Carlene Carter, as she was June's daughter from a previous marriage. They were there to watch Carlene perform and, of course, Garth Brooks. Carlene performed well, and then came Garth! His performance was outstanding - the crowd embraced him as warmly as just about any I have ever seen. Even his imitations of Willie Nelson surprised everyone. I was astonished - not a word I often use, but the best one to describe my reaction! As a disc jockey in the '70s, for KLUC in Las Vegas, I was privileged to see over seventy acts with every major entertainer performing there: Elvis, Sammy Davis Jr., The Carpenters, many rock 'n' roll groups, Steve Martin, Cheech and Chong, Buddy Hackett, Johnny Carson, etc. I have seen many performances throughout the years, so I believe I have a solid basis for comparisons! Garth is among the best!

After Garth's performance, we all went backstage to meet him. He was there with his first wife, Sandy. Buddy and I and our wives thanked him for the outstanding show. Garth was a bit shy but very kind. He kept asking if there was anything he could do for us. "Another show would be nice," we replied, laughing. I then added to our brief conversation that Merle Haggard had recorded a song I wrote called "Losin' in Las Vegas" - he seemed genuinely impressed! Before leaving, I told Garth that other than Sammy Davis Jr., he was the best I'd ever seen in Las Vegas. This embarrassed him a little. He was very humble in his thanks.

A couple of years passed, and Garth was racking up the awards and the hits. On March 7, 1994, I went down to the Crazy Horse Steakhouse in Los Angeles to see Merle play. The venue only held about seven hundred people, so it was relatively intimate. I arrived early to visit Merle and was hanging around his bus visiting with Don Markham when a white limo pulled up. Out stepped Garth and Sandy. The minute Garth saw Don, he ran over and put his arm around Don's shoulders. They laughed and hugged like old friends. After reminding them of our meeting in Las Vegas and my association with Merle, I invited Garth to say "hi" to Merle on his bus.

He replied, "No, that's his *home!*"

I said, "Are you crazy? You've come to his show; you should probably come up and say hi!" He agreed with that and timidly climbed aboard as I led them onto the bus. Sandy took a seat in the bus' lobby area, and Garth walked in circles, taking in every little thing - the pictures on the wall, the "Merle" motif, etc. He kept repeating, "Cool... cool... cool." After a couple more "cools," it was time to let Merle know he had company. I walked to the back and announced the lucky couple. Merle said, "Come on back!" Merle's fiddle player, Abe Manuel, had been visiting with Merle, so I didn't join them, feeling it best to let the four of them visit in private.

Garth and Sandy were gone for maybe seven minutes when suddenly they were back up front. Over the years, I've invited scores of people to enjoy the thrill of meeting Merle Haggard on his private bus. Some of those people nearly knocked me over upon their exit, without so much as a "thank you." That wasn't the case with Sandy and Garth, real fans and genuinely kind people. They both grabbed me by my shoulders and said, "THANK YOU FOR GETTING US ON MERLE HAGGARD'S BUS!" They were delighted and most sincere.

Merle took the stage with his excellent band, The Strangers. Garth and Sandy stood by me, having a great time watching from the back of the room. About halfway through the show, Merle told the audience an exceptional guest had come to see him. Then he invited Garth to the stage, something I've rarely seen him do. Garth was stunned - he couldn't move. I gave him a playful nudge to 'wake him up,' and he ambled on up to the stage as the crowd went crazy! Merle, surprised by the crowd's reaction, said, "Now I know how Bob Will's felt when he called me onto his stage!" (back in the '60s). Merle and Garth embraced, and then Garth left the stage. He didn't say anything to the crowd, nor was he asked to sing. But Garth had a "Moment of Forever," as Kris Kristofferson famously wrote.

It was one year later that I ran into Garth at the ACM Awards in Los Angeles. Merle was to be presented with the 1995 Pioneer Award and had invited me to go. I drove to LA from my home in Las Vegas to join the festivities, arriving early enough to visit and watch rehearsals. Merle had arranged two tickets and one backstage pass for me, so I took my older brother, Bobby. I was surprised to learn when we got there that Merle wasn't attending. The producers saw my pass and asked if I could call and plead with him to reconsider. I said I'd try my best. But I called his cell phone for over an hour with no response. That was it; he wasn't coming! Buck Owens accepted the prestigious award for Merle.

A few days later, Merle told me why he had not attended. (Call me, and I'll let you know what he said - I'm not going to put it in print.) After the show, I ran into Garth backstage, holding the five trophies he'd won that evening. I reminded him of where we had met.

I said, "Remember, I told you I have a Merle Haggard cut? All I've got is a Merle Haggard cut, and you've got five trophies!"

He said, "I'll trade you all five for a Merle Haggard cut!" I believe he meant it!

On October 21, 2012, Garth Brooks, Connie Smith, and Hargus "Pig" Robbins were inducted into the Country Music Hall of Fame. Connie Smith asked Merle if he would welcome her into the ranks with an official induction speech. He gladly accepted. Soon we headed out for Nashville; by this time, I had been Merle's lead driver for two years.

I was not invited to the ceremony. Instead, I spent my evening about a hundred yards away in Merle's suite at the Hilton Hotel, keeping an eye on his little dog Fannie Mae. We had a fantastic time watching the San Francisco Giants win a World Series game. When Merle returned from the ceremony, Frank Mull and Lance Roberts were with him. I asked how the ceremony went, and he said Garth Brooks had certainly surprised him. According to Merle, George Strait presented Garth, but George was not Garth's first choice. He wanted Merle, but Merle had already been enlisted by Connie Smith. During Garth's award acceptance, in front of all those people, he pointed to Merle, who was sitting in the front row, and proclaimed, "Here is the greatest country music singer-songwriter in history."

That statement coming from Garth, at that moment, significantly impacted Merle. He continued to explain that many people had told him Garth had made similar flattering statements, but this was the first time he'd been in his presence when he said such things. Merle told Lance Roberts, his booking agent, to get on the phone with Garth's manager the next morning to arrange a tour with Merle opening for Garth.

I understand Garth's manager did get the call, but when he presented Garth with the idea, Garth merely said it couldn't happen, explaining he didn't feel qualified to follow Merle Haggard, so he wasn't going to do it. I hope it's the truth; it sure sounds good - that's what you call 'respect.'

Along came Jones - Curly Jones - a new and elite bus driver. Eddie Z, another elite driver (who drove Frank Mull's merchandise bus), introduced Curly into the Haggard camp. When Merle purchased his new Prevost from the Hemphill Brothers (out of Nashville), he wanted to hire a second driver to oversee the bus starting from the day he owned it. Curly worked for the Hemphill Brothers at the time. After a closed consultation with Eddie Z and a few others, Merle asked me to interview Curly for the driver position.

We spoke for about an hour by phone, and I was immediately impressed by his relaxed tone and genuine laugh. Knowing he had driven professionally for over forty-five years, I inquired about some of his former clients. From his first job driving the Oak Ridge Boys to many who followed, including Jimmy Buffett and a kid named Keith Urban, he had significant experience! And Curly happened to be good friends with Garth Brooks and family. Garth hired Curly to drive his parents in their private bus to every concert they wished to attend and any other trip they desired.

Curly got the job, which would begin by overseeing the building of the bus. Merle was not only pleased to have a pro driver but one who'd know every square inch of the bus - every detail inside and out, front to back and top to bottom. I called Curly back to tell him the good news. Without even meeting Merle Haggard, he got the job! Curly was elated and then shared with me that Merle Haggard was the one man he had always hoped to have the privilege of driving for. His wish came true because of his reputation alone.

So one fine day in June of 2015, Merle was waiting for the delivery of his new bus to a Walmart parking lot in Chattanooga, Tennessee. We chose that parking lot to allow plenty of space to switch out the old bus to the new. Suddenly Curly appeared from around the corner, driving the most spectacular bus I'd ever laid eyes on. Merle had the Santa Fe logo affixed on the sides in tribute to his dad, who worked for the railroad back in the 1930s. The silver body shimmered with paint sent from another galaxy, made with the dust from thousands of stars - the envy of any space ship!

Merle always wore a smile, but the smile that broke across his face when his new home pulled into view was wider than the Chattanooga River! After taking some time to admire this masterful piece of machinery, we got to the task of switching everything out. The brothers Hemphill arrived on board the bus and gave Merle about one hour of tutelage on his new ride. I took notes, too, but was increasingly overwhelmed by the thought Merle would let me drive his new embodiment of perfection. Sure, I'd driven his MCI for about six years and around a half-million miles, but this felt different. The Prevost was a work of art that deserved to be in a museum. The thought of driving his 'Super Chief' severely intimidated me!

Merle was on his way in his new bus to perform for a crowd of 112,000 people. Curly drove us to the outdoor concert venue and site for the annual festival held in Chattanooga. Everyone had cleared off the bus except Merle and me. I was sitting in the driver's seat, trying to familiarize myself with the controls. Suddenly I realized a man was standing over me. It was Merle dressed and ready to go onstage - three hours early - with his boots, pleated trousers, perfect white high collar shirt, Merle Haggard stage jacket by Manuel, and a big smile. He didn't look at me; he just stared out at the river and said, "Ray, I just took a shower on my bus. I've never had a shower on any of my buses!" His hair was wet, combed back, and he looked magnificent! He'd earned that shower! After fifty years on the road, he could now relish in the luxury his new bus provided, including the fantastic onboard shower he had just enjoyed. From that day forward, given a choice, his Prevost always won over a hotel room - he loved it!

Merle performed energetically for the large crowd that night near the banks of the Chattanooga. I could see it coming, his *joie de vivre* (exuberant enjoyment of life!), and desire and dedication to give it all up for his fans every time he took the stage.

After the show and on the road again, I asked Curly to drive us to Nashville. Still feeling intimidated, I wasn't about to touch that steering wheel. About thirty miles from Nashville, we stopped for fuel. Curly wanted me to drive the new machine into town, but I said, "No, I ain't touchin' that steering wheel, man!" He laughed and pulled out of the station to stop at a red light. He calmly told me to take over driving so I could get the feel. I said, "It's a red light, and it's gonna turn green, so you better keep driving." He told me the trucks behind us could wait and got out from behind the wheel. Realizing it was now or never, I took over the driver's seat. To my surprise (and relief), it was just like driving a bus - any old bus. It operated so smoothly and handled one hundred times better than the old MCI bus. I drove into Nashville and parked in front of the downtown Hilton that always saved a special space for Merle Haggard.

Curly Jones became fast friends with Merle and his family. We became friends, too, as I spent many hours sitting up front next to him, chatting about his life and career. I learned that Curly Jones, the legendary bus driver, was also a great storyteller! Now I was learning about other entertainers (he really loved Garth!) and their life on the road.

Garth Brooks performed on a CBS television special from the Wynn hotel in Las Vegas - just Garth and his guitar. Garth spoke of two artists who were honored in his home when he was a kid. His dad preached that George Jones (one forearm thrust up vertically) and Merle Haggard (the other thrust horizontally, creating a cross with both forearms) were sacred in his house.

These two artists held a special place in Garth's heart because of their songs and the vivid memories of his dad's religious fervor for them. I had watched the CBS special then telephoned Merle to ask if he knew of it. He had not seen it but was delighted to hear about it. Curly rounded up a copy of the special so we could give it to Merle. I don't know if he ever watched it, but I suppose he did. Merle was very private in his analysis of music in general, so I never asked him. He was not doing well in early 2016 when we gave it to him. I'd like to think he watched the tribute from Garth, and hopefully, enjoyed it. Garth sang quite a few George Jones and Merle Haggard songs during the television special. I'm sure millions of fans enjoyed and appreciated the show.

The Marty Stuart Show

CHAPTER 29

Marty and Merle sharing the stage October 12, 2013
Photo courtesy of R.J. Shearin

MARTY STUART IS A COUNTRY music dynamo, recently inducted into the Country Music Hall of Fame's class of 2020 in the Modern Era Artist category. As a teenager, his talents earned him a place in the famous Lester Flatt and Earl Scruggs bluegrass band. He's a phenomenal guitarist, mandolinist, singer, and showman who is also very handsome. For confirmation, just ask any woman or man who has ever seen Marty. Since Moses, he has the most incredible head of hair and is well known for this 'crowning glory,' which adds at least six to twelve inches to his already near six feet in height. (chuckle) Marty is one of country music's great historians who is as well-spoken about the topic as any professor. He was Johnny Cash's son-in-law at one time, and Merle considered

Marty one of his best friends - a friend he adored along with everything Marty stands for.

Merle and Marty recorded a bluegrass album together down in Tennessee. *The Bluegrass Sessions*, released in October of 2007, climbed to number one on the bluegrass charts. They hired the great Ronnie Reno and a host of other incredible bluegrass musicians, and Merle 'laid it down.' Merle was not known as a bluegrass man, but he could play and sing any music genre, including jazz, rock, blues, western swing, Dixieland, and pop tunes.

Merle mentioned Marty Stuart frequently in his live performances all over America and Canada. He'd tell the story about Marty's phone call that led to a song Merle wrote called "Workin' in Tennessee." Here's the story. Marty called to ask Merle if he was watching television and, if not, to turn on the news. He told Merle there was a flood down in Tennessee, and the Country Music Hall of Fame had been a victim of the overflow from the Cumberland River. Marty broke the news that the beautiful Merle Haggard signature Martin guitar Merle had donated to the Hall of Fame was last seen floating down the river. Then Merle would tell the audience how Marty had jumped in the river to save his guitar and got his hair wet. That always brought a big laugh from the crowds. The vision of Marty Stuart with wet hair remains hilarious no matter how many times it's told. Merle had a talent for bringing humor to a so-called tragic event, which was indicative of his nature. After telling this story, Merle had his fiddle ready to kick off "Workin' in Tennessee."

AIn 2008, Marty began hosting his television show, *The Marty Stuart Show*, featuring traditional country music. (Currently, Nashville's RFD-TV airs old episodes as *The Best of the Marty Stuart Show*). Merle frequented Marty's show as a guest, and on one of those occasions, I had permission to invite some friends to the taping session. As Merle

Haggard's primary driver, certain perks were available and begging to be used!

I phoned Rickey Wasson to invite him to go to the taping. Rickey is a fine man. He recorded a bluegrass version of my song "Losin' in Las Vegas" that Merle recorded in 1989. Upon its release, Rickey's version became the most played song on the Sirius XM bluegrass channel. Anyone who loved Merle's music as much as Rickey deserved an invitation to watch him at the taping of Marty's television show. Rickey was elated and asked if he could bring his son and when I said "sure," he then asked if he could bring some friends. Affirmative. The names he gave me to present to security were Mo Pitney and Alison Krauss. I'd never heard of Mo, but Alison is an American music icon. Alison asked to bring her ten-year-old son, which I was more than happy to add to the list. Alison has more Grammys than any other female artist in the history of the Grammys. She is the epitome of an artist with no limits to what she can do. Her voice is angelic, her violin sublime, and she's an astounding entertainer.

I drove Merle to the studio for the show. We were waiting in the lobby of the studio when Alison showed up with her son. Rickey introduced us. The first thing she said to me was, "I wasn't going to wash my hair today, but when I found out I was going to see Marty Stuart and Merle Haggard, I *had* to wash my hair!" Now that last revealing sentence is not meant to embarrass Alison, only to expose the humbleness of a great lady. (By the way, her hair looked fantastic!)

Merle was in the lobby when Rickey, Alison, Mo, and their guests arrived. Now Mo, who was an aspiring singer, had never met Merle. I remember him as a kind and considerate young man - tall and lanky, with a big smile. When introduced to Merle, he was momentarily speechless. Imagine meeting your all-time hero. What would you say? How would you act? Mo was in awe. They shook hands, and Merle gave him a warm hello, then turned quickly to head down the long hallway to the stage. I had watched Merle meet hundreds of people over the years - they were always so thrilled. You could see in their eyes how being in his presence would be remembered for a lifetime. You certainly could see it in Mo Pitney's eyes!

Mo had a regular 'day job' pouring concrete, so he had to take time off work to see Marty and Merle. Rickey told me Mo was also a songwriter and the next day sent an email with a recording of the song Mo had just written called "I Met Merle Haggard Today." I played it for Merle on the bus, and he got a huge kick out of it. A few years later, Mo released his first album featuring "I Met Merle Haggard Today." Mo is a rising star in country music and a fine singer-songwriter in the classic mode. About a year after meeting Merle, he performed an excellent solo opening act for him. One of the songs in his set was "I Met Merle Haggard Today." He told the story, then sang it, and the audience went wild!

Mo has one photo of himself with Merle. (In his song "I Met Merle Haggard Today," he mentions forgetting to take a picture of his idol!) The photo was taken somewhere in the Appalachians when Mo was opening for Merle. Mo had asked if I could arrange a photo, so I told him to be ready at all times because the right moment might come and go. When that moment arrived, I politely asked Merle as he was about to go on stage if I could snap a shot of them together. Mo has that picture now.

Alison Krauss and Merle were friends. They had worked together, and Merle was a big fan of hers. Rickey sent me another song via email, this time from Alison Kraus (Alison and Ricky were childhood friends). She had given Rickey permission to share a song from her upcoming album, with the express understanding we were not to share it with anyone. I listened to it and immediately brought it to the back of the bus, where Merle was quietly relaxing at his dining table. I told him I had a special song for him, sent from Alison Krauss. His eyebrows raised in anticipation. I brought my trusty Jam wireless speaker so I could turn up the volume. The song was so beautiful; he dropped a tear or two. Being so passionate about life, music, lyrics, and incredible vocals always moved Merle; he could rarely contain his emotions.

The title of the 'mystery' song is "Losing You." My God! Merle had me play it about four consecutive times. You can find "Losing You" on Alison Kraus' masterpiece LP, Windy City. I politely ask the reader to listen to this touching song to feel what Merle experienced that lovely afternoon as he listened to Alison's new song for the first time.

Legends in Bronze

CHAPTER 30

Raymond McDonald (on right) and sculptor Bill Rains, with his Merle Haggard bronze statue, on display in the Crystal Palace in Bakersfield, California. *Photo courtesy of Raymond McDonald*

"LEGENDS IN BRONZE" WAS ONE of the coolest concert events Bakersfield had ever experienced. Buck Owens and his family of employees and friends worked hard to produce it. The inspiration for the musical gathering was the unveiling of ten bronze statues, nine of which Buck was commissioning to honor and celebrate some of country music's exceptional artists. The idea grew from a gift Buck received from his children: a life-size statue of himself for placement in his Crystal Palace steakhouse and concert venue. Buck was so pleased with the artist's work, he ordered one in the likeness of Johnny Cash, and both statues stood in the Crystal Palace's lobby for a few years. Sometime around 2004, he decided to commission another eight statues depicting more of the greats in country music, including a few modern artists he determined worthy of the honor - George Strait and Garth Brooks. There was no discussion, I'm sure, about who Buck wanted to honor.

During the months required to produce these bronze statues, Buck had plenty of time for planning the major concert event to coincide with their unveiling. The brilliant Bill Rains, a sculptor out of Montana and creator of the two previous statues, was honored again with the commission. He had his work cut out for him and wasted no time getting started! In addition to Buck Owens and Johnny Cash, the list of deserving individuals being immortalized in bronze for their talents and accomplishments included: Hank Williams Sr., Bob Wills, Elvis Presley, Willie Nelson, George Jones, George Strait, Garth Brooks, and of course, Merle Haggard. Buck was spending $50,000 apiece for the statues. I had my five-year-old grandson do the math for me. He said, "That's about half a million dollars, Grandpa."

Bill and I spoke on many occasions about the project – he had asked me to take the precise measurements needed to begin Merle's statue. Bill Rains required meeting with the honorees for measurements that facilitated getting the close, true to life resemblance of his subjects. Merle was privy to all of this and agreed to have his measurements taken. Buck Owen's crew asked me to take on the task!

I lived in Las Vegas when I got the call asking me to drive the 650 miles to Merle's home in Palo Cedro. I was to retrieve the overnighted calipers Bill Rains had FedExed to Merle's and then proceed with the measuring. I agreed to this last-minute request (on my own time, with my own funds) and left almost immediately for the ranch. Fortunately, the calipers came with detailed instructions. Bill had explained it was a tedious chore and would take around thirty to forty minutes. Can you imagine how I felt taking on this task? I enlisted the help of Brooks

Liggat, a good friend of the family and longtime local drummer and bartender. Since Merle knew him well, I thought Brooks would be a good distraction.

My directions from Bill were to start with about thirty measurements of Merle's head using the calipers. Invasive? Oh yeah! But when I described to Merle what Bill Rains wanted, he remained utterly cool. We started with measurements from the tip of his nose to the edge of his chin, ear lobes, eyebrows, top and bottom lips, forehead at his hairline, the middle of his crown, and both of his eyes. Then we measured the distance between both eyes, the width of his nostrils, and the length between his nostrils! Through it all, Merle didn't even flinch.

While Brooks was doing a fine job visiting with Merle, I began wondering how and why I got involved in this process, which even required me to measure Merle's mouth. And they sent a special tape for measuring his neck - this made me nervous because I had visions of him wrangling it from my hands and then using it to strangle me! However, he was so compliant, and all worries proved laughable.

I measured the length of his hands and then his head as if I were fitting him for a custom cowboy hat. The next part was easy. Just like measuring someone for a suit, I recorded his sleeve, leg, and torso length, shoulder-to-shoulder width, and his height of five feet eight inches. Instead of measuring his foot length, I to recorded his shoe size of men's eight and a half. I was meticulous in all my measurements, making sure to jot them down accurately – we could not have Merle Haggard's statue resembling a Picasso.

Bill Rains wanted a description of Merle's preferred pose. When asked, Merle described precisely how he wanted to be portrayed: holding his beloved "Tuff Dog" Fender Telecaster in a playing position, wearing the cowboy hat and boots he had on that day, and with a cowboy shirt, blue jeans, and a big smile. Merle got exactly what he wanted. The sculptor did an excellent job – the bronze statue is very true to life and with all Merle's requested details. From May 25, 2005, onward, his statue stands with nine of his peers in Buck's Crystal Palace lobby. If you're ever in Bakersfield, stop by the Palace and take a look!

The 'head Buckaroo' decided to ask, months in advance, if the honorees (live ones, of course) could be there to perform during the celebration. They all agreed, except for George Strait. Buck also added two musicians who were getting a start in country music, Dierks Bentley and Joe Nichols, along with Ray Benson from Asleep at the Wheel fame. Buck's fabulous Buckaroo band would back the guests, with Merle bringing along his award-winning band "The Strangers" for his part of the show.

The concert and unveiling were staged in the back parking lot of Buck's Crystal Palace. Buck had thought of everything, including a complimentary dinner and drinks for his approximately three hundred guests who gathered inside the Palace. The five thousand tickets for general admission sold out quickly at the ridiculously low price of $10 per ticket. All ten statues were draped, then each one unveiled with an introduction honoring the person represented for his contributions to the world of country music. This emotional and historical gala was the sort of ceremony you'd find in Nashville, not Bakersfield.

The phenomenal evening proved full of surprises, especially during the unveiling of Garth Brooks' statue. Garth was dating the talented singer, Trisha Yearwood, who was standing on stage by his side. As everyone cheered, Garth knelt on one knee, pulled an engagement ring from his pocket, and proposed to Trisha on the spot. My girlfriend nearly fainted; the crowd went wild - the moment was electric! Trisha said, "Yes, of course," and the crowd cheered more as Garth kissed his now official fiance. It was a touching and romantic moment.

After the unveiling, all the artists were scheduled to play music. With the Buckaroos backing him, Garth entertained the crowd playing a few of his mega-hits using a red, white, and blue guitar that Buck, I suppose, loaned him. Dierks Bentley, Joe Nichols, and Ray Benson followed Garth, with Buck playing next. While Buck was on stage, I headed inside the Palace for some more free whiskey. While walking along an aisle, two guys named George Jones and Merle Haggard approached me. George knew I was working for Buck that night (unofficially) and said, "Tell ole Buck I'm a takin' her home," which meant, in his Texas drawl, he was going home! He was scheduled next on stage, so this surprised me. Stunned, I didn't say a word. I looked at Merle, who just nodded, then I told them both I'd inform Buck. George turned to leave for home on a private jet, Merle headed to his bus to get ready for his performance, and I immediately went out to the parking lot where Buck had just finished his part of the show. He was in high spirits – everything he'd planned, so far, had been perfect. I hesitated to relay the news that Mr. George Jones had decided to leave early, especially at this particular moment, but I had to let him know. When I told Buck that George had headed home, he seemed unconcerned and simply said, "Okay," and that was it.

Merle and the Strangers performed a ninety-minute concert that anchored the night. The crowd roared for every song as Merle brought all his magic to his hometown! It makes a huge difference when you play at home, and this was his family's home. Tonight's experience would not be repeated anywhere, ever. It was legendary.

Later, I watched an interview with Trisha Yearwood regarding the unique **Legends in Bronze** evening at the Palace. She said something like, "Bakersfield is the most romantic city in the world." Apparently, Trisha had never visited Oildale.

Willie 'Pancho' Nelson

CHAPTER 31

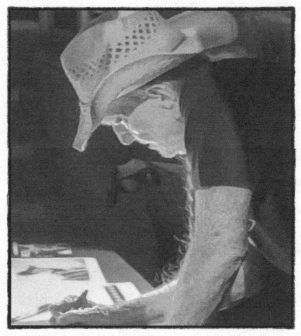

Willie Nelson signing posters and albums for charity
Photo courtesy of Raymond McDonald

IMAGINE YOURSELF STANDING IN FRONT of a great Indian Chief, wisdom in his eyes, surrounded by an aura. His face of chiseled features proudly displays the lines of years etched across his brow. Long braids lay gently against his shirt. His peacefulness is apparent within his warm brown eyes, and his voice is clear and resonant. His presence is commanding, yet not intimidating. He shakes your hand and kindly says hello. You have just met Willie Nelson, Indian Chief - Chief of country music, and ambassador to the songs of America.

Willie is a national treasure and a friend to everyone. Among talents other than music, this man started "Farm Aid" in 1985 together with Neil Young and John Mellencamp to help support America's independent farmers. So now, imagine Merle Haggard, another American icon has just introduced you to the incredible Willie Nelson! I never dreamed it could happen, but it did. Merle invited me to a Merle Haggard/Willie Nelson concert in San Diego, California, sometime in the mid-1980s. These two great chiefs were widely known as "Pancho and Lefty." I went to greet Merle on his bus, and he immediately took me to meet Willie. This would be the first of many memorable encounters with Will (that's what Merle called him).

The incredible music these two musicians have made individually is unsurpassable; to watch them on stage together was enthralling. Magnificent doesn't even come close to describing their talents.

After meeting Willie, I had the privilege of enjoying both his and Merle's company in the coming years. They were good friends who admired one another's work. The following episode from the year 2001 is a small window into their friendship.

I was working as Merle's assistant and office manager at his home in Palo Cedro, California. It was late morning, and Willie called Merle for some help. Will had a bad cold he couldn't shake and knew that Merle was adept and informed about herbal medicines. Willie asked Merle to bring him a concoction before his concert that night in nearby Clearlake, California.

Merle was honored to help the great Indian Chief. He immediately checked his wide array of herbal supplements and began mixing up a healing concoction for his friend, Willie "Pancho" Nelson. Immediately after Dr. Haggard brewed up a full quart of liquid, which used numerous health-promoting ingredients, we drove the roughly 150 miles to Clearlake in Merle's Ford Expedition. Upon arrival, we were ushered onto Willie's bus. Willie greeted Merle with a semi-urgent tone.

"What have you got for me?" he asked. Merle handed him the quart of healing liquid, and Willie drank half of it and stopped.

Merle said, "You've got to drink it all!" Without hesitation, Willie finished the concoction. Willie may have asked what was in it, but I don't remember. He was just relieved that his old pal Merle had made an effort to help him out. And it seemed to have worked - Willie started feeling better soon after drinking it. Merle and Willie then began to pass around another type of herb. Everyone on the bus participated in this 'healing ceremony' and felt the benefits immediately.

We all listened to Willie's newly released album, "Rainbow Connection," previously was nominated for the Country Album of the Year Grammy in 2001. Standing in front of me, without saying a word, Willie offered me a CD. Without saying a word, I accepted it. Willie sang the gripping title song "Rainbow Connection" later that night in concert.

While we were enjoying more of the 'healing herb,' Willie brought out another gift - his own brand of whiskey called Old Whiskey River, made as a tribute to him by a family-run distillery in Kentucky. Of course, we had to try it and found it to be very, very smooth. You could say we were all feeling quite mellow after the smoke and Willie's special whiskey.

It was time for the concert. Willie asked Merle if he'd mind playing and singing, and Merle happily agreed to join the band for the evening. They headed for the stage while I left to find my proper place in the audience. The crowd went wild when Merle walked on stage unannounced. They knew who this guy was! Willie handed Merle a strange-looking electric guitar to play - something that might look more at home with Kiss or Metallica. But Merle played it perfectly and remained on stage with Willie and his band all night. The two men performed each tune flawlessly. I literally couldn't believe the brilliance of their performance together. About halfway through the show, Willie announced that the man who typically sings their tribute to Merle every night was stepping aside so the original artist could sing his own hit song, "Workin' Man Blues." What a show!

On the drive home, Merle jokingly told me that Willie must have added some heroin to his Old Whiskey River. We laughed about that for many miles; I still do.

Merle made two unforgettable remarks about his great friend, Willie Nelson. His first: "Willie is my mentor." And the second: "Every time I'm around that man, I think: this is the MF who wrote 'Crazy!' "

Tribute to Willie Nelson

CHAPTER 32

Segment of the Corn Palace murals in Mitchell, South Dakota - corn and other grains were used to create this mural of Willie Nelson

Nagel Photography / Shutterstock.com

YESTERDAY, EARLY IN THE MORNING, I had a dream. Willie Nelson was singing a song I'd never heard. He was singing live in a small bar-like room. I believe I had the dream because I'd read a quote from Willie concerning the children of immigrant families. Simply put, he believes it is wrong to separate those children from their parents. He's so right, of course. This dream inspired me to write a tribute to Willie Nelson on the morning of June 19, 2019.

The Father of Song
By Raymond McDonald

To be in his presence
Is a sweet melody
Songs flow like a river
Sweet as can be

He treats us like children
With a kind gentle hand
He guides us through troubles
He's the heart of the land

He's been given a gift
That he shares every day
Every night, every morning
Every step of the way

It's an honor to know him
The Father of Song
Even children know
What's right and what's wrong

Everyone's an immigrant
Everyone's the same
The earth belongs to the immigrant
In the home of the brave

Fuzzy!

CHAPTER 33

Fuzzy Owen, Merle Haggard and Bonnie Owens at the Del Mar
Racetrack in California in early 1990
Photo courtesy of Raymond McDonald

MY MOTHER AND I WERE watching television together on a warm
August California day in 1959. I was nine years old, and this would
be the first time I witnessed a man playing what turned out to be a
steel guitar. That man was Fuzzy Owen. Fuzzy's face set the standard for
the show. His smile was warm and wide, and his eyebrows matched his
smile. His hair was slicked back, blacker than black. Seated behind what
looked like a machine, FuzzO effortlessly made that contraption sing.
I'd never heard or seen anything like it! I was so impressed!

Like most everyone in the San Joaquin Valley, we watched *The
Tradin' Post TV Show* every afternoon, Monday through Friday. This

local variety show was an excursion set in the valley, with a cast of royals in the land of farms and oil fields. Everyone dressed in fine western clothes that mirrored their respective talents. It was mesmerizing. The somewhat portly but vivacious Cousin Herb Henson, who played his part in developing country music's Bakersfield Sound, hosted the program.

Over the years, with my near-daily dose of Herb Henson's country music variety show, I became familiar with many country musicians and their talents. The first time I visited my friends Mike and Buddy Owens at their home, I had the surprise and pleasure of meeting thier mother, Bonnie Owens, the female singer and regular on *The Tradin' Post TV Show*. Already familiar with her talents for about a year, I was utterly star-struck meeting her in person - a glorious, beautiful woman inside and out. Her boyfriend at that time was Fuzzy Owen (steel guitarist from *The Tradin' Post TV Show*)! Meeting celebrities was rare for me, and I will admit, exciting.

Fuzzy and Bonnie were a charming couple with enchanting verbal inflections. Bonnie's Oklahoma twang and Fuzzy's Arkansas twang, both uniquely natural and melodic, attracted people to them, including me. These two talents would soon be highly instrumental in the success of Merle Haggard. Fuzzy, as his manager, and Bonnie, as Merle's wife and singing partner.

You might wonder if Merle 'stole' Bonnie away from Fuzzy? I suppose the answer would be "yes," but that's country music! However, the three of them remained great friends, traveling the world with their talents. It was my good fortune to witness much of their success from a close and personal perspective.

Fuzzy was a funny, witty man, slim, and standing about six feet tall. He was striking with the blackest hair you can imagine and always had that perfect smile. At the tender age of ninety, he decided to write his life story. I visited Fuzzy in his home during preparations for the release of his book in June of 2019. I asked him why he waited so long to tell his story. He directly responded that he wanted his children, grandchildren, great-grandchildren, and all who followed to know that he had been a part of the historic Bakersfield Sound. He wanted country music fans to have an inside look at this significant evolution in country music and some of the people who made it happen. The title of Fuzzy's book is *Merle Haggard, Bonnie Owens, and Me*. It is an insightful and entertaining read, available on Amazon.

The pastor of Fuzzy's church helped him write his book. Pastor Phil Neighbors is a tall drink of water from Oklahoma and a fine man who wound up in Bakersfield, preaching the Lord to the fine people of the San Joaquin Valley. After he and Fuzzy invited me for an interview about my recollections of Merle, Bonnie, and Fuzzy, we became fast friends. They were kind to include some of those memories in Fuzzy's remarkable book.

Fuzzy had a calm, strong guiding hand in Merle's career. In silence, I watched in the recording studio as he helped produce many of Merle's greatest songs. When Merle hired me to drive his band bus in 2009, it was an eighty-year-young Fuzzy, and Norm Hamlet, not far behind Fuzzy in age, who taught me how to drive. I was embarking on my new career at age fifty-nine, and they were patient, especially Fuzzy, considering I'd never driven a bus before. Fuzzy and Norm taught me well and soon were able to sleep - with both eyes closed - while the bus was moving.

Merle promoted me to his bus driver after a year of experience driving the band's bus. Fuzzy and Norm vouched for my capability and responsibility. I was grateful for the vote of confidence but knew I'd miss all the great times on the band bus. Scott Joss, an incredible musical genius, was so supportive of me in my new role. He often sat in the jump seat (the seat next to the driver), engaging me with an enlightening conversation. Scott was a marvelous entertainer, and I miss him a lot. As I recall, Scott was the only one who ever thanked me, every time, for driving all night and safely delivering the band.

Fuzzy and Raymond *Photo courtesy of Raymond McDonald*

The great Fuzzy Owen passed away in early May of 2020 at the age of ninety-one. He was as important to the Bakersfield Sound as anyone could be. In June of 2019, when I visited Fuzzy at his home in Bakersfield, he asked if I'd like to go out for lunch. Of course, I said yes, not wanting to miss one opportunity to enjoy the company of my highly entertaining gentleman friend, Fuzzy. He said, "I'll drive," so we headed out to lunch in his Lexus SUV. At ninety years old, Fuzzy looked more like fifty and drove better than most who were younger. I asked if he could attribute his longevity to anything in particular. He replied in his melodic Arkansas drawl, "Well, Raymond - I chew my food thirty-three times, and I laugh at everything."

Mayor Buddy Cannon

CHAPTER 34

Musician, Songwriter, Producer, Buddy Cannon
Photo courtesy of Jeff Fasano

BUDDY CANNON, FROM LEXINGTON, TENNESSEE, is a prodigious producer of country music tunes. I met Buddy through our mutual friend, Merle Haggard. Buddy had been producing music for Kenny Chesney, Alison Krauss, and Willie Nelson, amongst others, when he got the job of producing the Willie Nelson and Merle Haggard collaboration for the album "Django & Jimmie." The project was a tribute to the great French-Gypsy guitarist Django Reinhardt and the father of country music, Jimmie Rodgers.

Merle, Willie, and Buddy got together for a few days down in Austin, Texas, to record the album. They had a band playing with them that included some of the best players in America. If you'd like to know more, I'd suggest you google it at your convenience.

Buddy Cannon relaxed completly around these two musical icons, and his Tennessee drawl seemed to set the tone for the whole session. He listened intently to what anyone had to say about an arrangement for any of the songs. He always had a great open attitude and, of course, didn't want to deviate from what Merle and Willie had in mind. To get an idea of my assessment of Buddy Cannon and his work ethic, you can check *YouTube*. There are many videos of this recording session supplied there for us all. My favorite song is "It's All Going to Pot" (Buddy co-wrote it). Yes! That pot! The kind you smoke that makes you high and makes your day. The last time I looked, the video had over seven million views.

I hadn't met Buddy, so Merle called me to the back of the bus where they were meeting.

Merle said, "Buddy, have you met Ray McDonald?"

Buddy answered, "Not yet."

Merle said, "Well, it's about damn time you did!"

I was wondering about Buddy Cannon. Merle had mentioned him many times on our way to Texas and was most impressed with the fact that he played the bass guitar. Everything he said about Buddy revolved around that bass guitar.

After a few days and a lot of fun, they only had to mix the masterpiece down. Sony Records released it, and in June of 2015, it became the number one country music album in the world. Merle was so pleased. He worked hard on his part and wrote some great songs, as did Willie. Their friendship helped mold the project into a new house to enter musically. Buddy played a vital role. He was like the Mayor of Django and Jimmieville.

I noticed that Buddy didn't hesitate to point out to Merle or Willie if one or the other didn't quite hit a note or word right on. They were very appreciative of his kindness and honesty. They simply did as many takes as it took to get it right, and they didn't need anyone "smoothing their fur," as Tommy Collins would say.

After news that the album had hit the top of the charts, I mentioned to Merle that this was one record that will probably never be broken.

He asked, "What record?"

I said, "Well, is it possible that Toby Keith and Tim McGraw, for example, will come along when they are both damn near eighty years old and make a duet album that goes to number one? I don't think so." He just smiled a satisfied smile. The age record is the one I was referring to. It's only fair to mention that both of these men, at this point in their lives, could still write, sing and play their guitars as well as any artists half their age. Have I mentioned that Buddy plays bass? Have I mentioned that he's a youngster? He was only in his sixties when they cut that baby in Austin.

Don Markham - Trailer Park Genius

CHAPTER 35

Don Markham and Tim Howard outside Bass Hall, Ft. Worth, Texas *Photo courtesy of Raymond McDonald*

DON MARKHAM WAS A GENIUS! This man's most remarkable aspect was probably his ability to complete *The New York Times* daily crossword puzzle, usually in less than an hour. He could transpose music from a recording to paper in minutes. Merle would give him a song he'd written as a recording, and Don could write it out on staff paper with all the proper notations: the time signature, the correct key, the melody with note and rest values - everything in perfect order. This particular skill made Don the ideal man for Merle's stellar band, The Strangers. Not only did he have the gift to transpose, but his sax and trumpet playing soared. His musical talents were nothing short of amazing.

Don and I were good friends for fifty years. Even though he's not with us anymore, I'm sure he wouldn't mind me calling him the strangest Stranger. Don lived in a trailer park in Oildale for decades. He made more than enough money to have purchased a beautiful suburban home, but he was content to be in a most humble spot by the railroad tracks!

Don was passionate about life, especially his sports teams: The San Francisco 49ers, the San Francisco Giants, and to a lesser extent, The Oakland Raiders. If you wanted to upset him, all you had to do was insult his sports teams. I'm a fan of all California teams, so I did not run that risk.

Once I witnessed a few teenagers insult his teams, intending to draw his ire. They got a well-deserved tongue lashing from Don each time, which they found humorous. These kids did not know how to play baseball, football, or basketball. I had to explain everything about each sport. They didn't even know the "three strikes, and you're out" rule in baseball! How could they not know this?! What they did know was how to annoy a guy like Don. I must admit, I loved it when he chewed them out. He was earnest about his sports and his teams!

I visited Don and Wanda Markham's home one Sunday afternoon when their beloved Oakland Raiders football team played a home game. (Bay Area teams held a special place in his heart.) When I sat down on the couch, the other team intercepted a pass, which became my fault - Don had superstitions.

He asked, "WHY did you come over here today? You're a JINX!"

I politely explained, "I didn't throw that pass; I'm sitting here on the couch!"

His wife, Wanda, sat amused as always by Don's animated moves. He was on the living room floor, waving his arms in front of me, ranting and raving! "WHY? WHY?"

On the very next play, the Raiders intercepted a pass and returned it for a touchdown! As Don and Wanda celebrated the happiest time of the day, a touchdown, I rose from my seat and started acting like Don. I took the floor ranting, raving, and preaching, "Every time I come over to your house, something good happens! Every time!"

With that, Don asked in a tender tone, "Can I make you a drink?"

"Of course!" I replied. He brought me a large vodka and pink grapefruit over ice, perfectly blended by hand.

Don and I played golf together two-hundred times, at least. We were bitter rivals and always had a bet going. Fortunately, we were evenly matched, both of us shooting around eighty and sometimes sneaking into the seventies on a typical county course. Don was a powerful man and kept in good shape by lifting weights and riding his bicycle. He loved shooting pool and always enjoyed the competition with a gin and tonic nearby. Oh, how he hated to lose at anything! I loved it when I beat him!

Don rode on Merle's private bus for decades and enjoyed every minute of this wild character's company. They would converse for hours on topical subjects and argue just as long. Their combined history of country music was so advanced they could lecture any college student. I like the sound of Professor Haggard and Professor Markham because that's what they were.

Another favorite topic was the national pastime of baseball. Don was a master at this subject, so Merle generally let him have the bus's dais, Merle's dining table. Don once showed me a book he'd compiled of the stats of major league baseball players. He had hundreds of pages, all written in longhand. I was amazed! I asked him why he hadn't published it. He simply said, "No one would understand it."

Don was an atheist - Merle, an avowed Christian. They didn't argue about that; they both respected the other's opinion. I was witness to a very tender moment between the two men concerning the subject. We had just returned home to Merle's ranch in Palo Cedro, California. We were in Merle's living room with Merle relaxing in his favorite chair, and Don, anxious to get home, standing and saying his goodbyes. As he turned for the door and the 450-mile drive home to Bakersfield, Merle stopped him with his goodbye. Merle said, "Don, I know you don't believe in God, but I do, and I want you to know that I love you, and I'm praying for you always." That stunned Don. Don was a strong-minded and strongly opinionated soul, but he could behave like a gentleman with a comment like that. He simply uttered a soft, "Thank you" and left. Merle's prayers were always answered. Don drove 450 miles to work and 450 miles home for decades and never had an accident. I should mention that he drove 450 miles per hour.

Everyone in the Haggard organization had a Don Markham imitation. Don loved it. He had a whimsical, melodic speech pattern. It started high and got higher in pitch, usually ending with many exclamation marks!!!!! Don's favorite word was simply, "WHY!!!" followed by, "I DON'T KNOW!!!" His bandmates, The Strangers, adored him.

Merle and The Strangers had a date at Buck Owens Crystal Palace in Bakersfield. The soundcheck was over in the early afternoon, so Don took off to his trailer park home about two miles away. I noticed he didn't ask any of his fellow Strangers to visit, so I asked a few of the guys if they'd ever been to the home that Don shared with his wife, Wanda. They said no, but they were more than interested in having me accompany them to his house. As usual, I didn't call. I brought the Manuel brothers, Abe and Joe, and Eddie Curtis. They acted like I was taking them to Elvis Presley's house. That's how much admiration they had for Don. When I pulled up to his very modest trailer, they weren't a bit surprised. They seemed relieved that this wasn't some over-sized brand new home in the suburbs, with a big lawn and two-car garage.

Don and Wanda were thrilled to have their company, and the boys felt very much at ease in Don's home. We had interrupted their daily Scrabble game - Don and Wanda had a running tournament between them for years. They played on their tiny kitchen table with Don keeping score in a ledger. He was ahead of Wanda by ten thousand words or so.

They always had a drink for their guests, usually vodka with pink grapefruit juice. Abe, Joe, and Eddie were from Louisiana, so they knew how to party - and party we all did! It wasn't so crazy that they would drink knowing they had a performance that night nor that they were all as marvelous as usual. Of course, before we left, we had to watch Don and Wanda's two favorite shows: Wheel of Fortune and Jeopardy. Did Don dominate those shows? Oh yes, you bet he did!

The 'Sirius-ness' of Renato Caranto

CHAPTER 36

Promo photo of Renato Caranto

THIS IS THE STORY OF Renato Caranto and his saxophone. We'd just left Merle's ranch, headed out for another concert tour of America. It was a pleasant sunny California day as we traveled south on Interstate 5 toward the Sacramento Valley. Merle was sitting up front next to me in his jump seat, looking and feeling good.

Typically, I'd turn on SiriusXM, tuned to Willie's Roadhouse, which plays classic country music twenty-four hours a day. Yep, it's Willie Nelson's Roadhouse. You'll hear Johnny Cash, Patsy Cline, George Jones, Merle Haggard, and, of course, Willie, along with a host of others. Occasionally a guy like me, who enjoys many music genres, prefers other SiriusXM channels such as their classic rock channels or the Sinatra channel. On the last tour, I'd been listening to B.B. King's channel, so Sirius was still tuned to that station when we turned on the radio.

Knowing Merle also had a wide variety of music tastes, I left it on B.B. King's channel to see how he would react. He listened to a cool R&B tune and didn't say a word until the song was over. Then he said, "What the hell channel is that?" I didn't know if he liked it or not. I couldn't tell.

I replied, "It's R&B man, B.B. King's channel."

He said, "Well, don't ever change it!"

I declared, "Yes, sir!"

Completely captivated by the tunes, Merle praised the vocals, the guitars, the production, and the melodies. Then a song played from an unknown group out of Portland, Oregon, and Merle exclaimed, "That's really good!"

Merle had let go of his longtime sax player and good friend, Don Markham, about a year earlier and missed him. Don had played with Merle for decades but was starting to have health issues (Don was inching up on eighty years old). That concerned Merle deeply, so he asked Don to consider retirement, and Don agreed. He even told Merle, "Well, if I'm officially fired, now I can get unemployment!" Merle was relieved Don could put a positive and humorous spin on the rough transition for those who have enjoyed a long career and are not quite ready to 'let it go.' Now Merle faced the dilemma of where to find someone good enough to replace Don. He found him on the R&B channel!

Merle's ear was so uncanny. He had the ability to hear every note by every instrument in any song. He was so 'in tune' and 'tuned in' when he listened to this particular song by the Portland group, he immediately asked who the sax player was. Our co-driver was sitting behind us, and we told him the name of the group when it scrolled across the radio's digital readout. He found the name of Renato Caranto online in minutes.

Renato's life was about to change. Fortunately, for both Merle and Renato, Portland isn't far from Redding. We obtained Renato's number after researching his group online and calling the nightclub where the band worked regularly. Merle called Renato a few weeks later and invited him to his ranch in Palo Cedro near Redding. Renato accepted the invitation and was soon auditioning with Merle's legendary band, "The Strangers." He blew Merle's mind and immediately became the newest member on the band bus!

Renato fit right in. He was a full-on gentleman and totally professional. He had been raised in the Philippines, in San Carlos City, by a father who was also an excellent sax player. Renato would occasionally share memories from his childhood. It was unexpected and surprising to discover Merle Haggard had been a favorite of the elder Caranto. Renato recalled when, at age thirteen, the first song his dad ever taught him was "Silver Wings," a Haggard standard. Renato came to the United States in 1981 as a member of a six-piece band, The New Exiles. He played with The Strangers for the remainder of Merle's career and became a close friend of the family. Once I asked Renato what his favorite radio station was, thinking it might be the B.B.King channel on SiriusXM. I was right!

Kern County
Sheriff Donny Youngblood

CHAPTER 37

Merle Haggard, Harold Youngblood, and his son, Sheriff Donny
Youngblood Kern County Museum, July 2015
Photo courtesy of Raymond McDonald

THE FIRST TIME I MET THE future Sheriff of Kern County was when
he and his family started tossing money into my guitar case at the Kern
County Fairgrounds, as I played and sang Merle Haggard songs. They
call that money tips, and it wasn't just a few coins, but several bills
totaling nearly forty dollars.

Donny Youngblood was running for sheriff and had a booth
promoting his candidacy near the spot where I was busking. When it
was time for a break, I met Donny, his family, and some of his supporters
who had been listening to me sing. I told Donny, "I'll announce your
candidacy on the microphone if you'd like."

Donny Youngblood said, "That'd be great! I've got a booth nearby. Would you like to have a look?"

I said, "Sure," and went over to his booth to check out his qualifications. It was apparent he would become the next sheriff, judging by his experience alone. With thirty years working in the sheriff's department, he had come out of retirement to run for sheriff. He won easily.

Donny Youngblood and his immediate family, in-laws, girlfriend, and friends were like a big posse – a perfect name for the group. I didn't tell them I had known Merle nearly all my life. That would come later. I just kept playing every Merle Haggard song I knew. They were happy to have me nearby and often stopped to listen the next day, and the day after, and kept generously tossing money into my guitar case!

Finally, Donny asked, "Maybe you can help me by playing and singing at some of my fundraisers. You can bring your band or just play solo or whatever."

I said, "Okay, great!" then called him about a week later. "Hey, I'd love to come work for you!"

He asked, "How much do you charge?"

I replied, "For just me, two-hundred bucks, but if you want a whole band, it's five-hundred." He was good with either, and I did go on to play a few fundraisers for him, both solo and with a band.

Donny won the November 2006 election easily over the incumbent. He and his supporters were elated and asked me to play at Buck Owens' Crystal Palace the night of the election as results trickled in. The Palace said, "That's great, but we won't have Ray McDonald play here." Buck had me play at the Palace with my band on many occasions, and sometimes I even sat in with his incredible "Buckaroos." However, I'd had a little tiff with the guy who booked the talent. Buck had passed away earlier in 2006, and with him gone, I had lost all my 'juice.'

However, Donny Youngblood stood up for me. He wasn't the sheriff yet, but would soon be elected. With confidence, he informed the Palace if Ray McDonald wasn't allowed to play for his election night party, then he'd take his business elsewhere. Well, that was settled quickly! I put together a terrific band, including Merle Haggard's former pianist, Mark Yeary, and some other outstanding musicians. The election night party at the Crystal Palace was a success, as was Donny's bid for sheriff! The evening turned into a victory celebration, with ample television and press coverage.

The next day Sheriff-elect Donny Youngblood called and asked, "Do you think Merle Haggard would come to my inauguration?"

I said, "I don't know. I'll give him a call and find out."

He'd told me the date was in January, only a few months away. Donny had enlisted Charlie Napier, a well-known character actor, to help persuade Merle to come down to Bakersfield for his inauguration. Charlie and I each called Merle the next day. Merle told me he sure was getting a lot of calls asking him to come to Bakersfield for the inauguration, but he hadn't yet committed. Merle's sister, Lillian, sealed it when she told Merle what a good guy Donny Youngblood is, and that was that. So in January 2007, Merle, who had never met Donny, drove the 450 miles from Palo Cedro to Bakersfield just for Donny's inauguration.

The ceremony took place in one of the old buildings at the Kern County Fairgrounds. It was a big deal. Hundreds of people, including dignitaries, friends and family, and various press agencies, attended Donny Youngblood's well-advertised ceremonial induction into office. Donny and I were anxiously awaiting Merle when he pulled up in his bus. Resplendent in his new sheriff's uniform, a very excited Donny and

I headed onto the bus. Donny and Merle hit it off immediately. Merle was very impressed with Donny's former service in the U.S. Army and the fourteen months he'd spent in Vietnam.

Donny is a funny guy, very honest, unassuming, and extremely bright. He held various college degrees - not what you'd expect to find on a typical sheriff's resume. He delivered his inaugural speech with the eloquence and thoughtfulness of a preacher. Donny wanted everyone to know that Merle Haggard, his all-time idol, was sitting in the front row, supporting him. He explained how much it meant to him that Merle had traveled all the way to Kern County to attend, especially since he had only met Merle that day. Then with deep appreciation, he thanked me, Charlie Napier, and some other people who had helped persuade Merle to come to Bakersfield.

After Donny had finished his speech and the event was drawing to a close, Merle suddenly jumped up on the stage, took the microphone, and said, "I got one thing to say - we need more cops in Lamont!" The crowd laughed· and cheered as he jumped off the stage. Now we had somewhat of a dilemma because everyone wanted a picture taken with Merle. With much experience in these situations, Merle took charge and said, "Let's all get together over here and take one big photo." Probably fifty people gathered around Merle, who stood in the middle after someone made that suggestion. Nearly everyone in the picture was a uniformed policeman or deputy sheriff from all over the county with a smattering of dignitaries such as mayors and city council members. I was standing off to the side with Sheriff Donny Youngblood. I said, "Donny, it looks to me like one important person is missing from this photo here. I believe it's you."

Donny responded, "No, it's not my day. It's his." That one thoughtful comment revealed what sort of a man Kern County had for its new sheriff! This was Donny's inauguration day - he'd worked his entire life to become the Sheriff of Kern County - yet he viewed it as Merle's day because Merle had come to Bakersfield to support him.

In the years following Donny Youngblood's inauguration, he and Merle became good friends. Whenever Merle was in Bakersfield, he took time for a visit with Donny. He and his posse, who became like an extended family, were always welcomed onto Merle's bus for a visit.

Anytime Merle needed help with an issue a sheriff might resolve, he would just call Sheriff Youngblood. One year, Merle desperately needed assistance with the Canadian Mounties. We had arrived at the border, just above Detroit, Michigan, for the beginning of Merle's tour in Canada. The Canadian border police would not let Merle Haggard into the country because of his previous felony conviction. Merle explained how Governor Ronald Reagan (California's governor from 1967-1975) had fully pardoned him. However, the Canadians wanted proof. Merle was becoming increasingly agitated – we had now been detained for about four hours. Finally, someone remembered how Donny Youngblood had approached the current California governor, Arnold Schwarzenegger, to secure a second unconditional pardon for Merle (the first one apparently didn't cover firearms). We contacted Sheriff Youngblood, who fortunately had a copy of the new pardon in his vault, which he faxed immediately to the Mounties.

At last, with proof in hand, they let us into Canada. It took a little time for Merle's demeanor to switch from a livid Mr. T back to the docile Mr. Rogers after that frustrating ordeal. Merle and his incredible band went on to play about a dozen sold-out shows to his adoring Canadian fans who would have been sorely upset if his concerts had been canceled on a technicality. It's worth noting, when we returned to our beloved United States, we were warmly welcomed back into the country, passing smoothly through the border checkpoint.

The sheriff made friendly calls to Merle often. One call brought both men to tears when Donny contacted Merle regarding the aforementioned second pardon from 'Ahhnold.' Donny wanted Merle to know the minute the pardon had been signed, and Merle could own guns again. This proved an emotional moment for both.

In early 2016, while driving back to Northern California, Merle phoned Donny from his bus to tell him he'd been a great friend and that he'd come by to see him soon. Donny knew he was calling to say goodbye. Merle died not long after that last conversation.

Donny was such a popular sheriff he was easily re-elected with no opponent four years later, and four years after that! After twelve years, someone decided to run against Donny Youngblood, but lost! On the night of his first re-election, Donny mentioned Merle during his speech. He wanted everyone to know how much Merle and his friendship meant to him. Donny said it was critical as sheriff to be popular and well-liked, and his friendship with Merle had certainly helped with that. Donny often mentioned how his association with Merle had aided his career, but, more than anything, he valued their close friendship and how comfortable Merle made him feel. Merle valued Donny's friendship, too. He didn't invite just anyone to his home for dinner - Donny Youngblood and his girlfriend had been guests in his home in Palo Cedro and probably would have gone more often had they not lived 450 miles apart.

Once I called Merle to ask if, in addition to Donny, I could bring two other people for a visit - Stan Ellis and his business associate. I explained that Stan was a friend and much admired successful Bakersfield businessman, known for providing underprivileged kids in Kern County with gifts at Christmas. He gave them bicycles, shoes, and whatever they needed to bring a little joy into an otherwise bleak holiday. Stan also helped the kids in Oildale throughout the year, every year.

Plus, it didn't hurt to mention (knowing Merle's appreciation of guitar players) that Stan played guitar for a fine country band in Bakersfield. That did it! We all flew up to visit Merle in his home, where he would autograph a few guitars and photos Stan brought before we headed to Lulu's (Merle's favorite downtown Redding diner) for an enjoyable lunch.

Merle so admired Donny Youngblood. Donny was and still is well-known for his integrity, which given the politics involved when you're sheriff, is not always easy to uphold. Donny Youngblood is a real-life Andy Griffith.

Q-Ball and a Pitcher of Whiskey

CHAPTER 38

Glenn Queen and Merle at Merle's home recording studio
Photo courtesy of Raymond McDonald

GLENN QUEEN AND I ATTENDED Beardsley Junior High School together. Glenn was one of the funniest, nicest guys I'd ever met. He was athletic, smart, not much for rules, and a friend to everybody - an affable character, as John Lennon might say. When I lived in Merle's household during my sophomore year, Glenn was just a fourteen-year-old kid. He'd come over to hang out along with many neighborhood kids and even some we knew from junior high school. Mike Owens, Buddy Owens, Merle, and I were gracious to all of them. So, Glenn knew Merle from his early teens.

Many years later, when Glenn was forty, he wanted to see Merle's concert at Whiskey Pete's in Primm, Nevada, near the California border. When Glenn arrived, we headed backstage to visit with Merle. After the show, we got on Merle's bus and noticed a few people were smoking marijuana (and inhaling!). There were about seven people in the back, so it was a little crowded. Merle was loudly playing some music he'd just recorded and passing around a joint. Glenn was known to take a toke along with the rest of us – we all agreed that smoking pot was for pleasure, enlightenment, and medicinal value. Medicinal is a word Glenn could never quite pronounce correctly. He'd say, "Medicimal." We'd say, "No, it's medicinal! me-dic-i-NAL." But our efforts failed to change his pronunciation!

I'd smoked Merle's pot before and knew it was a little more potent than most marijuana in those days. I neglected to tell Glenn that Merle's cannabis might be stronger than what he was familiar with. Glenn had a couple of tokes and very quickly got very high and very paranoid. He was trying to get out of the bus, but I was blocking the narrow hallway with really only enough space for one person to walk at a time. He looked at me with his big, baby blue eyes that subtly revealed his trusting soul. He felt trapped, but we managed to get out of the hallway and into the front, where there was more room. I said, "I gotta go home now (to Las Vegas, about 45 miles away). I'll see you later, Glenn. Enjoy your evening," and left.

The next day, Glenn headed home to Bakersfield. He called and told me that he'd been up all night, on Merle's bus, just the two of them listening to music and talking. He was so excited - it was a day and a night he treasured completely. I asked, "All night long? Wow. Good for you!"

He replied, "Well, we were about halfway through the night when Merle decided we needed some whiskey."

Merle had said, "Glenn, I want you to go to the bar inside the casino and tell 'em you're with me. Tell 'em to put it on my tab. I want a big bottle of whiskey. Bring it out here to the bus, and we'll have us some whiskey." Glenn approached a bartender and relayed Merle's request. The bartender said, "We can't give you a bottle, regardless of who you're with. Sorry friend, but it's against the law; we can't sell packaged liquor, man."

While pondering the situation, an intriguing notion surfaced - his instincts had sprung into motion, which was indicative of the way Glenn thought. He had noticed a large pitcher of beer and politely asked the bartender if he could pour a pitcher full of whiskey and sell that.

"Hmm," the bartender replied, "Ya know what? That I can do." The bartender poured the entire bottle - probably a fifth - into the pitcher. He trusted that Glenn was with Merle, so he put the bottle on Merle's tab.

Delighted, Glenn continued, "Now, I'm walkin' out to the bus with the pitcher of whiskey, while Merle's watching me with a big smile on his face." Glenn described boarding the bus and how Merle chuckled as he said, "Looks like you got some whiskey there, Glenn." Glenn explained the dilemma and his solution to Merle, who was quite impressed with Glenn's problem-solving skills. There's a famous magician by the name of David Blaine. Even he would be hard-pressed to magically turn a pitcher of beer into a pitcher of whiskey!

So, that's where the pitcher of whiskey came from. Did they drink it all? Oh, I doubt it. Merle wasn't a big drinker. He wrote songs about it, but he really didn't drink much - maybe a couple of shots now and then for social or medicinal purposes.

After the whiskey episode, Glenn complained it was hot and getting hotter out in the desert. Merle said, "Well, go jump in the pool over there then."

Glenn replied, "Well now, ya know what, Merle? That's a good idea." He jumped in the pool fully clothed, cooled off quickly, and returned to the bus dripping wet. Merle laughed at his antics. Q-Ball (the nickname earned from the first letter of his last name and his penchant for the game of pool) had a knack for making folks laugh.

Sadly, our great friend Glenn Queen passed away from a heart attack on March 19, 2009. When I called Merle to deliver the sad news, he asked me to pick a yellow rose from my back yard, put it in a vase, and take it to Glenn's memorial service. He wanted me to let his family and friends know the rose was from Merle to his friend Glenn.

Ray Wills' Dream is Answered

CHAPTER 39

The John Lennon Educational Tour Bus and Merle's bus both parked at a truck stop in Barstow, California.

Photo courtesy of Raymond McDonald

RAY WILLS AND HIS WIFE Barbara, owned and ran a bar and music venue five miles west of the Las Vegas Strip. I first started rollin' into the Idle Spurs in the 1980s. I quit my job in '86, drove down to the bar, and watched the band for a while. Soon I realized that I could easily sit-in and sing with the band. I just needed a little more time to practice. Luckily, I was no longer burdened by steady employment, so I started playing at home, and before too long, I was working with the house band. I ended up heading the Idle Spurs house band for four years on Thursday, Friday, and Saturday nights, from 9:00 p.m. until 1:00 or 2:00 in the morning. On Sundays, we had an afternoon jam session, from about 3:00 until 7:00 p.m., when anybody could walk in and sing. So, we were working four days a week for four years.

Ray Wills was this little guy in stature, but he had a generous heart, and he was an emphatic storyteller. He told me he was a nurse in the Korean War. He didn't talk about that part of his life, but he did mention it a couple of times. Ray, Barbara, and I used to have a few drinks together - that's what you do in a bar - and we had a wonderful time.

After four years of playing music, I left the Idle Spurs and got a real job as a land surveyor. We got paid on Fridays, and the Idle Spurs was only a couple blocks away from my office. So I'd head down to the bar to get my check cashed every other Friday. There would almost always be a hundred people in there cashing their checks, drinking, playing pool, shuffleboard, and slot machines, with the jukebox going crazy and televisions playing. There was everything you'd expect to see in a barroom in Las Vegas. One Friday, I expected to go in there and fight to get my check cashed.

But on this particular Friday afternoon, the entire tavern was empty, closing-in on five o'clock. I thought, "What in the world is goin' on here?" Then I checked the back door and saw cables running from the outside to the inside, and literally everywhere. I spotted Ray, Barbara, and one bartender. I said, "Ray, uh, what's goin' on? There's nobody in here on a Friday afternoon. How could that be?"

"Raymond," Wills always called me Raymond, like I was his son or little brother. "Look, they're filming a movie here tonight. Sharon Stone, Robert DeNiro, and Joe Pesci are here, and all the crew. They have been here rehearsing today. They picked my joint to do a scene in the new movie, *Casino*." He was nonchalant. Not bored with the situation, but he didn't let on that it was the highlight of his week.

"Oh?" I said. But really, I was thinking about how cool it was. "Well, can you still cash my check?" I asked casually.

So, Ray Wills cashed my check. He bought me a couple of drinks, and then he bought me a couple more. Before I knew it, we were havin' a grand time! He really didn't have to work that night. It was just me and Ray sitting at the bar talking.

"You know, all those movie stars are out in their trailers right now, and the crew is out havin' their dinner," he said rhetorically, his eyes glassed over ever so slightly. "They're gonna come in later and shoot a couple of scenes. All these worldwide, famous movie stars are here in my joint tonight," he paused a moment, "but the one guy I wanna talk to is not here. He's my all-time favorite hero, my all-time favorite celebrity, Merle Haggard."

I knew where Ray was going with this. He was fishing, and I was feeling a little saucy. So I took the bait, "Well, you know - I know Merle."

If he were pulling a line, it would've snapped clean-off, "Yes, I know that you know Merle very well, and I want to talk to him." He reacted as quickly as I'd ever seen him. He was smooth but determined.

"You mean, you wanna talk to him? When?" My eyebrows were up so high that my forehead shrunk in half.

"Well, I wanna talk to him now." I wouldn't say Ray was demanding, but he was coarse and a little lit-up by then.

"Okay, let's just call him then!" I was now attempting to psyche myself up for the inevitable.

"Would you do that for me?" Ray implored.

I nodded and voiced in the affirmative, pretending I was comfortable with the idea, as if Merle welcomed random calls from friends to field questions from strangers at any time of day.

"Would you tell him that all these movie stars are here?" Ray Wills was as animated and excited as I had ever seen him. "And I don't wanna talk to them. I wanna talk to HIM! He's my hero, not them. Oh, I like 'em, but not one of them is my hero. He is."

I called Merle's home number from Ray's landline telephone in his little tiny office in the back of his Idle Spurs Tavern. Ray was giddy. I was less anxious than I should've been - we were both a little drunk. Caller ID was starting to make the rounds at that time, but I didn't know whether Merle had it. He picked up the phone, and I said, "Merle, it's Raymond."

"Ray, how ya doin'?" Merle asked. I didn't call him a lot in those days, so he probably thought it was important. Certainly, he was not expecting this call.

"I'm doin' fine, man," I was talking pretty fast. "Uh, hey listen, uh, I've got a really good friend down here in Las Vegas. He lets me sing at his tavern, he's a good friend of mine, and he wants to talk to you really, really bad, just for a minute."

"Ray, I am eating my DINNER!"

His reaction to this silly request was not unexpected. He was a busy guy, and here I am, half-drunk, calling him while he's having dinner just so my friend can say hello. I said, "Look, all these movie stars are here tonight: Robert DeNiro, Sharon Stone, and Joe Pesci. They're filming a new movie, right here, where I'm standing. But this guy is not a big fan of theirs. You're his hero. Can you give me just sixty seconds, please?"

"Alright, put him on," Merle said. Clearly, he was not thrilled, but he obliged.

Ray Wills' face lit up like a little kid, "Hi, Merle."

I could hear Merle faintly, "Hey, Ray. Whattaya doing?"

"Oh Merle, I'm a big fan of yours; all these movie stars are here: Robert DeNiro, Sharon Stone, and Joe Pesci. They're filmin' a new movie here, but you're my all-time favorite celebrity. You're my favorite singer, and you're my all-time favorite hero, and it's just so great to be able to talk to you on the telephone."

I couldn't make out what Merle said after that, but it made Ray laugh. Merle gave Ray about a minute of just back and forth chatter, and then Ray handed me the phone.

I said, "Bye, Merle."

Merle said, "Bye, Raymond." And that was it.

I was way up on the list of heroes now for Ray Wills, my friend, and boss at the Idle Spurs. As far as I knew, Ray Wills was always a decent, caring person. He gave me a job for many years. I got to play my little guitar in the tavern every Thursday through Sunday, and I enjoyed it very much. He was kind to me, and I knew he was always respectful, so I had taken a chance. My friend Merle Haggard, Ray's hero, was sympathetic enough to get on the phone with him and give him a moment that he'd never forget.

Ray Wills had a bad heart, and it finally failed him on February 17, 1995, just two or three years after his conversation with Merle. I sang at Ray's funeral. I chose "Swinging Doors," naturally. I told Merle about it, and soon after, I brought Ray Wills' daughters to his show at the Hard Rock in Las Vegas. Before the show, I introduced them to Merle and told him who they were. He was pleasant, attentive, and appreciative. Before we headed out to join the crowd, he gave them some guitar picks from his pocket. Hell, that's like giving somebody an Academy Award if you're a country music fan!

Those two ladies so enjoyed seeing Merle live and meeting him that night. Later, as Merle sang "Swinging Doors," he took his hat off (during the song!) to pay his respect to their father, Ray Wills, to whom Merle had only ever spoken once in his life. This indicates a man with a real solid heart who knew the story, who knew that those ladies were there. He didn't forget, and then he took off his hat because he remembered that it had been sung at Ray's funeral, which may have been a first. When the song was over, he put his hat back on and continued with the rest of the show. This is the kind of man Merle was. He was so kind and sincere.

On February 17, 1996, I dreamed I was in a room with Paul McCartney. I knew it was a dream because, although I was confused, I was calm. (Even then, I knew I could never be calm around Paul McCartney!) Paul was sitting at a piano, and I was standing there wondering why I was in this dream and this room with Paul McCartney. Suddenly, the phone rang, and I answered it.

"Raymond?" the voice said in a tone and Scouse accent that I've loved for nearly my entire life. It was the unmistakable speaking voice of John Lennon.

"Yes?" I was still confused but now elated.

"It's John. I'm thinkin' about puttin' a new band together."

"Okay. What?" I was a bit confused.

"Yeah," John paused, "You're an affable character." Affable character? I didn't even know what 'affable' meant, but I thought it must be something positive by the way he said it. I remember talking to him very briefly, and then I woke up. I immediately realized that it was him. I'd heard his voice, his speaking voice, since I was a little kid.

"What in the world was THAT?" I thought for a minute. "WHAT in the world was that?" I questioned aloud to myself.

I recalled that John Lennon had been gone from this world since December 8, 1980, and then I thought about my friend, Ray Wills. I had kept the program from Ray's funeral on my refrigerator. I couldn't go back to sleep, so I went downstairs to see if it was the anniversary of Ray's death. Well, it was, to the date! I remember standing in the kitchen, staring at that funeral program in the middle of the night. It'd been up there for a year because I didn't want to forget him.

It was at that moment, as I stood alone in my kitchen, with my wife and two children sleeping quietly, that I thought ole Ray Wills called in a favor. I believe Ray looked up John Lennon, on the other side, and said, "Could you, um, could you call a friend of mine? He called Merle Haggard for me one day, and it was the thrill of my life."

"Would you mind calling' him in a dream and gettin' him on the phone and sayin' Hello?" I imagined Ray saying.

I think that's what happened. I told the story to Merle Haggard when we were in Bakersfield, driving around, looking for his friend's apartment. Merle really liked that story, and I think he believed it was true. At the urging of Ray Wills, who owned the fabulous Idle Spurs Tavern in Las Vegas, Nevada, John Lennon called me from the other side.

Dean Holloway, Merle's Best Friend

CHAPTER 40

Dean Holloway and Merle *Photo courtesy of Scott Holloway*

THE YEAR WAS 2001. MERLE and I drove into Redding nearly every workday for lunch from his ranch in Palo Cedro. He loved taking the twenty-minute drive into town. Merle had a 2001 Ford Expedition then and enjoyed driving, so the lunch trip became a sort of ritual. We usually met his lawyer friend, who was very bright and witty, yet humble. Merle enjoyed his company, and they visited a few of their favorite restaurants often. Merle loved fish and usually ordered some every day. His favorites were catfish, bass, trout, and salmon. (Merle had stopped eating beef years before.)

The Ralph Stanley song "O Death" was from the hit movie *Oh Brother Where Art Thou*. The movie had a down-home, hard-core, country music soundtrack that won a Grammy. Ralph Stanley won a Grammy for his vocals on "O Death," sung a cappella, a purely vocal performance - no instrumentation (Andy Griffith's deputy Barney Fife thought differently). One day Merle and I took my Mercury Cougar to town because his Ford was low on gas. While I was driving, Merle started rifling through my CDs and found the soundtrack for *Oh Brother Where Art Thou*. He had never heard it and was surprised to learn it was awarded country music's highest honor. So we popped it into the CD player so he could have a listen. After a few songs, "O Death" began playing. Merle was stunned. He listened intently to every word. The song had him on the verge of tears, and it completely blew his mind.

We listened to the entire album on the way to lunch and back to his ranch. Merle loved every song! I had no choice but to gift him the CD. If not, he would have just taken it! You might wonder why I would say that, but there is a bit of truth to it. Let me explain. Dean Holloway was Merle's best friend starting in sixth grade at Standard Elementary in Oildale, California. Two narratives have surfaced about how Merle and Dean met. Both agree they met in the sixth grade, they got in a fight, and most importantly, they became best friends for life.

Dean's son, Scott Holloway, told this first story. According to Scott, Merle and his dad first met at Standard School in Oildale, when his dad's older brother, Franklin, got into a fight. Franklin and Dean had arrived from Arkansas, wearing Khaki pants. The Oildale boys, who wore blue jeans, didn't like the Arkansas boys or their Khaki pants. This led to Franklin fighting with some older boys. Then Merle asked Dean if he wanted to wrestle or box, and they agreed to wrestle.

They wrestled each other, and from that day forward, they were best friends.

Merle told a different account of how they met. He said they were in the River Theater's lobby when some older boys wanted Merle and Dean to fight each other, probably for their own amusement or maybe to gauge how tough the younger kids were. Per request, they began fighting. After the fight was over, they became best friends for life.

Through years of close friendship, Merle began to view Dean as a brother. No one could have predicted that eventually, Dean would become Merle's first bus driver. He drove Merle and his band all over America for millions of miles and to thousands of shows. He co-wrote "Big City" and a few other Merle Haggard notables. Merle could never replace a friend like Dean. After his passing on February 24, 2009, with a heavy heart, Merle delivered a beautiful eulogy for his friend who had become his brother, Dean Holloway.

Dean's widow, Sue, remained in their home located in a little town just east of Sacramento, California. That little town happened to be Folsom, the place Johnny Cash made famous with his song about the nearby state prison, "Folsom Prison Blues." When Merle played two sold-out shows at a community college there, Sue came to visit one afternoon. She brought with her a small box of some of Dean's belongings. She told me there were two items she wanted me to have, then handed me a beautiful silver and turquoise ring and a silver pocket watch. I was thrilled! Dean had been my hero!

I went to the back of the bus where Merle was sitting and showed him my treasures. He said, "That's my watch!" and took it from me. I was shocked but ultimately not surprised. Merle explained how he had given the watch to Dean. Therefore, under the rules of the Oildale brotherhood, the beautiful watch rightfully belonged to him. I didn't say a word, took my ring and went to the front of the bus. Sue gave Merle everything else in the box, including the watch, as it turned out. That's why it's best to simply give someone whatever it is that brings them so much enjoyment. I bought another CD of the soundtrack, *Oh Brother Where Art Thou*. Merle kept his gift and listened to it often. The album that is, although I'm sure he heard the pocket watch too.

Shared Dreams

CHAPTER 41

Cousins Louis and Fuzzy – promo photo, Cousin Herb's Tradin' Post show

MERLE ONLY SHARED TWO OF his dreams with me, which isn't many considering I knew him for fifty-two years. But I remember the dreams just as he told them. The first dream he shared was in 1986, the year his great friend Lewis Talley died. Lewis was a great singer, guitarist, record producer, and comedian. He was one of the biggest stars to emerge from Bakersfield in the 1950s. Lewis had his own band, "The Tallywhackers." They whacked their way through the honky-tonks of the day and left the patrons slashed.

Lewis, along with his cousin, Fuzzy Owen, discovered Merle Haggard and signed him to their small record label, Tally records.

Lewis became a mainstay throughout Merle's career, acting as a record producer, a press agent, a musician, and many other facets of Merle's life.

I spoke with Merle maybe a month or so after Lewis died. Merle told me he was having a tough time dealing with the loss of his friend, the affable Lewis (Louie) Talley. Finally, one-night, Louie came to Merle in a dream. Merle described it as such: He appeared to me in a dream looking much younger, in his thirties maybe (Louie died at age fifty-eight). He was wearing a beautiful bright yellow shirt, as bright as the sun. The sky behind him was a brilliant blue. Louie spoke to me, saying, "Merle, don't worry about me; I'm fine and happy where I am. Look! (Louie rolls up his pant leg) My scars are gone!" (He'd had bypass surgery.) Merle said he asked Louie, "Can you smoke up there?" Louis replied, "If you want to." Merle said the dream allowed him to see that his friend was just fine, which gave him great peace of mind.

In the year 2001, I was working in Merle's living room/office. One morning, immediately after I arrived, he described for me his moving and thought-provoking dream. Merle said, "I don't dream much, but I had this dream last night. I dreamed I died. I was lying on a raised concrete platform in the middle of a room with high ceilings, no windows, and no pictures on the wall. I opened my eyes, and a nurse lookin' lady was standing over me. She asked if I knew where I was. I told her, 'I believe I've died.' She said, 'That's right.' She told me my dad was waiting for me at the door, but first, we must get you prepared." (Merle's father died when Merle was nine.) When I got up to meet my dad, he said, "Hurry up, son, we're late!" I said, "Late for what, Dad?" "The concert!" his dad replied. "What concert?" Merle asked in his dream. His dad said, "Jimmie Rodgers, Lefty Frizzel, and YOU!" That's when Merle woke up. End of dream!

Merle was kind enough to share such personal dreams with me. I shared a couple with him and now will share one with you. My younger brother, Danny Joe, died of a heart attack at the tender age of forty-five. His wife and three kids asked me to speak at his funeral service. I had nothing prepared, but I did ask if we could play some of the great music we grew up with. They obliged, and we played some of his favorites: The Beach Boys, Beatles, and Jim Croce, to name a few. Danny and I played each other in all the games: baseball, football, and basketball. He matured into a kind and gentle man until you got him angry, and like most older brothers, that was my assignment.

I was in Las Vegas when I got the news we lost Danny. Incredibly heartbroken, I immediately left for Bakersfield, where Danny had lived for all but the first seven years of his life. I walked the streets of Bakersfield alone, where we had roamed together, picking fruit, rummaging for pop

bottles (redemption price was two cents a bottle then), and where we had visited the local swimming pool every day in the brutally hot Bakersfield summers (admission was only ten cents in those days). We shared a great time together as kids and brothers.

Born September 22, 1952, Danny Joe passed away on July 1, 1998. I stayed with him during the entire visitation period until his service

Danny and Raymond McDonald

on July 7th. He was not alone; a continuous stream of friends and family came to pay their respects every day. Story after story conveyed the remarkable love shown to his fellow human beings through his involvement in coaching, playing sports, and his high profile in the sports card community. He loved those Los Angeles Dodgers and Los Angeles Rams. He would occasionally lease a bus to take Bakersfield's Dodger fans to their home games.

The morning of his service, I had the dream. It came to me just past midnight. I was playing the guitar for Jim Croce while he and his band performed a concert for a huge crowd. I knew it was a dream, and I wondered why I was there since I didn't know how to play any of his songs. He played portions of a few of his hits, then finally played a song all the way through: "I'll Have to Say I Love You in a Song." After the band finished, Jim Croce introduced me to the crowd as a guest in his band. The crowd cheered - I felt embarrassed and astonished, still aware I was not supposed to be there. This was a dream, and I knew it. I was startled awake, but not by a nightmare - this was a vision and a message!

Danny Joe NEVER told me he loved me. Our family was like that - we knew it, we just didn't say it. The lyrics of "I'll Have to Say I Love You in a Song" explain it all. It's the most beautiful song, and I am sure Danny Joe was sending a message to me. Knowing this helped relieve my pain and immense grief. I was still in a state of shock but comforted knowing he was looking out for me from his new home.

Danny and I used to listen to Jim Croce often - he was among our favorites. Jim Croce died in a plane crash on September 20, 1973, just two days before my brother Danny's 21st birthday. Jim Croce was only thirty years old when he died. I believe they reside in heaven, where Danny has most likely thanked Jim repeatedly for his music and for letting his brother, Raymond, sit in with his band, even if it was just once… in a dream.

Movie Stars and Movie Songs

CHAPTER 42

Sinking of the Titanic, Illustration by German artist Willy Stower 1864-1931 *Stock photo*

I WENT TO SEE THE movie *Titanic* five times! I had never been to any movie more than once at any theatre. If I didn't see a film when it first came out, I'd rent it later and sometimes rent movies to watch again at home – especially great ones like Jaws, Rudy, or The Godfather. But I had never returned to a theater to watch the same movie five times. It's hard to believe this happened, but Titanic was so thrilling and unique, I couldn't help myself. The acting, the love story, and the special effects were all brilliant and perfect! The first time I saw it, I immediately shared my enthusiasm with Merle by calling him in Palo Cedro from

Las Vegas. I wasn't working for him then but phoned him nearly every day just to visit. "Man, this is the greatest movie I've ever seen! You really might want to go see it - you'll like this one!" I told him, hoping he'd take my advice. To my recollection, that's the only time I ever made a movie suggestion to Merle.

Going to the movies did not particularly excite Merle for several reasons: movies take a lot of time, they require staying seated for a couple of hours, and being famous made it difficult to venture into public. But he had to go! For the full experience, I strongly recommended a large-screen theater. So after the fifth time I had seen Titanic, he finally decided it might be worth the effort. It surprised me a little that harping on it finally paid off, and he risk a matinee. If anybody had noticed or recognized him while in that small-town theater, he never mentioned it.

I asked him, "What'd ya think?"

He said, "Well, I fell in love with those two."

That's all he said after watching this incredible film that took home eleven Academy Awards! *Titanic* was by far the most phenomenal movie I'd ever seen (and I've viewed many)! After hearing his comment, it struck me how differently Merle thinks than most people. He was such a sap for love, and what a gripping tale of love that movie told. It doesn't matter that the romance was fictional; we know the fate of the 'invincible' ship was not, and that it could have been the stage for many poignant stories of love and loss, stories no one will know. I will never forget Merle's response nor how he was able to distill all his thoughts and emotions about the film into one concise statement: "I fell in love with those two!"

Merle was a big fan of the movies despite his reasons for not wanting to go. Sometimes he'd talk about the films he had seen as a kid, or the few movies he did see in theaters over the years. Based on comments he made, my opinion is that his favorite was *A River Runs Through It.* He mentioned favorite actors such as Steve McQueen, John Wayne, Jimmy Stewart, Gene Autry, Dean Martin, Humphrey Bogart and Lauren Bacall, and many more. He thought the movie *Bonnie and Clyde* was fantastic and became friends with Faye Dunaway after its release. He actually wrote a song about the film using the same title, "Bonnie and Clyde," which ended up on the flip side of "Today I Started Loving You Again." So it can be said movies did have a little influence on his music.

Angelina Jolie and Merle were both scheduled to be on the PBS talk show, *Tavis Smiley*, for separate tapings. We were in Merle's dressing room, which was actually an outdoor cottage. I had just mentioned that Angelina's name was on the cottage door next to Merle's when we were surprised by a knock. It was one of Angelina's associates asking if Angelina could come to meet Merle. Merle said, "Of course!" Only a few moments passed when the second knock came. As we opened the door, Angelina peered around the door's edge to see if Merle was really in the room. I had never seen anyone so beautiful with her green eyes, perfect skin, and the prettiest smile - one that brightened the room. This was one of those moments I stopped to realize how fortunate I was!

Angelina's hair was long, and as she leaned to peer into the room, it nearly touched the sidewalk. The scene reminded me of a Norman Rockwell Christmas painting, where a little girl comes down the stairs peeking to see if Santa is there because if he is, he must be real. The painting comes to life when the child views Santa, and her eyes light up just as Angelina's did when she saw Merle – he's there, he must be real!

She stood up tall and rushed in to give Merle a big, warm hug. He was a little startled by her approach but happy to see her. Angelina immediately began telling him how much his music meant to her and how she had been a fan since childhood. She had brought along her photographer and asked Merle politely if she could have her photo taken with him and her friend. Of course, he obliged.

Angelina had walked over, and after a few seconds realized she was standing in front of me. She turned around, introduced herself, and shook my hand. I told her I was Merle's long-time friend, lead bus driver, and a big fan of her work. She said, "Thank you," and turned back around to face the others. As she was turning, I mentioned that I also admired her humanitarian efforts. She turned around again and said, exuberantly, "Thank you!"

Merle mentioned that he'd met Jack Nicholson once at the Pantages Theatre in Hollywood. Jack visited him on his bus, and Merle said the first thing they did was laugh at each other. Merle asked Jack to cast him in a movie, but Jack's response was, "No way! You're too damn pretty!"

Ernest Borgnine came to see Merle once in Las Vegas. After about an hour into his show, Merle stopped and said, "This has been a real hard show for me because one of the greatest actors in Hollywood is sitting right here in the front row. It's kind of tough to sing with him sitting here. This man is one of my heroes, Ernest Borgnine." The large crowd gave Mr. Borgnine a huge ovation. Merle had the spotlight turned on Ernest; he smiled that famous smile and waved at the audience.

Once, Merle shared his thoughts about movie stars, actors, and all the people involved in making films. He said they work harder than any other group in the entertainment business because of their long eighteen-hour workdays, after which they grab a little sleep before starting all over again the next day. They'd do that for weeks, sometimes months, with few breaks, if any. Merle knew this because he had been involved in several movies and television productions himself, so he fully realized the time and commitment it took. Merle was good at acting and could have had a second career as a full-fledged movie star if he'd dedicated himself to the craft. But knowing everything he knew about the business, he decided to focus on being a country music star instead of a guy burning himself out on two careers.

However, there were a few, like Kris Kristofferson and Dwight Yoakam, who did manage dual careers and were good at both. In fact, Merle believed they were the best out of all the country singers who had dabbled in acting. A few acted sparingly, such as Johnny Cash, Reba McEntire, Willie Nelson, Dolly Parton, Tim McGraw, and several others.

Merle had several stories about entertaining movie stars on his bus who had attended his shows in Hollywood. They would tell him, "The difference between a live performance and the movies is 180 degrees. You can always do another take in movies if you forget your lines or if you are not happy with your performance. But in your business, you don't get another take! It's live! It's right now! You perform in front of thousands of people who paid a lot of money to see you, and you only get one shot!" That's why movie stars have such an admiration for live performers.

Merle was always thrilled to contribute his music to a movie. On many occasions, a song from his extensive library would be added to a soundtrack, and a few times, he composed music for a movie. Merle has credits on over one hundred movie soundtracks. He appeared in hundreds of television performances, starting in the 1960s through 2019 when Ken Burns' documentary, *Country Music*, was released. Below I've listed some of Merle's music that found its way onto the movie soundtracks and then a few of his movie and television appearances that were not limited to music performances.

MUSIC

"Sing Me Back Home" – played in one episode of the Showtime series *Billions*

"Misery and Gin" and **"Bar Room Buddies"** - two songs recorded for the Clint Eastwood movie, *Bronco Billy* - the latter he sang as a duet with Clint Eastwood

"Okie from Muskogee" - this well-known song appeared in *Platoon*

"Wag the Dog" - Merle wrote and sang this song for the engaging movie *Wag the Dog*

"The Fightin' Side of Me" - you can hear this Haggard classic in the background during a scene in *Jack Reacher*, a 2012 Tom Cruise movie

"Big City" - this Merle and Dean Holloway tune rolls throughout the opening scene in *Fargo*

"The Man in the Mask" - Merle sings this title song in *The Legend of the Lone Ranger*

"Turn Me Around" - Merle sang this in the John Wayne classic, *Chisum*

"Rainbow Stew" - appears in *Six Pack*, a Kenny Rogers film.

"Mama Tried" - is included on the soundtrack of *Fear the Walking Dead* and also was sung in *Killers Three*

"I Guess He'd Rather Be in Colorado" - While playing the role of Cisco, Merle sang this song in the television film *Centennial*

"I'm Always on a Mountain When I Fall" - This played in the 2005 movie *Brokeback Mountain*

MOVIES & TELEVISION

Bronco Billy - Merle played himself in this Clint Eastwood movie

Centennial - For this television film, Merle played the role of Cisco

Killers Three - Merle played Charlie in this 1968 film

Huckleberry Finn - In the 1975 television film adaptation of Mark Twain's famous novel, Merle played the role of Duke

The Waltons - Merle played Red Turner in this well-known television series

Billy Mize & the Bakersfield Sound - a documentary interview and performance.

Country Music - Merle played a prominent role in this 2019 Ken Burns' documentary, both in interviews and performance

On December 2, 2014, roughly a year and a half before his passing, Merle accepted the first of its kind CMT Artist of a Lifetime Award at the ceremony in Nashville. Many testimonials praised Merle and his contributions over time, but I think the best was from the presenter and Merle's friend, Billy Bob Thorton, who said Merle Haggard "will be atop the *CMT All-Time Top 40*, a countdown of the most influential musicians of all time, among all genres, voted on by country artists." Then he told the audience that in addition to being among the greatest songwriters, Merle is a true storyteller alongside greats like John Steinbeck and Tennessee Williams. The art of storytelling, which has been somewhat lost, is making a comeback, "and Merle Haggard personifies the storyteller," Thorton said.

Merle humbly accepted the award with a very brief but thankful speech. As a final thought, he added, "Good music lives forever!"

Kennedy Center Honors

CHAPTER 43

Paul McCartney and Merle at the Kennedy Center Honors, Washington D.C., Dec. 10, 2010 *Photo courtesy of Jim Haggard*

MERLE HAGGARD RECEIVED NEWS OF his inclusion in the Kennedy Center Honors in June 2010, but I did not find out about it until August while visiting him in the back of his bus. He had inadvertently told someone about the award, assuming I already knew. But I didn't; this was the first I had heard of it.

I asked him, "When did you find out about the Kennedy Center Honors?"

He said, "Ray, it's a secret. I was supposed to tell no one until the official news was revealed in September." He asked me to keep it a secret.

"That's no problem, sir," I said. "Do you know who the other honorees are?"

He answered, "Yes, Paul McCartney and Oprah Winfrey." For me, this was startling news, and Merle knew why. When I lived in his home in 1965-66 with my friends, Buddy and Mike Owens, we regularly played the Beatles on his stereo. He would arrive home with the Beatles blasting, so Merle knew I was a huge Beatles fan and probably wondered if I could keep the secret.

This joyful news of Merle and his latest honor literally brought me to tears. He was somewhat surprised by my reaction and looked a little bewildered as he sat in his dining chair, looking up at me with his big blue eyes. I instinctively very lightly rested my head on his and said something like, "Merle, you really deserve this honor. You've dedicated an entire life to your craft, and you're being rewarded for it now in your golden years. For you to be honored together with Paul McCartney is staggering! Congratulations, my friend!"

Well, I had to share this incredible news with my son and daughter, who, in my euphoric state, were called immediately! My kids understood this was top-secret news and could not share it with anyone (even though I just had!). Merle probably knew I wouldn't be able to keep the secret, as elated as I was. With the Kennedy Center public announcement only days away, what could happen? I am fairly certain my son and daughter kept the secret - if not, it would only prove their excitement level was equal to mine.

A few days later, after they announced the honorees, Merle stated I would probably be attending the ceremony and then explained why. He was scheduled to fly first-class (all expenses paid) from Sacramento, California, to Washington, D.C. However, he wanted his bus nearby because that is where he feels safe and at home with his food, music, television, and his own bed. His privacy was paramount to his happiness. Merle's son, Benny, and Merle's nephew, Jim Haggard, were to assist with the long cross-country drive.

But there was another reason Merle wanted his bus in Washington, D.C. Merle had invited his longtime friend and manager, Fuzzy Owen and his wife, Phyllis, to the ceremony. However, Fuzzy wasn't able to fly due to problems from the airplane cabin pressure. He had lost his hearing years before, which left them overly sensitive to certain sounds. So Fuzzy rode with us the near 3000 miles, while Phyllis flew, compliments of Merle, so that she could enjoy the two nights of festivities with her husband.

We pulled into Washington, D.C., the day before Merle arrived at the airport. To pick him up, we rented a limousine from the hotel. He requested we drive the bus, but there were so many low bridges and overpasses between the Kennedy Center and JFK airport, it wasn't worth the risk. When I first met Merle at the airport, it looked like he had a case of pinkeye. He had no idea how he got it but did know he would soon appear on national television with pinkeye... for everyone to see. Merle didn't seem bothered – he was always lighthearted and comfortable with these kinds of situations.

One situation, however, did bother him. While going through security at the Sacramento airport, they randomly pulled him aside for questioning and a search. Merle complied even though he was irritated and angry with the security person who patted him down. Merle thought of himself as an elderly gentleman who had already gone through the metal detectors, but they still thought it necessary to search him. None of them knew with whom they were dealing: a legend on his way to receive one of the nation's highest honors for entertainers! The President of the United States, Barack Obama, would be placing a medal around this man's neck to honor his contributions to the arts of the United States. Merle never mentioned whether he said anything to the security guard about where he was going and why. Knowing Merle, I'm guessing he didn't - but he was furious.

Merle cooled off quickly as we drove him to the gorgeous five-star hotel, but he wasn't interested in going in. Instead, he boarded his bus and immediately summoned Willie Nelson, Kris Kristofferson, and Jamie Johnson to join him for a visit and maybe pass around a peace pipe. It was supposed to be a surprise that Willie, Kris, and Jamie were scheduled to play music in his honor at the Sunday night concert. Merle said, "I don't care about surprises. I know they're here, and I want them to come and have a party with me on my bus." And that's what they did! Merle needed privacy with his friends, so I never ventured onto the bus during our time there. But it's a good thing Jim Haggard did because he took some great photos of Merle, Willie, Kris, and Jamie.

A large contingent of national political leaders, entertainers, and artists from all spectrums attend the Kennedy Center Honors. Merle was asked to bring his wife, Theresa, and four other people to the occasion. He had initially invited his ninety-year-old sister, Lillian Haggard Rae, to attend. But she could not make the long journey because of her age and asked Merle to invite her only nephew, Jim Haggard, instead. Merle obliged, and that's why Jim was there and took the wonderful photos he did. They had informed Merle about the White House ceremony Saturday evening, hosted by the President and First Lady, Michelle and Barack Obama. The President would read a brief description of each honoree before presenting their medal. (Two additional honorees not mentioned earlier were the Broadway writer Jerry Herman and dancer Bill T. Jones.) A gala dinner nearby would immediately follow the medal presentations.

I stayed at the hotel while Merle and his party were having the night of their lives. The next day I asked Merle my only pertinent question: Did he talk with Paul McCartney? Yes, he did! At one point, they had a moment alone, and Merle asked Paul, "Would you like to step out on the White House lawn and burn one down?"

Paul McCartney took one giant step backward as his eyes widened, and he asked Merle, "Do you still do that, man?"

Merle answered, "Yes, sir! And I mean it!"

Merle left it at that, and I did not pry for an answer. Did they? Or did they not? I certainly wouldn't put it past Merle to enjoy a delightful smoke on the White House lawn, celebrating the occasion with none other than Sir Paul McCartney, a member of the greatest rock 'n' roll band of all time, The Beatles.

I often wondered what a security guard might have done had he discovered these two gentlemen having a 'smoke' on the White House lawn? Maybe they would have joined in – I know that's what I would have done! And if the President found out, he may have joined as well - he was, after all, a very cool President! When asked if he'd ever smoked marijuana, he said, "Yes. And yes, I inhaled. Isn't that the point?"

Merle admired anyone who told the truth; his dad hated liars, and so did Merle. I asked Merle if he'd had the opportunity to talk with President Obama at any time during the evening. "Yes," Merle said, and that he'd told the president they had something in common - each wife was taller than her husband. President Obama explained why this was only partially true: his wife was wearing high heels, and without them, he was two inches taller than Michelle. I'm sure Merle just laughed.

A formal dinner hosted in a nearby ballroom by the former First Lady, Hillary Clinton, followed the White House awards ceremony. Hillary spoke eloquently of the new honorees and the former members of this exclusive club, invited to the Honors every year to join the celebration donning their medallions!

While enjoying the dinner with his family and guests, Merle described how suddenly two large doors opened into the ballroom, and a fellow by the name of President Bill Clinton grandly entered. Everyone stopped eating as their eyes locked on Clinton while Secret

Service agents and friends escorted him into the room. A buzz followed as one might expect, especially in Washington, D.C.

Merle said Bill was smiling, waving, and saying hello to many of the guests as he bee-lined for Merle's table. Once there, he grabbed Merle's hand, shook it, and said to him, "Congratulations, Merle! I've been a fan of yours all my life." They had never met, and Merle was incredibly pleased and honored that Bill Clinton thought enough of him to stop by his table first *and* take time to chat. I am sure Merle introduced the former president to his guests and everyone else at his table.

As Merle told it, Julia Roberts surprised him by walking up to his table from behind. She placed her arms around his neck, gave him a big hug and kiss on the cheek, then told Merle she was a huge fan! Merle was a big follower of Julia Roberts, too. He liked her movies, especially *Erin Brockovich*. Julia received a Best Actress Oscar for her portrayal of Erin Brockovich in the film based on Erin's true story.

Before leaving for work one morning, I was watching the *Today* show on NBC, listening to an interview with an actress recently nominated for the Best Actress award. When the actress inquired about her competition, the interviewer began reading a list of the nominees. The second they announced Julia Roberts' name, the actress stopped the interviewer saying, "Contest over!" When I arrived at work and told Merle about the interview, he laughed so hard because he knew that the contest was indeed over, just as the nominee had known. If you've ever watched *Erin Brockovich*, you'll understand better why the contest was over before it even began.

The afternoon before the big dinner, Julia Roberts was in the lobby of the five-star hotel. Not wanting to bother her, I approached someone from her entourage as they entered the dining room. Tapping this gentleman's shoulder, I then explained who I was and how I knew beyond doubt Merle was a big fan of Julia Roberts. He promised to deliver the message when I asked if he could. If Julia knew Merle was a fan, I hoped it might inspire her to greet him warmly… as she did! The many famous people there were no doubt enthralled by their own idols and heroes in the crowd. Celebrities can be just as taken aback as non-celebrities when it comes to approaching their favorite stars.

A good example is when the fantastic Brad Paisley and his wife were in the lobby on their way to the Saturday night festivities. She, a movie star, and Brad, a country music superstar, looked stunning, dressed as expected for that sort of evening. They literally shined. I approached them in the lobby and (not known for being shy) offered my hand to Brad while introducing myself as Merle Haggard's assistant, bus driver, and longtime friend. They were kind and gracious when I told them I was a fan and only wanted to say hello. Then I inquired if they'd had an opportunity to greet Merle at any time during the weekend. Brad replied they had not. They were very aware of how much attention Merle gets and concerned about bothering him. I assured them Merle was a very humble man and one who would appreciate their greeting. With wide eyes, Brad said, "Man, I'm glad you let me know. I'll do it!" Brad was in the band when they honored Merle that Sunday night, and I don't know if he ever approached him. There is such profound regard for someone of Merle's stature; often, others feel the highest form of respect is allowing that person their privacy.

On Sunday afternoon, anyone with a ticket to the Kennedy Center Honors concert could use their ticket for the five-star hotel buffet. You know I would never miss that part of the event. Everyone at the noon buffet attended it dressed for the evening show, and since an evening jacket and tie were expected, I complied. Standing in the buffet line, I began to notice the crowd consisted of people I'd seen for years on television and in movies: Alec Baldwin, Smokey Robinson, Gwen

Stephani, Diana Ross, and many others. When I sat down to enjoy my buffet lunch, a fellow named John Kerry strolled by and said hello. (I liked that guy - he almost became President of the United States.) Once seated at my table, I began looking around to see who might be nearby. Sidney Poitier was dining at the adjacent table! Merle's publicity agent advised me NOT to take any photos of celebrities while at the function. Regardless, I had brought along my camera to sneak a picture if the possibility arose. I did snap one of Sidney Poitier laughing while enjoying his meal. I also grabbed a shot of Chris Rock entertaining Oprah Winfrey. Then I decided to do as advised and put the camera away.

As I was leaving the luncheon, a sudden commotion at the dining room entrance grabbed my attention. Sir Paul McCartney had arrived! I'm sure the look on my face was one of total wonder! I casually watched Sir Paul as fans engulfed him when he entered the buffet. His new girlfriend accompanied him, a beautiful woman he eventually married. A stout bodyguard helped move people gently out of the way so Paul could attend to his lunch. I pulled my camera out quickly, and the first photo I got was of a big hand in front of my camera. The bodyguard was none too pleased with me attempting to get a shot of my all-time hero. He said sternly, "No pictures!" But Paul was the one person in the world I wanted to meet!

The Beatles' music was so crucial to my happiness throughout my life - as I have mentioned in multiple chapters - that no matter how big the bodyguard, I would not be denied this opportunity. I quickly moved around the intimidating fellow to try approaching Paul from the side. The bodyguard realized I was no threat and eased up. Paul made a comical gesture when I offered my hand and tried to speak. He smiled and looking him directly in the eye, ready to deliver my heartfelt message, no words came forth! Suddenly it seemed everyone had vanished except Paul McCartney and me. No one else in the universe existed at that moment. Finally, after an awkward silence, I blurted out, "Longtime fan!" and dropping Paul's hand, turned to make a mad dash for Merle's hotel room, hoping he'd be there for my story. Merle was sitting in his room, eating lunch. My face communicated my excitement with a 'kid on Christmas morning' look! "Merle, I just met the one person in the world I wanted to meet. I just met Paul McCartney!" I exclaimed with much vigor as I told Merle how I'd been so excited I couldn't speak!

Merle responded, "Raymond, I'd be the same way if I ever met Chuck Berry!" His comment puzzled me.

"Chuck Berry?" I asked Merle, "Chuck Berry?" Chuck Berry is not a country music star. Chuck Berry invented rock 'n' roll, not country music (I didn't say this, but I was thinking it).

Merle said, "Chuck Berry is one of my idols. I've never met him, but I'm sure I wouldn't be able to speak if I ever did." Merle went on to explain that Chuck Berry had a profound effect on his music. I had known Merle for over fifty years, and only once had he ever mentioned Chuck Berry. While we talked about the lyrics to "Memphis," Merle explained that if it wasn't for Chuck Berry's music, he couldn't possibly have written, "Workin' Man Blues." "Couldn't I see how Chuck Berry inspired this song?" he asked incredulously.

I answered, "Not till now! Now I get it." I told Merle, "Thank you! If it weren't for you, I wouldn't have had an opportunity to meet Paul McCartney." I was genuinely sincere, and he knew it. Merle had endured years of the Beatles due to my love for their music. He understood because, as a teenager, he had similar feelings for his musical idols such as Jimmy Rodgers, Lefty Frizzell, Bob Wills, Tommy Duncan, Emmett Miller, Roy Nichols, Bing Crosby, Rose Maddox, and a host of others. And these feelings had lasted well into his golden years.

That evening, we took a limousine to the Kennedy Center for the concert (being filmed by CBS). The red carpet had been laid for the special guests. It was incredible to see so many artists, movie stars, and national political figures converging for this one event. I believe the word gala evolved to describe a night like this. The closest I had ever come to attending a gala was my high school prom!

The concert tribute lasted about five hours. All five honorees were introduced by other celebrities with a brief summary of their accomplishments, followed by a video production of their careers. After each introduction, the honoree received a rousing standing ovation, which lasted three to five minutes. It was remarkable the love and admiration these honorees inspired.

Vince Gill, who narrated a thirteen-minute clip of Merle Haggard's career, introduced him to the audience. Kris Kristofferson and Miranda Lambert performed his classic "Silver Wings." Brad Paisley and Vince Gill sang "Workin' Man Blues." Sheryl Crow and Willie Nelson beautifully delivered "Today I Started Loving You Again." Then with help from Jamey Johnson, the audience joined in singing "Ramblin' Fever." This incredible salute moved me to tears, not only because of the great musicians involved but from all the 'regular folk' mixed in with the celebrities - it was pure magic.

But that was just the beginning. Julia Roberts introduced Oprah Winfrey with a captivating salute. Wonderful tributes followed, honoring the multi-talented dancer, choreographer, director, and author, Bill T. Jones, and then Jerry Herman, the legendary Broadway composer and lyricist. Alec Baldwin introduced the last honoree, Paul McCartney. Surreal is the only way to describe watching my longtime friend, Merle Haggard, and my idol, Paul McCartney, so highly honored in person and live. When Paul's finale began, I stared at him standing next to the United States president - they were no more than one-hundred feet away. I couldn't have enjoyed the evening more and never imagined ever attending such an event. I deeply appreciated how Merle had made it all possible. What meaningful and lasting memories I have of this stellar concert tribute.

The last song of the evening was "Hey Jude." Everyone, including Merle and the audience, joined in singing, "Na na na nanana na, hey Jude." A line in the famous Beatles' song "Let It Be" mentions Paul's mother, who died when he was a teenager. Earlier in the tribute, I watched Paul as they sang "Let It Be." He placed his hands together in prayer mode and looked up towards the ceiling in remembrance of his mother, Mary.

The Grammys and Hollywood

CHAPTER 44

Photo illustration - R.J. Shearin

A FEW YEARS AGO, I drove Merle and his entourage - including their little dogs - from Northern California to the 56th Grammy Awards, held in the Staples Center in downtown Los Angeles. Merle and Willie Nelson, Kris Kristofferson, and Blake Shelton were scheduled to perform during the awards. We arrived a few days early for rehearsals and a special recording session, arranged by Jack White of White Stripes fame, for the documentary, The American Epic Sessions.

Upon arrival, Merle said, "Hey, look, I know you want to go to the Grammys, but you need to stay on the bus and rest up, and we need you to stay away from all the celebrities." Merle was particularly worried that folks in his camp might ask for autographs and photographs. We all understood, and we all agreed.

With these instructions, we began our several days amidst the famous. Fortunately, we were allowed inside the Staples Center to enjoy the music during the Grammy Awards rehearsal. Soon after, we headed to the Vox Recording Studios in Hollywood, located on Melrose Avenue across from the Paramount Pictures gate. The studio is said to be one of the oldest independent recording studios, operating continuously since the early 1930s. Countless musicians got their start using demos recorded there. As I understand, Jimmie Rodgers, father of country music, and Louis Armstrong, the jazz great, recorded together at Vox back in the '30s.

The multi-talented Jack White was an executive producer (along with T Bone Burnett) for The American Epic Sessions. This documentary film showcased twenty-three contemporary artists who represented music from diverse ethnicities and cultures. The recordings would be live, just as they were in the 1920s, and use the same equipment restored from that era. No musician had been recorded using this method in eighty years, and Merle and Willie were among those invited to participate. Together they sang "The Only Man Wilder Than Me," written by Merle just for the film. Merle was fascinated with the vintage set-up and pleased to record on possibly the very same equipment used by Jimmie Rodgers, his hero.

The story of how the original Western Electric recording system was restored and ended up being used to record the music in the film is fascinating and well worth the read (Wikipedia: The American Epic Sessions). For over ten years, an engineer scavenged parts from around the world. He was still missing a crucial piece (the Scully lathe) when he met the film producers who tracked it down after researching photos, which led to the inventor's family home where they found the old lathe in the basement!

I learned a lot about this special vintage equipment during the brief tour given to Merle, explaining the recording process and answering any questions he might have. We were warned not to touch anything because of the fragile and largely irreplaceable nature of the parts! Indeed, during one of the recording sessions, Jack White had to find an upholstery shop where he could have a broken leather belt re-sewn before recording could continue.

While Merle and the others were inside making music, someone asked, "Can you take this little dog for a walk?" It was Merle's dog, Fannie Mae. I agreed, and as we began our walk, we passed Willie Nelson's bus parked nearby. Suddenly, off the bus jumped James Caan, the actor who played Sonny in the Godfather. (If you don't know who James Caan is, you should!) He appeared to be alone, and knowing Merle was busy in the studio, I thought it safe to say hello and maybe even take a photo of this talented and famous actor.

"Mr. Caan, Mr. Caan," I called to him.

He replied, "Yeah?"

"May I shake your hand?"

"Sure! Whose ferocious dog is that?" he asked as I shook his hand, trying hard to contain my excitement.

With a chuckle, I answered, "That's Merle's dog, and I'm taking her for a walk - I'm Merle's bus driver and friend."

"Oh, cool!"

"I'm a big fan of yours, man. I've been watching your movies for a long time, and I really enjoy your work!"

"Ah, thank you."

Then I asked, "May I take your picture?"

"Sure!" he replied as though he didn't mind at all.

Only one day had passed since Merle asked us not to speak with celebrities or ask for photographs. But he was an actor I admired, and I had to do it. Somewhere I've still got that photo of James Caan and me, holding Merle's little five-pound dog, Fannie Mae. Merle knew nothing about this, and if he did, he never mentioned it.

At one point during the recording session, Merle and a few others took a break outside the studio. A few minutes before, I was standing with Willie's bus driver when Willie came out and walked over to join us. "Hi, Will, how ya doing?" (Merle called him Will). I'd met Willie many times and thought certainly it would be okay to greet him. We were talking about buses when Merle saw me from about fifteen yards away and yelled, "Ray, get over here!" Per instructions, I was not supposed to be talking to Willie, but Merle understood and never brought it up.

Later on that night, we drove to a swank restaurant on Santa Monica Boulevard, where the restaurant owner had invited Merle and Willie to dinner. With no room for both buses in front of the restaurant, I parked Merle's bus down the road near a shop that sold vintage items like records, signs, movie posters, posters of musicians, and pictures of, well, entertainers like Willie Nelson.

While they were dining, I thought I'd take a look in the shop, hang out, and talk with the owner if possible. She was curious about the bus. When I told her it belonged to Merle Haggard and I was the driver, she was smitten. "Oh my God, I'm a huge fan! Do you think you could get Merle to write something in a book for my son? He will be an Eagle Scout next month, and it would be perfect if he'd write something like, 'To the Eagle Scout.' "

"Sure!" I said, then she asked what she could do for me. I told her how much I loved the Beatles, and she found a special Beatles poster – a very expensive vintage poster. "You don't have to do that, but if you

give me one that doesn't cost a lot, I'll trade you. How's that?"
She happily replied, "All right!"

Merle signed the book with the requested message, and we sent it back to her probably a week later. About a month after that, she sent me a Beatles poster. I still have it on my wall.

Earlier, not long after entering the store, the owner showed me a poster-size photograph in the window display. It was Willie Nelson and his band playing on a bandstand in what appeared to be a little club somewhere in Hollywood back in the day. Now the shop had closed for the evening, and I was standing outside looking at Willie's poster-size photo when I saw Merle and Willie walking towards me, returning to Merle's bus after their dinner. Merle, walking two steps in front of Willie, had him in stitches all the way down the street.

I said, "Willie!" then asked him, "Have you ever seen this photograph?

Merle continued walking to his bus, but Willie stopped to look at the photo and said, "Yeah, yeah, I remember that night."
I asked, "Where was it taken?"

"Oh, it was right around here somewhere. That's a nice photograph!" Displayed not far from the nightclub picture was a poster of Honeysuckle Rose, a movie Willie starred in. I asked if he remembered the poster. "Sure, I remember that!" Then I shared with him how the owner of the vintage poster store had reacted when she learned he was on Merle's bus: "Well, sweet Jesus! You tell him hello!"

His eyes twinkling, Willie gave me that big Willie Nelson smile as he left to join Merle. So I broke the rules twice in one day but don't recall getting in trouble for either. Merle probably figured he'd give me some slack because it was Willie Nelson, whom I'd met several times before.

Merle and Willie had disappeared to the back of Merle's bus to smoke the peace pipe. My job was to be available if Merle needed anything, so I remained up front, allowing them privacy... but the smoke wafting up from the back smelled mighty enticing! Judging by their laughter, Merle and Willie were having a great time talking and listening to Merle's new album. Merle Haggard and Willie Nelson were just hanging out together as the two good friends they had become over the years.

A knock on the bus door interrupted my thoughts. I wondered who it could possibly be. James Caan was standing there when I opened the door. I hadn't known that he dined earlier with Merle and Willie. In a jovial mood, he asked, "Hey, are Willie and Merle up there?"

"Yeah, they're in the back of the bus."

"Well, can you tell 'em Jimmy Caan is here?" he asked.

"Well yeah, but come on up!" I replied.

"Are you kidding? You sure it's alright?" James seemed surprised.

"Come on up. Yeah, man, don't worry about it, it's all right! Just go on back."

"Thank you," he said, smiling as he headed back to join Merle and Willie.

Mr. Caan brought a Hollywood producer with him that evening who kept me company while James was visiting Merle and Willie in the back. He asked who I was, so I told him I was Merle's driver and had known him for fifty years, including when I was fifteen and had lived in his home my sophomore year in high school.

He said, "Well, now wait a minute. You've known Merle for fifty years? Have you written a book about this?"

"Nope!" I replied.

"Well, you should because there are a lot of people out there who want to know about Merle Haggard. You know stories they don't. I wish you'd write a book!" His wish is one of the reasons I decided to write this book!

Apparently, my day hadn't truly ended because another knock soon interrupted my thoughts! This time, it was the restaurant owner - Merle and Willie's good friend and multi-millionaire who produced movies. When I opened the door, he stood with two big tequila shots (very expensive tequila), asking if Merle and Willie were inside.

"Yeah," I answered.

"Can you just take these shots of tequila to 'em and tell 'em it's from me?"

"Sure," I said as I shut the door and walked back to deliver the shots and the message. Laughing, they said, "I think he wants us to get drunk!" I don't think they drank the shots, but later they gave their friend a big bottle of tequila. From what I know, neither Merle nor Willie drank much – I never saw either one of them drunk. They preferred the peace pipe.

The hour was growing late, and the long but eventful day was nearly over. I had broken the rules twice, talking with celebrities, and a third time (the following day) by slipping backstage at the Grammys when I was supposed to be on the bus sleeping. But I had to because I knew Paul McCartney was there and besides, I had to use my backstage pass at least once, if only for a few minutes. Yes, I was lucky enough to see Paul McCartney again! He was standing at his dressing room door, surrounded by the media.

I called out, "Hi, Paul!"

He heard me! "Hi," he responded softly.

The point of this story is: Sometimes, you just have to break the rules!

February 3, 1960 - A New Life!

CHAPTER 45

Merle in his hotel room in Washington D.C., December 10, 2010 *Photo courtesy of Raymond McDonald*

FEBRUARY 3, 1960, MERLE RONALD HAGGARD was released from San Quentin Prison. Immensely proud of this day in his life, he mentioned it often, especially on the anniversary date. Around 2007, I called to congratulate him on his accomplishments, knowing how much this anniversary meant to him. He was kind and sincere in his reply, "Thank you, Raymond!" Then he asked if I would call the local country music radio station in Bakersfield to make them aware of the date and the special meaning it held for Merle.

There were two DJs on the air when I called. One answered the phone off the air, so I proceeded to tell him of my association with Mr. Merle Haggard and the reason I was calling. He said, "I don't believe you!" and hung up on me. I explained that Merle merely wanted the great people of the San Joaquin valley to know that February 3rd was an honorable day in his storied career. The boss apologized profusely for his DJ's actions when I explained how he'd hung up on me. Then he asked if Merle would call the station for an interview on the topic of his anniversary. I relayed the message to Merle, and he agreed. They taped a five-minute interview and replayed it throughout the day, each time followed by a Merle Haggard song.

Merle spoke of the actual day of his release from San Quentin. With a few dollars in his pocket, he had said goodbye to his friends as he approached the main gates, filled with anxiety. The guards at the gates and in the tower were waving and shouting goodbye, but suddenly he stopped. The guards said, "You're free! You can go now!" Merle had stopped his waltz to freedom because he wanted to hear the song playing on the guard shack's radio. He asked permission to stop and listen to it before leaving; the dumbfounded guards granted this most unexpected request!

The song happened to be a Merle Haggard favorite, recorded years earlier by the great Hank Snow, titled, "The Last Ride." Merle froze in his tracks. His tracks to freedom... delayed by a woeful tale of a hobo who'd died in a boxcar with the promise from his pal to take him home and bury him with his kin.

Merle was thoroughly captivated by this song. I bought it through iTunes and had it ready to play anytime his mood turned sour.

The song took him back to that glorious day he left San Quentin and how he'd stopped to listen to Hank Snow before walking out through the prison gates. His bad mood could be erased by this favorite Hank Snow tune that had become synonymous with the sweet sounds of freedom.

In December 2010, I took Merle's photo in his hotel suite, dressed and ready for the Kennedy Center Honors. Merle was in good company with fellow honorees, Paul McCartney, Oprah Winfrey, dancer Bill Jones, and composer Jerry Herman (Hello Dolly). It would be fair to say that fifty years earlier, Merle began his musical journey the day of his release from prison on February 3, 1960, just about two months shy of his 23rd birthday on April 6, 1960.

Merle Loved Animals

CHAPTER 46

Merle's dog, Fannie Mae *Photo courtesy of Raymond McDonald*

IF YOU DIDN'T LOVE ANIMALS, then you didn't have a chance of being Merle Haggard's friend. He always had a few dogs around and was as loyal to his animals as his human friends. Merle preferred smaller dogs, although, over the years, he owned a German Shepherd and a few crossbreed mutts. His dogs would accompany him on the road, traveling all over America. He could be feeling the blues, and his canine friends would lift his spirits. Merle loved dogs - they warmed his heart.

Before leaving his bus to go onstage, Merle would give his dogs the sweetest goodbye, as affectionate and doting as if he'd never return.

But an hour or so later, when he did return, they were unrestrained in their joy, jumping and yelping as if they hadn't seen him in years! But honestly, Merle felt the same way. He always had the most warm-hearted, caring, and sincere greetings for his dogs.

Never once did I see a cat on Merle's bus. Several lived in and around the ranch but were more suited to staying at home, ridding the grounds of pesky vermin (which in turn helped keep the snakes at bay). His cats seemed quite happy staring out the window as Merle's bus pulled away - I did notice they watched a lot of television. Dogs aren't that naïve.

Merle lived about three miles off the main highway at his ranch in Palo Cedro. It was a very scenic, two-way, winding road with beautiful ranches spaced all the way to his ranch at the end of the road. He had made many friends through the years, and his neighbors were all delighted to see

him whenever he passed by. But none more so than his best friend on that road, Shadow. Shadow was the most beautiful mule I'd ever seen. I'm not sure how their friendship began, but every time Merle drove by Shadow's stable, she'd come running over to the roadside fence to see her friend. Merle had a Hummer, a mini-

Shadow, Merle's stubborn friend

cooper, and of course, his bus, but Shadow recognized all three, and she'd come running. He'd always get out and pet her and talk to her about a variety of subjects. It didn't matter if he was late somewhere or not; he was as excited to see Shadow as he was to visit his friends.

Once, heading back to the ranch from his favorite restaurant, Lulu's, Merle noticed a horse standing next to a fence about two miles from his property. He said, "Man, I think that horse needs help." I looked around for an animal in distress, but all I saw was the horse across the road - just standing there. Haggard pulled his Hummer to a stop, jumped out, and ran over to the horse. He grabbed the fence, untangled his new friend, and the horse ran free. How he could tell the horse's hoof was stuck in the bottom of the fence is beyond me.

Dozens of wild turkeys enjoyed the Haggard ranch. For some reason, Merle fell in love with one of them, and it followed him everywhere. He would hand feed it, pet it, and of course, talk to it. In the winter, he'd keep it warm, and, in the summer, I watched him spray his turkey friend with water to keep him cool.

Merle had a wolf, a real honest to God, one hundred percent wolf. I had introduced Merle to a friend who was a fantastic guitarist-singer in the Las Vegas area. The two were talking in Merle's suite at the Sahara Hotel one evening, and the subject of wolves came up. Merle had read wolves made great pets and wanted a wolf pup to raise along with his family. (He had a young daughter and son at the time.)

Terry, my friend, was originally from Washington State. He looked like a mountain man with a guitar and just happened to know how to obtain a wolf. So it wasn't long before Merle and his family would receive a new member of their family - a magnificent female wolf pup! They all fell in love, the Haggards and the wolf. When the children ventured out on the ranch grounds, the wolf would protect them. Some ornery critters lived on the property: skunks, opossums, raccoons, and such. But they knew to clear out when the wolf was around! She was smarter than any dog or cat and so gentle. The little dogs running all over the ranch also loved the wolf. Occasionally, they'd get a little too big for their britches. The wolf immediately put them in their place, and at times she'd put those little dogs in her mouth! She was firm with them but very gentle. The Haggard's wolf lived to be about nine years old. When she got sick and died, she broke the heart of each family member. They never wanted another wolf because nothing could replace her.

Merle passed on his love for animals to his kids. They loved animals so much they'd even bring them into the house. Once, we arrived home from a tour and walked into his living room to find his daughter and the baby goat she adopted standing on the carpet. He didn't get mad at his daughter or her goat but mentioned his house had turned into a zoo. Then he sat down and turned on his television. This same daughter eventually married and started her own zoo. She found a baby raccoon, probably abandoned or lost, and raised it.

American Diners

CHAPTER 47

Photo illustration - R.J. Shearin

MERLE SPENT MANY DAYS AND nights traveling all over America. He loved American diners, so we stopped to eat in just about every diner we could find. His favorite was in his second hometown, Redding, California. Lulu's, with tasty food and all the modern conveniences, can easily be located on Pine Street in downtown Redding. When you arrive, tell them Merle's bus driver sent you and ask for Merle's favorite booth in the corner (it seats five). You might even hear a Merle story or two. His picture is on the restaurant website - they were pleased and proud he frequented Lulu's.

Nearly every night on tour after the show, Merle was a very hungry man in need of a Denny's or its equivalent. Denny's populate the entire country and remain open twenty-four hours a day, every day of the year - you can always depend on good ole Denny's, and we faithfully did. As a precaution (because of his fame), Merle usually preferred to eat his meals on the bus. He'd check the parking lot - if it didn't seem too crowded, he'd try eating inside. One night, despite the fact this Denny's was only a few miles from the sold-out show he had just performed, for whatever reason, Merle decided to enter the restaurant. It was around midnight in this little Oklahoma town, and I am sure he knew a commotion was coming, but he was game.

Merle and I and four others had walked into Denny's together. About two minutes later, he looked at me and said, "I heard my name!" (Hard to believe someone recognized Merle Haggard in Oklahoma!) Well, the murmur was rising as the 'rumor' spread: Merle Haggard's sitting in a diner in Oklahoma with a full house of Okies! What a thrill for them, but not for Merle. He then informed us he was going to the bus to avoid being cornered by autograph and photograph hounds. All eyes in the diner followed him as he headed back to his bus alone.

Our food arrived. When I delivered Merle's, I asked nicely if he'd sign a photograph for our waitress. He said, "Sure!" He signed; I delivered - unfortunately, in front of fifty envious fans, who now each wanted an autographed photo! Nearly the entire crowd of on-lookers followed me out to the bus. I sat down with Merle while he ate his dinner (which was pancakes and eggs, his favorite breakfast).

He pointed out the window and said, "Now look what you've done!" The crowd from the restaurant was standing near the bus, having a grand 'ole time. Many had probably been to his concert earlier and undoubtedly had a little alcohol on board. But the crowd shared something in common - Merle was their hero, and they all wanted a souvenir! When asked if I could give each of them a signed photo, Merle smiled and said, "Sure!" Miraculously I found enough photos for the near fifty fans eagerly waiting outside. They were immensely pleased with their gift - those autographed photos of Merle sell for ten dollars a pop at his concerts. Merle didn't care, and thankfully, he didn't fine me for giving away so much of the tour's merchandise.

One of my favorite moments took place around five a.m. on the outskirts of Memphis, Tennessee. Merle surprised me with a 'good morning, and how about a breakfast' stop? We saw a Waffle House sign, so I parked the bus right next to the restaurant, and the two of us strolled in.

Merle loved beautiful women. It didn't matter what nationality; they grabbed his attention immediately. Our server was no exception. She was a stunning young Black woman wearing a perfectly fitted white dress – a captivating contrast! Merle was helplessly infatuated with this goddess whose clear and soft brown eyes, glowing skin, and a beautiful black wave of hair had mesmerized him. I recall her name being lovely, too, but sadly can't remember what it was.

Being the only customers at that moment, we were able to strike up a conversation. Chuck Berry was playing on the jukebox, and Merle asked if she knew who was singing. When she answered "no," he gave her a one-minute history lesson on the great Chuck Berry and his influential music. Now 'Professor Haggard' had captivated this young woman with his voice and eloquence. I was not surprised - women of all ages found Merle to be a handsome man.

Our lovely server asked what we did for a living. A cook and other staff were eavesdropping - I am sure they recognized Merle. I told her I drove the tour bus for the famous man sitting across from me. I glanced at Merle with my "do you want me to tell her who you are?" look. He gave me the "okay" look, so I proceeded to introduce her. This is Merle Haggard: the greatest singer-songwriter in country music history. Her beautiful eyes lit up as she smiled sweetly and gazed adoringly at the man she must have now viewed quite differently. Merle said nothing, but his smile said it all. They stared at each other, spellbound. I suggested to the young woman that she might want to tell her parents about her lucky encounter. I assured her they would know of this man from California, the legend, Merle Haggard. She had never heard of Merle - I hope she listened to a few songs on *YouTube*!

Merle always generously compensated the hard-working staff who served him. I had a business VISA card we used frequently. Merle instructed me to leave our lovely young lady a generous tip – 'he' gave her an additional $100 that morning on top of the $100 bill he left on the table.

Out on the road, we often dined at Cracker Barrel restaurants. The franchise has great food and service and convenient parking for RVs and buses. We all loved their food, especially Merle. He mostly ordered eggs over-medium, trout, biscuits, and pancakes with extra strawberry syrup. Comfortable with the atmosphere and the staff, he enjoyed dining inside nearly every time we stopped at a Cracker Barrel. He always picked up the tab for everyone in his group and never failed to leave a generous tip.

On one occasion in Ohio, Merle was ready to leave and asked me, "Do you remember the Lone Ranger?"

"Sure!" I said.

"Remember how he would all of a sudden leave without sayin' goodbye, but he'd leave behind his signature silver bullet?"

I replied, "Sure, I do!"

"Well," Merle said, "I'm leaving my guitar pick!" He left a $100 bill beneath his pick (a pick emblazoned with his name) and then said, "Let's go!" We hurried out of there like the Lone Ranger (Merle) and Tonto (me).

Whenever people approached Merle within a dining environment, they usually had a kind comment or two, and Merle appreciated that. I don't remember him ever barking at anyone for interrupting his meal. However, now and then, he did encounter a few weirdos. For example, one evening in Laughlin, Nevada, a fellow walked up and asked if Merle Haggard was at the table. Two of the four people sitting there were our wives, which left Merle and me.

Merle said, "I'm Merle."

The man said, "No, you're not!" then spun around on his heels and left.

Another time, it was two in the morning at a lonely diner in North Carolina. The only other guest in the room was watching us. He finally walked over and asked, "Are you Merle Haggard?"

Merle replied, "Yes."

The strange man exclaimed, "No, you're not!" then turned abruptly and left. Those two oddballs must have been related – or it may have been the same rude guy!

Buffalo, Missed It by That Much!

CHAPTER 48

Raymond at a truck stop in Amarillo, Texas
Photo courtesy of Raymond McDonald

WE WERE RETURNING FROM A concert tour in Canada. After leaving Toronto late at night, we arrived in Buffalo, New York, around 6:00 a.m. during rush hour traffic. Traveling east through the city on a four-lane thoroughfare, I began to notice the vehicles in front of me turning out of our lane quickly as if to avoid something. (Sitting up high in a bus has its advantages.) Maybe a car had stalled in our path, or perhaps a ladder had fallen out of someone's truck. Whatever was happening, I realized being in the second lane from the right, left no escape should an unexpected stop become necessary. Suddenly within seconds, it became clear why cars had been darting out of our lane: a car was approaching head-on toward us at an alarming rate!

Ordinarily, no one from the bus would be in the front at 6:00 a.m., but this morning was an exception for whatever reason. I told everyone to hang on tight because we were on a collision course with a misguided, fast approaching vehicle! Assessing the situation, I had no recourse but to slow my speed, wait for a moment to see if the oncoming car was going to swerve out of our lane, then decide whether I should gently move to the left or right – neither a great option. I waited a few seconds and realized the car was veering right and out of our lane, to my relief. Once confident, I eased the bus to the left, feeling quite lucky no one was in that lane. It was also a stroke of good fortune that no cars were on the right, giving the crazed driver a clear path as he whizzed past. He may have intimidated all the other vehicles he ran off the road, but a large coach like ours more than likely helped him make the wise choice to 'move it on over!'

However, as I glanced in my rearview mirror, hoping maybe the reckless driver had figured out he was on the wrong side of the road, it appeared his luck had run out. Sadly, I caught sight of the pile-up of crashed vehicles that I am sure he was in the middle of. Suddenly, as if from nowhere, a dozen police cars sped by on their way to assess the dire situation. I'll never know what happened; I did not research it. But this type of incident pumps you with adrenaline! I was ready for anything now, and of course, eternally grateful for having avoided a head-on collision!

As luck would have it, after exiting the thoroughfare and still high from that nerve-wracking incident, we had about fifty miles of winding two-lane road between the hotel and us. When driving a bus on such a road, the only way to keep everyone from shifting around is to go slower, and Merle was a stickler for that. To not upset him or anyone else on the bus, I reduced our speed to 35 mph. This meant slowing down a hundred cars behind me, including people dropping off kids at school, trying to get to work on time, or whatever their situation demanded. However, this could not be my concern as I drove cautiously, at 10 mph under the posted speed limit (just the way I had learned) for the entire fifty miles of winding road.

Merle himself taught me to drive 10 mph under the speed limit, especially around curves. It didn't matter how fast or slow I was going; that was his recommendation. And, I'd go a lot slower if I thought it would keep Merle from waking up; he needed his rest. Slowing down added to our time on the road, but after what seemed an eternity - fifty miles of a winding road at thirty-five miles an hour - we finally arrived at our destination.

Upon arrival, Merle walked up front to sit with a few of the guys already there. He was usually unhappy in the morning - either due to the driving or the location - and on this morning, it was the driving that had prevented a good night's sleep and provoked a cranky mood. I explained how there wasn't much I could do about a winding road but go 10 mph under the speed limit, as he taught me. I did what I thought was safe for my passengers and all the cars behind me. Merle wasn't interested in hearing my explanation, so to escape his abrasive demeanor, I excused myself to go pick up the hotel room keys.

Usually, I would be the only person awake with no one else in the front when we reached our next destination. I would fetch the hotel keys, then come back and level the bus so it would be ready for Merle by the time he woke up - usually sometime between 10:00 or 11:00 a.m. Merle and everyone else would get their hotel key, and everybody would be happy. But this particular morning, everyone was up already, thanks to the winding road.

When I returned with the room keys, Merle was still sitting in the same spot. Someone had told him of the near head-on collision, which put him in a most apologetic state. From one of the couches, he said, "Ray, I believe you saved our lives this morning. I had no idea you had to avoid a head-on collision. I want to apologize for talking to you the way I did. I am sorry, and thank you for saving my life."

Feeling undeserving of the praise, I reminded Merle I was just doing my job: I was wide-awake; I saw what was going on, and we were fortunate. I apologized again for the winding road. And again, Merle told me he was sorry. He could let you know his level of sincerity through the tone in his voice. Moments earlier, when Merle told me he was sorry for the second time, he spoke with the same tone used each time he sang a heartfelt song. I honestly didn't think I had saved anyone's life - I was just cautious, and it had paid off. My friend, Merle, was very kind. After the near-miss, he was much happier for about a week when he ventured up front in the morning.

More than anyone, Merle knew the extreme danger of driving a forty-five foot, twenty-four-ton bus, especially at night. We often traveled in darkness for three to four hundred miles, nearly every night, fourteen consecutive days with no break. Driving with this intensity requires total concentration. Night driving barely offers three hundred feet of visibility. Many roads aren't in good condition, and most are not well-lit. Weather is unpredictable and, with little notice, can create hazardous driving conditions. Crazy truck drivers, regular drivers, and drunk drivers abound en masse. With rarely a moment's relief from the burden of responsibility, driving a tour bus is challenging. Without exception, each leg of every tour left me utterly exhausted by the time we pulled into our destination.

Merle did explain the rigors of tour bus driving when I first started learning (but there's nothing like experiencing something to truly understand it!). He was an exceptional driver with such control and experience that he could drive his bus like a little car. So, I listened intently to his instructions on how to drive a forty-five foot, twenty-four-ton bus: what speed to travel under different conditions, which lane to use, and when, and short of listing them all, he taught me to watch out for everybody and everything! It was not only my job to learn how to drive the bus safely for everyone on the bus, but everyone outside the bus, too. Merle taught me well and that together with some good luck along the way, I managed never to wreck the bus or cause harm to anyone, for which I am eternally grateful. I have to mention, too, that Dean Holloway, Don Markham, and Biff Adams, who also drove Merle's bus millions of miles, managed the same clean record.

Once, we were driving through Kansas on Interstate 70, from Topeka to Denver. Merle was anxious to get home to California, about 2000 miles away. While holding the speed limit in the preferred, faster and smoother left lane, for some reason, I decided to move over to the slower, rougher right lane. Roads all over America suffer from right lane ruts and potholes due to heavy truck traffic.

Moving to the right lane proved a good choice, despite the bumps. Rambling along at 70 mph, I caught a glimpse of something in the middle of the left lane. It was an enormous dead deer - so large it could have fed a family for a year. There's no telling what could have happened if I had not changed lanes. My reaction would have been to swerve, but one of the first things I learned about driving a large bus is to never swerve! Just hit whatever it is! Yet, what kind of damage could that have caused both passengers and vehicle? Instead, luck still with me, I just rolled on past in the right lane without a worry.

I didn't tell anyone about what happened and how good fortune had once again saved the day. I saw no need to inform them about close-calls. Besides, by this time (near midnight), Merle and the others were probably enjoying some tunes by Bob Wills and His Texas Playboys. Everything was calm, and very soon, we would be stopping in Denver.

It was time to fuel up, so we pulled into a Flyin' J Truckstop just outside the city. A localized, torrential downpour had left giant pools of water in the parking lot. As we left, I thought the pool in our path looked hazardous and was definitely one to avoid. But someone encouraged me to drive through it, saying, "You can make that!" I thought, "Well, I know I can't! And who's this backseat driver without the courage to drive but with no problem offering his advice?" Unfortunately, I listened to him and not my instincts and dropped the right rear tire into a three-foot hole hidden by the water. We were stuck, and I couldn't get us out. Fuming, I let fly a string of swear words - not my standard response to a minor fiasco. We assessed the situation and decided that calling a tow truck was the only option. Three hundred dollars later, plus an hour of waiting for the truck and the tow out of the hole, we were on the road again. Merle was only mildly upset.

I suppose I could have mentioned how much worse things could have been had we not avoided the deer about two hundred miles earlier, but I didn't. Despite this being the only time I got stuck at a gas station or anywhere else for that matter, I was still a little angry for not following my instincts just to negotiate our way around the puddle. I was also infuriated with these truck stop gas stations for not filling holes deep and wide enough to swallow a large bus tire! Giant trucks drive through these stations all day and all night, seven days a week, fifty-two weeks a year - there is no excuse for such a state of disrepair.

To summarize this chapter, when you get up in the tour bus driver's seat, and if you hope to always "miss it by that much," you must be wide-awake while keeping your eyes on the road at all times, watching for every single thing! To be this alert driving all night, getting plenty of sleep (at least eight hours) the day before is essential. To do this, you need earplugs, blackout drapes, and prayers for a quiet hotel (which is nearly impossible). Sometimes I'd get a little drowsy despite my efforts, so I'd drink Coca-Cola for a good shot of caffeine. Once I tried a five-hour energy drink, but it was too strong. Even over the counter drugs were too much - luckily, Coca-Cola and I got along very well!

When first hired, Merle told me he knew I was lucky and that being lucky was one reason I got the job. His comment brought to mind one of his songs, "I Always Get Lucky with You," which has absolutely nothing to do with driving a bus but everything to do with luck.

Modern Technology

CHAPTER 49

Stock photo

MERLE WAS AMAZED BY MODERN technology and, in particular, the iPhone. Many people around him used an iPhone, I used an iPhone, and he was very intrigued and curious. One day while sitting in his living room, he kept talking about Gene Autry and "That Silver Haired Daddy of Mine." It was one of Gene Autry's biggest hits from 1935.

I told Merle, "I can play that song on my phone within a minute."

Merle said, "Show me!" It probably took forty seconds total to find the song on iTunes, purchase, and download it before we began listening.

I said, "That's how you buy your records nowadays, Merle. You don't have to go to a record store. You don't have to do anything but own a smartphone, then download a song, and it will be saved to your phone forever, waiting for you to play it. And the songs you purchase are not confined to your phone - you can listen on larger speakers, send them to someone, save them on different devices - you can do anything you want because you own them."

He asked, "How many songs do you have on your phone?"

I said, "I think I have about seven hundred now."

"You bought 'em all?"

"Yeah, I bought 'em all. You're able to buy the entire album if that's what you want. I could buy everything you ever recorded right now." He was flabbergasted!

From my phone, I showed Merle video clips of Roger Miller on the *Nashville This Morning Show* Ralph Emery hosted - a wonderful black-and-white television program that aired in the 1960s. We watched an episode from 1966. Roger had won various Grammy awards but still made time for his live morning show in Nashville. Merle was in stitches as he watched Roger sing two or three of his monster hits. He told me that of all of his show business friends, Roger was his closest.

Roger Miller was at the pinnacle of his career when he and Merle met back in the sixties. Among his Grammys was a Song of the Year award, which he won over The Beatles, no less! But it wasn't Roger's achievements that amused Merle this morning - it was his lively humor that had Merle laughing uncontrollably, pointing at the screen. "That's exactly how he is - funny and witty, and, of course, his music was just unbelievable." Some of Roger Miller's music during that period included "Dang Me," "Chug-a-lug," and "King of the Road."

Merle loved his iPhone (which he acquired soon after my demo). He became a big *YouTube* fan, and before long, he'd mastered FaceTime. Merle adored his baby granddaughter, who lived thousands of miles away. Using FaceTime, he'd make funny faces, laugh with her, and talk silly to her as though she were in the room directly in front of him. Merle was a wonderful, warm-hearted man who appreciated new technology like the iPhone and the apps, Skype and FaceTime, which allowed him to stay close with loved ones far away. Believe me, once Merle learned something, he never forgot it. He learned to use his iPhone quickly, and it brought him much pleasure.

Shortly after he started purchasing music, Merle became interested in buying other things. He'd ask, "How do you do that, Ray?" So I showed him how to make purchases by inputting his credit card information and shipping address. He was off and running!

Merle was in awe of the technology multiplying rapidly around him. He was smack in the middle of a technological revolution during his golden years but quickly learned how to use and enjoy it like any modern teenager.

My Three Songs

CHAPTER 50

Photo illustration - R.J. Shearin

SOMETIMES I THINK I'M THE luckiest guy in the world because Merle Haggard recorded three songs I wrote: "Losin' in Las Vegas," "I Wish I Was Santa Claus," and "It's Too Lonesome for Me." I wrote the first two songs on my own. "It's Too Lonesome for Me" is more complicated. Before continuing with the stories behind my songs that Merle recorded, I'd like to share my perceptions about his talents. Merle Haggard was one of the greatest songwriters ever in any genre. His awards and induction into the Songwriters Hall of Fame and his Grammy legend status are testaments to his talents. Merle Haggard wrote nearly all of his giant, iconic songs without collaboration. It was my incredible privilege to have witnessed his exceptional creative genius over time. It began upon first meeting in 1964, when he and his wife, Bonnie Owens, became my legal guardians for a year. How fortunate could a young fellow and fledgling songwriter be?

LOSIN' IN LAS VEGAS

I wrote the song "Losin' in Las Vegas" in 1986 while traveling with my kids and wife, Kathy, to Merle's Silverthorn Resort, located on pristine Lake Shasta in Northern California. My family and I were headed there for the Thanksgiving holiday. Our vehicle was an orange 1984 Dodge van. We'd squeeze a queen-size mattress in the back, fill a cooler of ice with beverages and snacks, and take off. My daughter, Alison, was ten years old, and my son, Benjamin, six. Traveling in this manner to such destinations produced countless unforgettable memories.

It was twilight as we left our home in Las Vegas for the 750-mile trip to Merle's resort. We were always astonished at the beauty of Las Vegas at night. Soon, our rear view encompassed the entire twinkling city. I suddenly felt compelled to write some song lyrics and asked Kathy to write down these words: "I'm livin' in Las Vegas, but the only thing I'm losin' is you." I had written a few songs in my amateur career, and most of them were really bad! But this one felt different; it showed promise! Kathy wrote the rest of the lyrics as I dictated them, and I kept the country music melody in my head.

On the way to Merle's Silverthorn Resort, we stopped in Bakersfield to visit Kathy's mother and brother. When we got there, I pulled out my guitar and added the melody to my lyrics. I liked this song and hoped (maybe even believed) that Merle would, too.

This was the first time I had approached Merle with a song I had written. Oh, wait! I'm forgetting "Russian Waiter," written while in my high school wood-shop class when I lived with Merle and Bonnie.

He liked the song and told me he would include it on a comedy album, sort of like the one Johnny Cash had recorded (*Everybody Loves a Nut*). He never recorded the album, but we had many laughs over the years about the song, "Russian Waiter."

While at Lake Shasta, Merle lived on his houseboat, not far from his resort. I had reserved a cabin there without informing Merle we were coming. We arrived around 10:00 p.m., having left Bakersfield in the early afternoon. It was Thanksgiving Eve, and Merle's bus was parked and waiting to take him to his mother's house - she was living near the California coastal town of Pismo Beach at that time. I did get to speak with Merle for a few minutes; he was apologetic for rushing off to his *mama's* house for Thanksgiving. I didn't mention my song - the timing wasn't right - but my family and I had a grand Thanksgiving holiday on the lake, as one might suppose.

A few weeks after Thanksgiving, Merle came to Las Vegas to play at the Sahara Hotel. Whenever possible, I'd go see him perform with his consistently excellent band, The Strangers. Since our trip to Shasta Lake, I had cut a demo of my song initially titled 'Livin' in Las Vegas,' at Buck Owens' studio in Oildale with an excellent back-up band. I copied it to a cassette tape and gave it to Merle's best friend and bus driver, Dean Holloway. I suggested to Dean, "One of these days, when you're rolling down the road, I'd sure appreciate it if you'd listen to my song."

He said, "Fine, I'll do that." Much to my surprise, Dean called a few weeks later, asking, "Did you really write that song?"

"Yes," I replied. Dean told me that he and Merle had listened to it, and Merle wanted to record it! I was stunned into a moment of silence. I finally heard, "Ray! Are you there?"

"Yes, let me compose myself because this blows my mind," I replied as calmly as possible.

Dean explained that Merle wanted me to sign a one-song contract with Inorbit Publishing (Merle's company) and that I needed to come back to the resort on Lake Shasta to sign the contract in person.

As soon as humanly possible, I headed to Lake Shasta! I arrived early in the evening and learned Merle and the Strangers would be performing later that night at Merle's resort, and the guest artist would be the wonderful Tammy Wynette! Merle introduced us backstage - she was gorgeous and genuinely kind to me. Since the early 1960s, I had been listening to this talented lady sing, and I absolutely loved her voice.

After meeting Tammy Wynette, the night couldn't possibly have held more surprises. However, Merle led me to one of the dressing rooms backstage for yet another! The room was full of strangers. I mean Merle's entire band, The Strangers, all sitting around the room. I knew all these musicians, starting with the original group in 1965 and the additional members over the years since then. Dean Holloway was sitting right next to Merle when they handed me a guitar and said, "Play us your song." Just me, in front of my musical idol, his best friend, and his stellar band, which included the legendary Roy Nichols and Norman Hamlet, and I was on! Was I nervous? No, because I knew them all and had practiced the song dozens of times. When I finished playing, they all smiled in unison as if to say, "We've known this kid since he was fourteen years old, and he did it - he wrote a good song!"

Then Merle said, "You've got one word wrong."

I nearly froze! I thought, "Oh my God, what have I done? Which word is wrong?"

Merle explained how the word livin' in my song's title would now be losin' (the song's original title was "Livin' in Las Vegas"). He continued his reasoning as I listened intently. He said, "Raymond, nobody *lives* in f-ing Las Vegas, but everybody *loses* there. Now, use losin' in place of livin' as you sing it this time."

I sang "Losin' in Las Vegas," and the whole gang approved. Relieved and grateful, I thought this was the end of it, but Merle wanted me to perform in front of two hundred fifty people on his nightclub stage with his band! I pleaded with them, "Man! I can't do that! I never, ever sing with bands, and I'll blow it, big time!" They all heard the sincerity in my tone and let me off the hook. I went outside and breathed a huge sigh of relief.

Three years later, Merle was in Las Vegas performing at the Golden Nugget again. In the afternoon, at Dean's invitation, I met with Merle and Dean in Merle's suite. Merle explained that my song 'didn't make the cut' for his latest album, *Chill Factor* (1989). They played one song from the album, "Twinkle, Twinkle Lucky Star," which was to become another number one song for Merle, making a total of about forty since 1965!

Now they assured me that "Losin' in Las Vegas" was coming soon. But it wasn't until six months later I got a call from Dean telling me that Merle had just recorded my song! Wow! Dean explained how Merle and The Strangers had been recording new songs for his next album when Merle spoke into his microphone, "Anybody got a song?"

Dean immediately replied, "Losin' in Las Vegas."

"Let's do it!" Merle said. And that they did! I couldn't believe my ears when they played it for me over the phone. I was elated! Merle told me this: "Raymond, this song will be on my last Columbia Records album. It's forever, and no one will be able to take it away from you." I was so grateful and fully realized the true gift Merle had given me.

In later years, Merle shared how he'd lived that song. In the early sixties, he lived in Las Vegas, playing bass and singing in Wynn Stewart's band at the Nashville Nevada Club. He reminisced about one day when he came home, and his wife, Leona, had packed up their kids, loaded a U-Haul trailer, and moved back to Bakersfield. Now the other small part he changed in my song made perfect sense: he had changed the words 'you walk' in the line 'as you walk out of sight' to 'as U-Haul out of sight.' What a visual and another lesson for me - one word can make a huge difference!

The song was eventually released in 1989 on the album *5:01 Blues*. My family and I were in Topeka, Kansas, for a family reunion when we stopped by a record store to find the album. We gazed in astonishment at my name in the credits. They were so happy for me; my nine-year-old son, Ben, proudly carried the album to the cash register, loudly announcing that his dad had written a song on the album!

Back in the days of vinyl, Merle had another surprise in store. He'd decided the flip side of his 45 rpm "A Better Love Next Time" should be "Losin' in Las Vegas." This was fantastic news because it meant I would make more money - I received a royalty check about a year later for $4,500! That was quite a thrill because, around that time, it took four months of labor to make the same amount of money working outside in the harsh desert with a survey crew. In the following years, whenever a royalty check arrived, I'd call Merle and Dean and thank them profusely. They got a kick out of that.

Life is never perfect, and some minor repercussions came my way in the form of envy. A few close friends I'd known for quite some time had paid their dues working hard in the country music business, but Merle had never recorded any of their songs. They hounded me relentlessly with, "Why did you get a Haggard cut? We've got better songs than that!" Merle explained years later why he had never recorded anything written by them: he could not relate to the songs they submitted. Mine, he said, he could.

One night while driving Merle's bus down the road, he asked me how many songs I'd written. I told him forty or so. Then he asked how many were about my life, and I replied, "All of them." Merle said,

"That's what I mean! I want real-life songs, man!" He added, "That's why I don't record songs that aren't real to me."

In 2007, I was searching the internet to see if anyone had covered "Losin' in Las Vegas." To my surprise, I found a cover! Rickey Wasson, a Bluegrass legend, had recorded and released it as a single on his latest bluegrass album. Bluegrass? My song was a country ballad! But Rickey and the great JD Crowe created a wild up-tempo version, which I liked. Rickey sent me a copy, and I played it for Merle, who loved the bluegrass version...and then I loved it more!

Years later, Rickey and JD came to watch Merle's concert in Kentucky. I had the approval to bring them on Merle's bus, and he was as gracious as always. They engaged in some conversation about the good ole days and took a few photos together. I even shot a video of the three of them. Rickey's version of "Losin' in Las Vegas" became the most played bluegrass song on Sirius XM - that's worldwide!

I WISH I WAS SANTA CLAUS

A friend once told me, "It's not what you know; it's who you know." That was his (somewhat envious) response upon learning Merle had recorded a song of mine. I couldn't agree more. And because I knew Merle, it was tempting to call him about my music, hoping he'd like another of my songs. But, I would only call if I thought a song would meet with his approval, and there were only a few he'd heard that he liked.

One crisp, sunny California day in early December 2003, I called Merle. I was living in Bakersfield, bumming off my brother-in-law Donnie Hughett because I had no money - no money for rent, food, fuel – I was flat broke. Donnie and I were good friends; I'd helped him out in a similar situation years earlier, so he was returning the favor. We lived in a funky two-bedroom apartment on the shady side of town. He said I could stay for a couple of weeks; I stayed for a year!

I had started playing guitar and singing songs at a bar in downtown Bakersfield belonging to my pal, Kipp Sullivan. He paid me fifty dollars a night with free drinks, so I drank. One afternoon, I thought, "I don't have any dough, so I can't buy presents for anyone. I sure wish I was Santa Claus." Then I said it out loud, "I wish I was Santa Claus," thinking it just might make a good title for a Christmas tune. I wrote the song in five minutes, sang it a few times to myself, and thought, "Here's my present to everyone! My gift is a song, and it didn't cost me a dime!" Very pleased with my latest attempt, I called my friend Merle Haggard at his home to see if he'd give it a quick listen.

He answered with a loud, "Now what!" I could hear the sarcastic tone in his voice as he laughed when he said it. I knew this might be a good time to introduce my tune, so I mentioned I had just written a Christmas song.

He replied, "Sing it to me."

I did, and he reacted immediately, saying, "That's wonderful! I'll record that! Now, go get Don Markham out of his trailer park, and bring Don and your song up here, pronto. Then we'll record a whole Christmas album!" This astonished me.

"Thank you, sir!" once again, stunned by my good fortune.

The following day, Don and I were off to Merle's ranch in Palo Cedro. When we arrived, Merle and his entire band were waiting in his living room. With everyone gathered around, he said, "Sing us your song, Ray, but play it in the key of D instead of C; that way, it'll be brighter." I played it in D (for the first time), and they loved it. Merle's piano man, Doug Colosio, pulled me aside to tell me it was the prettiest Christmas melody he had heard in years - his kind comment certainly boosted my confidence.

"Boys, go on out to the studio and cut me a demo of this song. (Merle had built a recording studio next to his house). I'll be in to overdub my voice later. While you're at it, cut a demo of my song 'Santa Claus and Popcorn.' Oh, and 'White Christmas,' too!" After about two hours of recording with the Strangers in the studio, they thought the takes were good enough for Merle to hear. We summoned him to the studio to listen, and he was pleased. Upon hearing my rendition of "Santa Claus and Popcorn," he even said, "Man! That's Ray McDonald!" He was genuinely impressed. I just sat there like a little kid, not knowing what to say, but what I did know was that my song, "I Wish I Was Santa Claus," sounded great.

The next day, Don and I returned home to Bakersfield. For the next month, Merle and his band added songs to his new Christmas album, and by the end of January, they had finished. A record company in Texas heard the album and wanted it. *I Wish I Was Santa Claus* was released on October 26, 2004.

I called a local record store in Las Vegas and asked if they had a new Christmas album by Merle Haggard. They said, "Yes, the album, *I Wish I Was Santa Claus*, is in stock." My daughter, Alison, and I hurried to the store, and there it was! Now, around fifteen years later, wouldn't it be great if a filmmaker or maybe a new artist would come along and record it? This often happens with Haggard's songs. Or perhaps Chevrolet,  Ford, or Microsoft will decide it would work perfectly in a marketing campaign. I still like to believe this will happen.

Here's to Santa Claus - his name is Merle Haggard! He gave me the greatest gift of all by recording "I Wish I Was Santa Claus," not to mention choosing it for the album title!

IT'S TOO LONESOME FOR ME

In 2001, while working as Merle's office manager and personal assistant, another gift came my way. Merle's office was in his living room, and I reported there for work every morning at 9:30 a.m., per his instructions. One fine morning minutes after my arrival, he stood up, pointed at me, and said, "Raymond, I've got a song title, but I don't have time to write the song. If you'll write it, we'll split it."

I asked, "What's the title?"

He answered, "It's Too Lonesome for Me."

Merle knew I missed my ex-wife because we talked about it every day. We had recently divorced after being together for thirty-two years and married for twenty-eight. He had already recorded one of my songs, so apparently had confidence in giving me the honor to write another.

That night after work, I hurried home to begin writing the lyrics and the melody using my very nice Takamine acoustic guitar (Garth Brooks model) I owned at the time. I chose the key of A-minor because of the beauty of that particular chord and how well it suited the tune. I don't read or write music - I just fit the words and melody together with chords, then remember what I've done. It only took fifteen minutes to finish the song, or so I thought.

The minute the opportunity arose, I played the song for my son, Benjamin. He said, "Dad, you're not singing about yourself." Ben was a promising songwriter in his own right, and when he suggested forming a new bridge – one that better fit my situation – it made a big difference. However, I didn't yet feel confident enough to play it for Merle.

It was not until twelve years later (TWELVE!) and pure happenstance that I finally debuted the song for Merle, stopped somewhere during a tour in America. I had walked to the back of the bus where Merle and his talented son, Benny, were trying to find songs for Benny to record. Merle asked if I had anything similar to what

Hunter Hayes might write. "Hmm, maybe," I said as I pulled out my trusty iPhone. With the speaker pressed to his ear, he listened intently to my version of "It's Too Lonesome for Me," then surprised me by saying, "Hell, I'll cut that! Benny can find something else!"

Merle had me play the song a few more times, during which I reminded him of the day in 2001 when he gave me the title. I reminded him that we were splitting it fifty-fifty. He said, "Well, that makes it even better!" When I told him of my son's input, Merle said, "That's fine. We'll each take a third." My son took care of the BMI (Broadcast Music Incorporated) register work, and we signed a one-song contract with MHMI (Merle Haggard Music, Inc.).

In 2014, Merle recorded "It's Too Lonesome for Me," and mastered it in 2015. Mayor Buddy Cannon produced this beautiful version of the song, and the talented Vince Gill and Sonya Issacs sang harmony. Merle changed a few words here and there while giving it that undeniable Haggard vocal, which truly was another gift for my son and me. We shall always treasure this association with Merle - how many songwriters in Nashville would have loved a Haggard cut? I suspect all of them!

On this same album, which sadly turned out to be his final studio album, Merle recorded Roger Miller's "King of the Road" and Kris Kristofferson's "A Moment of Forever." Merle honored the late Blaze Foley on this album by recording two songs Blaze wrote, "Clay Pigeons" & "Oooh Love." At this writing, in 2020, the album has not been released. If you're interested in listening to my version of "It's Too Lonesome for Me," and other songs I wrote, they are available on my *YouTube* channel, "Raymond H. McDonald."

Merle Haggard Interview

CHAPTER 51

Photo courtesy of Dannie Ray Spiess

IN 2014, I WAS HONORED to interview Merle about some of the great songs he had written and recorded. The following are his answers, transcribed verbatim from the interview recording.

MAMA TRIED

"Mama Tried" was written on the Kern River, Ray. I wanta' say, 1967 or '68, and uh, most songs that I've written I can take you back and give you a blow by blow description, but I don't remember much about writin' this. It's been over forty years. (with a smile) We recorded it: Glen Campbell was singin' harmony with Bonnie Owens, Roy Nichols was playin' the lead guitar, James Burton was playin' the finger pickin' guitar. They often played both of em' on my records. It would be hard to tell which one was which, but both of em' were on that record. It's been a wonderful song for me, and the kids tattoo it on their neck, and I guess if I had to choose which song would be my favorite of all the songs I've written - it would probably be "Mama Tried."

RAMBLIN' FEVER

I wrote "Ramblin' Fever" when I was livin' in Nashville in 1976, and my house butted up to Charlie Walkers' house. Our backyards were right next to each other, and I was out there doin' somethin' in the yard, and Charlie stuck his head over the fence and said, "Hey Merle, I'm recording tomorrow." He said, "Why don't you write me a couple of hit songs?" Well, as luck would have it, I went back in the house, and I thought, you know... I think I'll try to write him something, and I sat down and in about two hours I had really...two good songs. He recorded both of em' "Ramblin Fever" and "I've Had a Beautiful Time," and both of em' are in my million play stringer. (big smile) But, he went on that next day, he recorded "Ramblin' Fever" sort of swing style. And then, later, I recorded the record that I did with The Grady Martin Band. It was a memorable session. I've even got a picture of that particular band. Dave Kirby and Red Lane were playin' rhythm guitars. Grady was on the lead. Bunky Keel was on piano, and Joe Allen was playin' bass, and Jim Isabell was playin' drums, and I might mention that Jeannie Seely and Bonnie Owens were singin' harmony on that. And recorded it at Fireside Studios, Porter Wagoners' old studio.

MISERY AND GIN

Well, they asked me to sing it in a Clint Eastwood movie, *Bronco Billy*, and also we recorded "Barroom Buddies." That was out of that movie that also went to number one, I think, with Clint Eastwood and I. I didn't write the song, but I tell ya, there was I think forty-eight players, which was a sizable group compared to the ones that I normally used. But I went in there, and there was four famous guitar players that I had used one time or another on my sessions, and they was all four sittin' way back in the back among all these array of musicians. There was Clarence White and Billy Walker and Phil Ball and James Burton, all sittin' back there fannin' rhythm guitar. (big smile) They counted it off, and we sang it through one time. John Hobbs was playin' piano, but there was just an array of musicians, every kind of an instrument in the world on that record. (soft laughter) And it was a number one record that did real well. (I ask him to tell the Clint Eastwood grocery store story) Well, a lot of people told me that Clint lived up here close by, and I'd go in the little grocery store down here, The Holiday Market. People would say, "Hey, Ole Clint just left" or somethin'. I didn't pay much attention to that. I didn't know he really did live up here. One day, I walked in the store, and he kinda' walked right in ahead of me. I said, "HEY WESTWOOD," (Merle laughs loudly) and he turned and just kept on goin' a little faster, and I said, "HEY WESTWOOD! DAMN IT!" (laughs at the memory) He turned around and said, "Haggard! I'm glad I broke that bottle over your head." (Merle laughs)

YOU TAKE ME FOR GRANTED

You know I can't really tell ya'. I know when it came about. Leona Williams and I were married at the time. (he leans forward) That means we LIVED together. We lived together, and she came off a tour that she'd been on, and she sang me that song. And, we'd written several songs together, and a lot of people might've thought that she was, you know, leanin' on me because I was more famous than her, but not true. She's really a great songwriter and great musician and a great harmony singer. And she and

I wrote a song called, "Someday When Things Are Good," that had done real good. And we wrote other songs that made album cuts, but "You Take Me for Granted" was written solely by Leona Williams, and it was a great song. I'm glad that she allowed me to hear it first.

LET'S CHASE EACH OTHER 'ROUND THE ROOM TONIGHT

"Let's Chase Each Other 'Round the Room" was a boat song. We wrote it while we were out here, livin' on the boat. I lived out here on the houseboat for eight years, out here on Lake Shasta, and I still get out there much as I can. But Sheryl Rodgers was stewardess that was Freddies' current girlfriend at the time. (Freddie Powers, co-writer) We got out there one night and got to writin' that song. She had couple of good words, so she's on the song. Sheryl Rodgers, Freddie Powers, and Merle Haggard song recorded by Thompson Square.

I'M A LONESOME FUGITIVE

Well, it was written by Liz and Casey Anderson, who at the time lived in Sacramento, California, and the "Fugitive," or "I'm a Lonesome Fugitive," was my first number one song. I'd had several chart records. I'd had a couple that got into the top five. "Swingin' Doors" got into number one in one magazine, but "Fugitive" was the first one to go in all three magazines; back then, we had *Cash Box, Record World*, and *Billboard*. And she was the lady that gave me my first chart record. She wrote, "All Friends Are Gonna Be Strangers." I say my first chart record, my first top-five record. She also wrote a song that Bonnie and I had on the charts for thirty-one weeks called "Just Between the Two of Us," which was a wonderful song that was really what got me out of Bakersfield. I started bookin' other night clubs. "Just Between the Two of Us." "I'm a Lonesome Fugitive." She brought it to me in 1967. I think

I recorded it three or four times, once in Nashville, in Ohio, and once at Capitol in Hollywood. And, of course, the one in Hollywood is the one that we used, and that's the end of my story.

THE FIGHTIN' SIDE OF ME

"The Fightin' Side of Me" was recorded live in Philadelphia, as a follow up to "Okie from Muskogee." And the writing of "Fightin' Side of Me"...I was riding with good friend Lewis Talley. I had the song completely written, and I sang it to Louie in the car, comin' over the Ridge Route. (between LA and Bakersfield) He said, "Merle, I think you're using the wrong word on the title." I said, "What do you mean?" He said, I think, "I was calling the song 'The stubborn side of me.' I think you're trying to say 'The Fightin' Side of Me,' " and sure enough, of course, he was right, went on to record it, it sold a lot of records real quick. And I remember on that record, that was one of the few times in the history of my knowin' Bonnie Owens, where she forgot the words - remember she forgot the words to Philadelphia Lawyer? I don't know whether she was actin' or if she really forgot the words. It was a live recording, "Fightin' Side of Me."

GOIN' WHERE THE LONELY GO

Well, you know, that's one of the songs that was on what we call the *Big City* session. We did twenty-three sides, down in Tom Jones studio in Los Angeles, in I believe, 1980. "Goin' Where the Lonely Go" was a number one song. "Big City" was a number one song. Both of em' came off of that seven-day recording session we had down there. (I asked him if he remembered writing it) No, I don't, I don't remember actually writing that song. Most of 'em - I could tell you about it. But it was just a - I'm sure I wrote it on the boat - on the houseboat. We had a nightclub out by the houseboat at that time, and I could take new songs and go up and try 'em out on the crowd - you know. We had a little lounge that seated about two hundred people. We'd go up and play if we so desired. There was always a band there.

ARE THE GOOD TIMES REALLY OVER FOR GOOD

Well, you know, I wrote that song out on the boat. It was part of the seven songs I had when I signed with MCA. And it was Jimmy Bowens' pick of the litter; he thought that was the greatest thing he'd heard for a long time. I could say this, that I still do that song every time, and that opening line, "I wish a buck was still silver," always brings an applause. If a man could still work and still would. (Jason Aldean picked the song) Well, he picked a good song. It's probably one of the top two or three songs of mine.

I THINK I'LL JUST STAY HERE AND DRNK

Hey, you know what? Hank Jr. just recorded that, too! And Suzy Boguss just recorded that. So we've had three cuts on that here lately. I tell ya, I wrote that up here at what we call the 'big house.' Leona Williams and I was up there one mornin' writin' songs, and we worked all night on somethin' that didn't work. We tried to write this song, and in about ten minutes, I wrote that song and turned around and sang it for her. And it was done, and there was nothin', no work left to do on it. And she said, "How come you didn't ask me to help you on it?" I said, "I didn't need ya." (I mention Don Markhams sax is blowing wild, and he's got Reggie Young) Reggie Young has got the guitar part on it. I think the record was about five minutes long; it was way longer than most records. I remember somebody said they started listenin' to it on one side of Bakersfield, and when they got over to Tehachapi, on the other side of town, it was still goin'! (I mention that it was long for those days) Well, you get somethin' goin and you hate to quit and sometimes three minutes is not long enough to express the whole deal. (I mention that he yells out at the end of the record, "We're gone!") Yeah, I was trying to get 'em to quit, so I could go outside to go smoke.

THAT'S THE WAY LOVE GOES

Well, in the mid-seventies, we were in Nashville and visiting with Lefty and Whitey Shafer (co-writer with Lefty) and Johnny Rodriguez. We were in a motel room down there, singin' songs to each other that we'd just released. It got around to, I sang somethin' and turned around and handed the guitar to Lefty. He was sittin' behind me on the bed. And he started singin', (Merle sings) I been throwin' horseshoes... and he got my attention boy! He sang the whole thing. I said, "Lefty, that's your Faded Love man, that's the song that'll bring you back in the latter part of your life here." "No!" he said, "I want you to cut it... make me some money." I said, "Not while you're alive!" Johnny Rodriguez was standing there, and he said, "I'll do it!" Johnny went and cut it, and he had a number one record on it on July 10th, 1975. Well, lo and behold, Lefty passed away, and I went and cut it ten years later, in 1985, and I got a Grammy for it and it was also number one to the day, July 10, 1985. So I got 'Vocalist of the Year' and a Grammy for it. Whitey Shafer had all the lines leading up to the title line and didn't have a title line. Lefty listened to him sing it... what he had, and Lefty said, "Yeah, it's obvious," "That's the Way Love Goes."

TONIGHT THE BOTTLE LET ME DOWN

Well, I tell ya. Let me tell you about that song. It was a follow up to a drinkin' song that we had called "Swingin' Doors." In those days, you categorized your music. We had three of 'em: "The Bottle Let Me Down," "Swingin' Doors," and "Wine and Roses." And it was the first session that we used James Burton on because Roy (Nichols) was booked on another session in Lake Tahoe and couldn't make the Hollywood session. I said, "What do I do?" and Roy said, "Well, hire James Burton." So Burton came and played that first session with us. We also had... that may have been the first time we had Glen and Bonnie, those two, singin' harmony... talking about Glen Campbell. I always say I can use the girls help on this, and they really get into it. It's a song for all drunks, and just here lately... there's been a couple of good records on that song. (I say that you sing "each night I leave the barroom when it's over") That's what you do when you're through drinkin'!

KICKIN' THE FOOTLIGHTS OUT

Kickin' the Footlights Out... Again, was the title of a George Jones/Merle Haggard album. It's been about three years since we done that. Since then, George has passed away, and I want to say that he was partial to this song, "Kickin' the Footlights Out." He called it, 'The Floodlights.'

SING ME BACK HOME

We're in the process of trying to come up with a film that has something to do with my time in prison and my association with Caryl Chessman, who was a condemned prisoner. Who I watched walked from his cell to the office quarters of Quentin many times, and that along with... There used to be a lady named Sister Mary that came into the jail with a little minstrel group and she used to allow me to put my hands through the bars and play the guitar at the Bakersfield jail. Between the thoughts of her, and the thoughts of the condemned prisoner that used to walk by and see us out in the yard playin' guitars, those thoughts brought about the writing of "Sing Me Back Home." Let me say this, it's a big song and I'm really proud to have my son, Benny (his son, Benny, sang it), participate in the Merle Haggard tribute.

MY FAVORITE MEMORY

(I lead with Joe Nichols recorded "My Favorite Memory") And Joe Nichols recorded, "Kickin' the Footlights Out" and he's a...they are calling him a traditional artist, and I'm proud to have him recording my songs. He does a real good job on 'em. Thank you for "My Favorite Memory." It was written on the houseboat, long around 1982. And it was right before the big blow-up (with Leona Williams. I ask about the line, 'Sleeping all night long on the floor.' Did that happen?) Well I'm not sure it happened with Leona. (wink) Yeah, it happened.

Until We Meet Again

CHAPTER 52

Photo courtesy of Raymond McDonald

IN THE YEAR 2012, JENNA Bush Hagar, of *The Today Show*, interviewed Merle while he was on tour in Tennessee. At the time, Merle was seventy-five years old. Jenna wanted to know if there was anything that could stop him.

Merle's response was, "I think when a man quits workin' - I don't know, he kind of gives up on everything - you know. So retirement's not in the picture at all."

Jenna stated, "It seems like music is just - really - a lot of who you are."

Merle replied, "That's about all I am. You know as, uh, as - that's what I'm for. That's what I do. I eat, sleep, and breathe it, and uh - people around me - if they can't handle it - they just have to get away. (laughs) This is how it is."

There's no doubt music was Merle's lifetime love and passion.

It was December 2015 in Palm Springs, California. Clad in a hospital gown, Merle was sitting in a wheelchair in the Eisenhower Medical Center emergency room. He pointed to the heavens as he looked toward us and said, "If this cancer is back, I'm not going to let them treat it! I'm going home to see my dad!" (His dad passed away when he was nine years old.) A few minutes later, his son, Benny, and I were standing next to Merle when a nurse came into the room. She said, "Merle, who are these men with you?" He replied, "These are my sons." Benny surprisingly blurted out, "But we're from different mothers!" Since Merle was my legal guardian when I was in high school, he thought of me as another son, and I thought of him as a second dad.

Now Merle was tired: tired of being sick, tired of being examined, tired of being poked and prodded, tired of fighting for his life, and certainly tired of not being able to sing. Merle was ready to go. He had even planned his last day on earth. A week before his birthday, Merle said he was going to die on his birthday. Who does that? Apparently, Merle Haggard - he died on his seventy-ninth birthday, April 6, 2016.

Merle always said I was lucky. I do feel very fortunate to have had a loving, lifelong relationship with the greatest country music artist of all time. Of course, as with any long-term relationship, there were ups and downs, but our tie could never be broken. He was truly a musical genius, and I, this Native American Indian kid from Kansas, had the great pleasure of being his friend.

Merle once told me, when referring to a song that I'd written and he'd recorded, "No one can take that song away from you, Raymond." I feel the same way about our friendship - it is something special that will last forever. I think of Merle often and miss him every day.

Here's to you, Merle!
With love, until we meet again,

◈ ◈ ◈

AFTERWORD

In 2006, soon after returning to my hometown of Bakersfield, California, I began a career driving limousines for Susanna and Troy Zandes and their fabulous company, Luxury Limousines. I obtained a Class B commercial driver's license and informed Merle of my latest venture. He was surprised and delighted to hear I'd found another job that kept me happy, but mostly he was interested in the fact I'd obtained a commercial driver's license and mentioned maybe it was time I became his driver.

A few years passed, and in mid-March 2009, sometime during the night, a phone call from Merle Haggard awakened me. He asked if I would fly to Dallas, Texas, the next day to drive his band bus! Apparently, his tour bus driver had quit in the middle of the tour. My employers kindly granted me a leave of absence - I arrived in Dallas the next day.

It took a full year of driving all over America before Merle called me into his private quarters in the back of his bus to confront me with a rumor. "Is it true?" he asked. "Are you considering quitting?"

I responded with a very firm, "It has crossed my mind."

His reaction was vintage Merle. He asked if I was ready to die, go to heaven, stand in front of Jesus, and have him look down at me and say, "You didn't quit Merle Haggard, did ya?"

I told him since he had invoked the name of Jesus, I would stay on, adding that the job was stressful and dangerous and driving three to four hundred miles every night was exhausting, not to mention the impossibility of eating right or resting properly. I asked him how he had managed to live such a life on the road for fifty years. His answer once again was vintage Merle and contained one word: GOD.

The next day I was promoted with a huge pay raise to the lead driver's position on Merle's private tour bus. What a blessing! Little did I know how much my life would change in the next six years in ways I couldn't yet imagine. Looking back, I realize those years were a blend of the challenges of tour bus driving, the hardships of life on the road, and time spent with many wonderful and talented people; but the best parts are those memories of my friendship with Merle Haggard.

Merle was diagnosed with lung cancer in 2008 and died of complications from double pneumonia eight years later on his 79th birthday. I had told him once that he was the kindest man I'd ever met, but he was also the orneriest. He just smiled at that.

ACKNOWLEDGMENTS

This book is dedicated to the memory and legacy of Merle Haggard. He was a kind and gracious soul. Peace to his memory. Much thanks and immense gratitude to Bonnie Owens, the Queen of the San Joaquin Valley. Peace to her memory. Mike and Buddy Owens provided me with a lifetime of fond memories. Their kindness was unsurpassed in the days of our childhood. I wouldn't have these stories without them.

When I started this project in November 2016, I called Merle's sister, Lillian Haggard Rae (she was 95 years old then), to ask her if she would approve of my memoir. She was most charming, as always, and wholeheartedly endorsed it. She mentioned that she'd like to hear the stories of her brother from another's eyes. That endorsement meant so much - thanks, Lil! Also, a huge thank you to Lillian and her nephew, Jim Haggard, for providing so many wonderful photos of Merle. And a special thanks to Grace and Jim Haggard for their help and support with the book.

Special thanks to my sweet Mother, Mary Virginia (Saylor) McDonald. Peace to your memory, Mom. To my daughter, Alison Brae McDonald-Marsh, thank you for the encouragement and support of my memoir. The books you sent me detailing how to write it were so helpful. To my son and sometimes editor, Benjamin McDonald, thank you for your help. I know that I had to impose on you and your career to help me, but you were kind and patient. All my love to Alison, Benjamin, and their families.

My wonderful sisters, Connie and Jolene McDonald, both were vital in their support. They constantly inquired about my progress and well-being. Connie temporarily abandoned the leisures of retirement to help edit the entire book. Thanks, big sisters; I'm a blessed little brother.

I enlisted help from some cousins of mine when I first began this journey. I asked them to type out my audio stories and send them back to me, as I wasn't capable of actual work. To cousins Parker and Katie Sayler, from the great state of Kansas, thank you. To cousin, John Ditmore, from the great state of Nevada, thank you, sir.

My ex-wife, Kathleen (Hughett) McDonald Leavitt, and I still love each other. We are not in love anymore, but share an affection for the 32 years we shared together. We have been blessed with seven grandchildren, Caitlyn, Kirsten, Madison, Daniel, and Zechariah from Chris and Alison Marsh, and Braden and Gage from my son, Benjamin, and his lovely wife, Faustin. I wrote this book for my family and the family of country music fans, as well as the many curious souls of this world.

I had a multitude of support from my friends from Oildale. Most notably, Steve and Donna York. My God, they even bought me a bed to sleep on when I had none. When I didn't have gas and grocery money, they supplied me with a helping hand I didn't ask for. I'm forever in their debt. Kipp Sullivan managed to remind me every day for years that what I was doing was paramount to the history of country music. The guy sent me a thousand emails on the how and why. Much gratitude to Kipper and all my friends, too many to mention, from Oildale and Bakersfield - they are golden, and I appreciate their kindness.

I'd like to thank my lifelong friend, Rebecca Shearin, for lending her immeasurable talents to this historic project. I appreciate her friendship, talent, and support. She designed the front and back cover and formatted all the interior pages, including dozens of photos. She also was extremely helpful in the editing process and in relentlessly researching dates and facts pertaining to the story of this remarkable American, Merle Haggard. Thanks again, Rebecca!

Thanks to the entire Townsend family of Woodrow Avenue in Oildale. Those people became a vital part of my happiness. Ernie and Jeannette and their children, Townie, Stuart, Barry, Jeff, and Jennifer, took me into their home and treated me with the kindness of the Waltons. The year I spent in their home (junior year of high school) was filled with laughter.

Thanks to Fuzzy Owen and Pastor Phil Neighbors for their guidance and inspiration. Fuzzy's book "Merle Haggard, Bonnie Owens & Me" was enlightening and educational. Peace to your memory, Fuzzy.

The man I adored from the first time I met him in 1965 has a title, "Merle Haggard's best friend." Dean Holloway is the man. Dean told me that he and Merle met in the sixth grade at Standard Elementary School. They were lifelong friends, and it was Dean who became Merle's first bus driver and drove millions of miles for decades. He was a gentle soul. Without my friendship with Dean Holloway, I wouldn't have had the opportunity of a lifetime. Peace to his memory.

Best friends, Dean Holloway and Merle Haggard